James Dewar was a  1950s when he began with the BBC in Br contributions to radio Later, as television ou he began writing for appointed a television his documentary inve produced and narrated.

He was the first Regional Television Manager of BBC West and, after taking the job in 1970, continued to make television himself. As executive producer he was responsible for four major series of documentaries from the regions shown on BBC2. A fruitful collaboration with the novelist Beryl Bainbridge led to two of these series, *English Journey* and *Forever England*. James Dewar, who lives in Bristol, is also the author of *The Rape of Noah's Ark*, an investigation into man's exploitation of animals.

'Brethren, nothing now remains, but, according to ancient custom, to lock up our secrets in a safe repository, uniting in the act of Fidelity, Fidelity, Fidelity' – Final words from the ceremony for closing a Freemasons' lodge.

THE UNLOCKED SECRET

FREEMASONRY EXAMINED

JAMES DEWAR

CORGI BOOKS

THE UNLOCKED SECRET
A CORGI BOOK 0 522 13535 6

Originally published in Great Britain by
William Kimber & Co Ltd.

PRINTING HISTORY
William Kimber edition published 1966
Corgi revised edition published 1990

This book is set in 10/11 pt Ehrhardt by Selectmove Ltd, London

Corgi Books are published by Transworld Publishers Ltd.,
61-63 Uxbridge Road, Ealing, London W5 5SA, in Australia by
Transworld Publishers (Australia) Pty. Ltd., 15–23 Helles Avenue,
Moorebank, NSW 2170, and in New Zealand by Transworld Publishers
(N.Z.) Ltd., Cnr. Moselle and Waipareira Avenues, Henderson,
Auckland.

Made and printed in Great Britain by
Cox & Wyman Ltd., Reading, Berks.

*For Diana and the other members of our secret society,
Andrew, John and Stephen*

Acknowledgements

The author and publishers are grateful to the Central Board of Finance of the Church of England for permission to reproduce extracts from *Freemasonry and Christianity: Are they compatible?* The report of the Working Group established by the Standing Committee of the General Synod of the Church of England (Church House Publishing 1987); to Grafton Books for permission to reproduce extracts from *The Brotherhood* by Stephen Knight, © Stephen Knight 1983; and to Harrap Ltd for permission to reproduce extracts from *Stalker* by John Stalker, © John Stalker Ltd 1988.

'What then is Masonry? If it could answer, I believe it would say: I am rooted in the midst of great antiquity, and point to God and eternity; I am the Past, Present and the Future; I belong to the ages; I circle the globe and stand at the cross-roads of the world; I am steeped in tradition and traced in the pages of history; I have rites and words that have beauty, symmetry and rhythm; I have knowledge, wisdom and secrets locked in my bosom, which I give to men who come to me desiring me in their hearts; I place upon my altars Holy Writ and turn to the Deity in prayer; I hold a Square and Compasses in my hands and contemplate a line from earth to heaven; I speculate with all the tools of operative masons, and I translate their use into moral values and spiritual building; I await all free men of lawful age and good report, but solicit none; I admit them of their own free will and accord, and teach them brotherhood and unity; I make builders of men of those who are willing, and give them my tools that they may work; I stoop to raise the fallen brethren and cast out the unworthy; I walk in the way of charity and travel the road of peace and harmony; I render aid to the poor, the sick and the distressed; I answer the cry of the orphan, and sustain the widow and the aged; I commit to the earth brethren who travel to that "Undiscovered Country"; I ponder at that moment on the ravages of time, as I stand at the door to eternity; I am a way of life that teaches immortality; I raise men from darkness to light.'

Wiley Odell May, Past Grand Master of the Grand Lodge of Tennessee, quoted in *The Empire State Mason*, September/October 1963.

'The point of a club is not who it lets in, but who it keeps out. The club is based on two ancient British ideas—the segregation of classes, and the segregation of sexes: and they remain insistent on keeping people out, long after they have stopped wanting to come in. At their best, clubs are still havens of disinterested friendliness where professions mingle. At their worst, they are havens of humbug.'

Anthony Sampson, *Anatomy of Britain*, Hodder and Stoughton 1962.

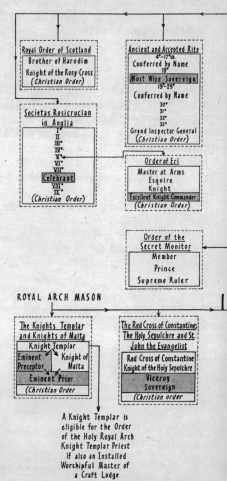

Royal Order of Scotland
Brother of Harodim
Knight of the Rosy Cross
(Christian Order)

Ancient and Accepted Rite
4°–17°th.
Conferred by Name
18°
Most Wise Sovereign
19°–29°
Conferred by Name
30°
31°
32°
33°
Grand Inspector General
(Christian Order)

Societas Rosicrucian
in Anglia
I°
II°
III°
IV°.
V°
VI°
VII°
Celebrant
VIII°
IX°
(Christian Order)

Order of Eri
Master at Arms
Esquire
Knight
Excellent Knight Commander
(Christian Order)

Order of the
Secret Monitor
Member
Prince
Supreme Ruler

ROYAL ARCH MASON

The Knights Templar
and Knights of Malta
Knight Templar
Eminent   Knight
Preceptor   of
                 Malta
Eminent Prior
(Christian Order)

The Red Cross of Constantine;
The Holy Sepulchre and St.
John the Evangelist
Red Cross of Constantine
Knight of the Holy Sepulchre
Viceroy
Sovereign
(Christian order)

THE INTER-RELATION OF THE VARIOUS MASONIC ORDERS AND DEGREES

Degrees and Chairs of each order [⌐ ¬]
Installation ceremonies not comprising
a degree ▓▓▓

A Knight Templar is
eligible for the Order
of the Holy Royal Arch
Knight Templar Priest
if also an Installed
Worshipful Master of
a Craft Lodge

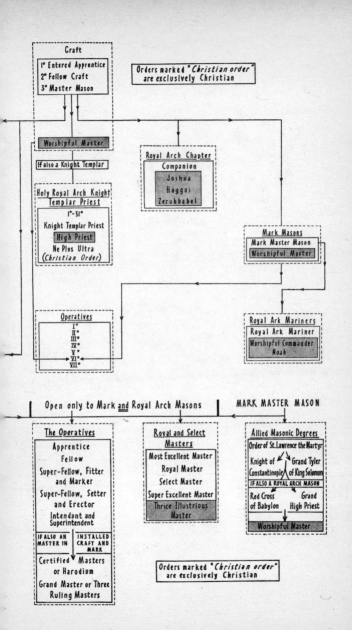

Craft
1° Entered Apprentice
2° Fellow Craft
3° Master Mason

Orders marked "*Christian order*" are exclusively Christian

Worshipful Master

If also a Knight Templar

Holy Royal Arch Knight Templar Priest
1°-31°
Knight Templar Priest
High Priest
Ne Plus Ultra
(*Christian Order*)

Royal Arch Chapter
Companion
Joshua
Haggai
Zerubbabel

Mark Masons
Mark Master Mason
Worshipful Master

Operatives
I°
II°
III°
IV°
V°
VI°
VII°

Royal Ark Mariners
Royal Ark Mariner
Worshipful Commander
Noah

Open only to Mark <u>and</u> Royal Arch Masons

MARK MASTER MASON

The Operatives
Apprentice
Fellow
Super-Fellow, Fitter and Marker
Super-Fellow, Setter and Erector
Intendant and Superintendent

| IF ALSO AN MASTER IN | INSTALLED CRAFT AND MARK |

Certified Masters or Harodium
Grand Master or Three Ruling Masters

Royal and Select Masters
Most Excellent Master
Royal Master
Select Master
Super Excellent Master
Thrice Illustrious Master

Allied Masonic Degrees
Order of St. Lawrence the Martyr
Knight of Constantinople / Grand Tyler of King Solomon
IF ALSO A ROYAL ARCH MASON
Red Cross of Babylon / Grand High Priest
Worshipful Master

Orders marked "*Christian order*" are exclusively Christian

Contents

List of Illustrations

The author and publishers wish to thank the BBC for permission to reproduce photographs from the television documentary Freemasonry, The Open Secret *broadcast on 16th March, 1965. They are also grateful to those members of the cast of non-Masons who agreed to publication of the pictures here and particular to the principals:*
Basil Henson (Worshipful Master); Malcolm Webster (Candidate); Michael Goldie (Junior Deacon); Maurice Durant (Senior Deacon); Ronald Russell (Senior Warden); Peter Andrews (Junior Warden); Bernard Padfield (Inner Guard); Roy Brimble (Tyler).

Ceremony of Initiation

'Whom have you there?'
The Inner Guard holds a dagger to the candidate's breast
The Junior Deacon leads the candidate around the lodge
The Senior Warden presents a candidate 'properly prepared to be made a Mason'
The candidate's right hand is placed on the Bible
The candidate holds the compasses, one point to his bare breast
He swears to keep the Masonic secrets
The candidate's head is directed towards the Bible
He seals his Solemn Obligation with a kiss
'Rise, newly obligated Brother among Masons'
The Masonic step, right heel in the hollow of the left foot
The First Degree sign
The First Degree grip, thumb pressing the first joint of the forefinger

Ceremony of Passing to the Second Degree

The Inner Guard holds a square to the candidate's breast
The candidate wears the apron of the First Degree with its triangular flap turned up
The candidate takes the oath of the Second Degree
The Worshipful Master demonstrates the sign of Fidelity and the Hailing sign
The Second Degree grip, thumb pressing the first joint of the second finger

Ceremony of Raising to the Third Degree

The Brethren stand holding the Penal sign
The Master Mason awaits his 'last and greatest trial'
A 'death' blow from the Worshipful Master's maul
The Master Mason is lowered to the floor
The Wardens 'bury' the new Master Mason
The Master Mason lies in his mock grave

Introduction to 1990 edition

When this book was first published in 1966 the worldwide membership of Freemasonry was estimated at six million and thought to be increasing in every country where the secret society was allowed to flourish. Today there are about four million men sworn to keep secret the rituals carried out in their temples.

The popular belief is that Freemasonry attracts a large number of men who undergo the bizarre initiation ceremonies only because they hope to benefit financially from their membership. There are fears that Freemasons, far from promoting ideals of universal brotherhood and service, are sworn to promote each other's interests and some lodges include Masons who are criminal and corrupt.

Fear of corruption among the many police officers who are Masons is a particular cause of widespread public concern. The most frequent allegations are that Freemasons in the police are preferred for appointments and promotions, are protected from disciplinary procedures, and may not be impartial when they investigate cases involving other Freemasons. More than a hundred MPs voted for a Bill presented in the House of Commons in 1988 which would have banned Freemasonry in the police.

There have also been demands that Freemasons should not be appointed as judges in future, and those judges and justices of the peace who are Masons should be required to make this known. Many local authorities have called for similar declarations of interest from officers and councillors.

One reason why the number of Freemasons has decreased so dramatically is that exposures of Masonic rituals by the media have persuaded many outsiders that the ceremonies are pretentious and humiliating. Another is that the

Methodist Conference in 1985 and a report by the Synod of the Church of England two years later advised members of serious theological objections to Masonic ritual and said that Freemasonry is not for Christians committed to traditional doctrine.

Abroad, a Masonic scandal in Italy brought down the Christian Democrat government in 1981 and is still having repercussions. Freemasons of a secret lodge were so powerful and influential that they conspired to be a state within the state. A membership list, found when police raided the home of the Master of the Lodge, recorded nearly a thousand names including those of Cabinet ministers, judges, military chiefs, leading businessmen and financiers who did business with both the Mafia and the Vatican. British Freemasons were embarrassed by the implications of the Italian scandal and speculation that Freemasonry could also be a danger to the state in this country.

Revelations of political intrigue by Freemasons on the Continent, and suspicions that Freemasonry is a threat to social justice and can be used to conceal corruption, have brought fresh attacks on the secrecy with which Masons surround themselves. This book removes much of that secrecy.

Introduction to first edition

Many people fear Freemasonry and this book is an attempt to bring their forebodings into the open and to examine them in the light of what may be discovered about the largest secret society in the world. With six million members, the movement is so big that it is not as secret as first appears and there is a vast literature devoted to Freemasonry, much in French, German and Italian; but a large proportion of it is from Masons themselves, or from detractors with a religious bias against the movement. I do not pretend to have read all those who have written on the subject; nor have I thought it necessary to do so, for the purpose of this book is to give a contemporary picture of the attitudes of Freemasons towards their organisation and to review the problem which its existence today poses to all concerned with social justice.

I have never sought to be a Freemason, nor am I a Roman Catholic: my credentials are those of the journalist and this book is offered as a result of an investigation started more than three years ago for a BBC television documentary. In spite of the folklore about their order and its secrets, I do not believe that Freemasons are a special kind of men to be examined as a separate species of humanity. I have met many Masons and I find them no different to the men one comes across on a Sunday morning when the churches are closing and the pubs are opening. Many men feel the magnetism of Masonry and think deeply about whether they should seek to join it or to oppose it, or merely to adopt a neutral standpoint. All too often they do not reach a considered decision because the secrecy of Freemasonry sustains the rumours and half-truths which have gathered like a fog around the subject.

It has been an essential part of my training to prize objectivity as the touchstone of good reporting and I have conscientiously sought to bring that quality to this book. Where I will be found to have failed, I can only plead that an ignorance encouraged by Freemasonry itself is partly to blame and I have fallen into the trap innocently.

None of us is without some prejudices but I have not considered this an excuse to avoid offering personal judgements. I have tried to make clear in the text where such conclusions are my own and to include all the evidence upon which they are based. I have gathered that evidence from books, magazines, reports, newspapers and personal conversations with Masons; and I am satisfied that most of what Masons would wish to say on behalf of their movement is contained in this book.

I make no apology for reproducing the Craft rituals. They are so readily available that no one can argue seriously that they are currently part of Masonic secrets. Their accuracy has been confirmed from many sources, including Masons themselves. A few Freemasons even pressed upon me copies of the books from which they learnt the ceremonies. These books are small enough to hide in the hand and bound in blue, the colour of the edging of a Master Mason's apron. The rituals they contain are described by Masons as 'Emulation workings' and derive from the Emulation Lodge of Improvement, established in 1823. There are other systems and local variations; but Emulation rituals are widely used and I have been assured the differences encountered are minor ones.

Freemasons protest that their rituals are a private concern and to expose them is unwarranted intrusion. I cannot agree. If people are to be given an opportunity to form considered opinions of their own about Freemasonry, access to such an important part of Masonry cannot be denied to them. It is a more cogent argument that the rituals are open to misinterpretation by those outside Freemasonry. On the other hand, much of the symbolism of Masonry and the teachings of the order are explained within the ceremonies which have the dual functions of initiation and instruction.

18

To avoid the intrusion of unusual spelling, I have sometimes adopted the word 'ancient', although it is taken from
many sources where it is spelt 'antient'. There existed from
1753 to 1813 the Antient Grand Lodge of England and the
present day Freemasonry movement in England is officially
styled the 'Antient Fraternity of Free and Accepted Masons'.
I have also used a capital 'M' for mason, masonic and
masonry, where these words are used to describe modern
Freemasonry and its members; when spelt with a small 'm'
the words apply to men employed as craftsmen.

I found it necessary to sketch fairly fully the historical
background of Freemasonry, because such facts as are now
established remove a great deal of popular mythology. I have
relied extensively upon the work of the Masonic historian
Robert Freke Gould, using the four-volume edition revised
by the Rev. Herbert Poole. Other authors whose works have
been particularly useful and so deserve special mention here
are Bernard E. Jones, F. L. Pick and G. N. Knight—all
Masons.

Two important investigations were made into Freemasonry during 1964. They were the inquiry into the
theological implications of membership undertaken by the
panel on doctrine of the Church of Scotland and the commission into secret societies in South Africa. Both are quoted at
length here. The South African Government's inquiry into
Freemasonry was carried out in private by only one man,
Judge Botha, but his terms of reference were comprehensive
and matched by formidable powers. Following the publication of his report, there have been no suggestions of which I
am aware that his work was in any way a 'whitewash'.

The chapter on the theological issues raised by the first
three degrees of Masonry owes much to the report presented
to the Assembly of the Church of Scotland in 1965 by its
panel on doctrine. I must also acknowledge a larger debt
to the report of the General Assembly of the Presbyterian
Church of Victoria in October 1958, and to the notes in
defence of Masonry which N. H. Symes contributed for the
consideration of Australian Presbyterians. I should also like

to say that these documents about theological issues were offered to me by Leonard Scott, the Church of Scotland minister who raised the matter in Assembly and pursued it without discourtesy or partiality.

Some of those clergymen who took part in similar, but unsuccessful, efforts to persuade the Church of England to debate Freemasonry in the 1950s showed little taste for reviving the issues when I approached them. I do not blame them for that; but I cannot go along with the burial party when there is no corpse. Freemasonry is not on the decline but is increasing. One reason for this may be that as more widespread prosperity removes from many men anxieties over the basic necessities of life they concern themselves more deeply with questions of status.

Status-seeking and social justice are matters at the heart of society today, and they are not unlinked with Freemasonry which has recruited one adult in every twenty-three of Britain's male population.

There is in Masonry a great deal that men undoubtedly find of value to them in their attempts to achieve a higher quality of life, not materially, but spiritually. Freemasonry is also full of half-truths and the seeds of menace. No man should join in ignorance.

CHAPTER I

History and Fantasy

About four million men throughout the world belong to the movement known as Freemasonry, a secret society which exists in every country where it has not been outlawed by the State, and whose members confidently expect to be greeted by fellow Freemasons as special strangers with whom they have been taught to exchange secret hand grips, signs and code words. Some aspects of the movement are attributed to the English craft guilds of medieval stonemasons, so today Freemasons call their organisation 'the Craft' and their ceremonies 'the workings'. Masonic rituals are carried out behind guarded doors in meeting places described as 'temples' by groups of Masons known as 'lodges'. The working tools and instruments of the stonemason provide the symbols by means of which the moral principles of Freemasonry are taught and illustrated; and a narrative thread for most Masonic ceremonial is woven from apocryphal events concerning the building of King Solomon's temple and the murder of its chief architect.

It cannot be conclusively established that modern Freemasons derive their organisation, beliefs and practices from the working stonemasons of medieval times. Indeed, there is virtually no evidence to suggest that the early stonemason attached any moral or spiritual significance to his trade or its working tools. It is true that stonemasons in the Middle Ages sometimes organised themselves within lodges; but the lodge was a workmen's hut on a large building site used for storing tools, taking meals and holding meetings. Medieval stonemasons also shared a legendary history of the craft and a tradition of fraternal and benevolent relations between masons, together with a rule of secrecy about what was discussed in the lodge. No modern lodge of Freemasons, however, can claim a continuous existence since the Middle Ages, and the practices of the stonemasons of that time are still largely a matter for conjecture.

Obscure, too, is the meaning, or meanings, implied in the 'Free' of 'Freemasons'. Many scholars are opposed to the suggestion put forward in the *Oxford English Dictionary* that the term 'Free' could refer to the medieval practice of 'emancipating skilled artisans, in order that they might be able to travel and render their services wherever any great building was in process of construction'. These scholars point out that at the time when the building of abbeys and churches was at its height there were too few, if any, town masons' guilds for these to be important.

The void of fact has been filled by speculation, but perhaps the most likely explanation is that the term Freemason originates from the words 'Free-stone mason'. There are other theories more fanciful than they are tenable: that working masons were made 'Free' by Papal Bull; and that the term 'Free' is a corruption of the French word *'frère'* deriving from years of mispronunciation of the appellation 'Brother Mason'.

The medieval lodges were for working masons, and they evolved legends, rules, initiation rites and secret signs. These lodges still existed in the seventeenth century, and by then had begun to admit as honorary members men who, although not connected with the building trades, were considered eminent architects or antiquarians. A distinction gradually developed between the 'operative' craftsmen masons and the 'speculative' Masons, whose main interest was in the social and moral aspects of the lodge ceremonies and activities; by 1740 secret, 'speculative' Freemasonry had progressed a long way towards its modern organisation. Grand Lodges controlling the Craft had been founded in England, Ireland and Scotland, and they were followed by others in Europe and America.

Undoubtedly, Freemasonry is a British product and it first emerged in the seventeenth century, by which time it was fashionable in this country for men to become 'accepted' or 'adopted' Freemasons. Before the end of the century Freemasons' societies were widely known as social groups given to banqueting on a considerable scale. It was, after all, the century that gave birth to the club. Today speculative Freemasonry exists in every country where it has not been banned by Communists or dictators, and the movement is to be found among men of the new emergent nations.

Modern Freemasonry, say the Constitutions of the United Grand Lodge of England, consists of three degrees and no more, those of Entered Apprentice, Fellow Craft, and Master Mason, including the Supreme Order of the Holy Royal Arch. The allied degrees of the Royal Arch are regarded as the completion of the third initiation ceremony, or Master Mason's degree. In fact, each Masonic degree is an initiation rite, and most men who join the movement are content to stop at the symbolic status of Master Mason. The central theme of these ceremonies is the building of King Solomon's temple and legendary events associated with the work. At the heart of this Masonic mythology is the hero-figure Hiram Abiff, the principal architect of the temple, murdered by three Fellow Craft masons because he refused to part with the secrets of a master mason.

Until comparatively recent years speculation about the origins of Freemasonry and its Hiramic legend has produced some of the most spurious and carefree of historical theorising; so much that those Masonic writers responsible for the more reliable and scholarly tradition which now prevails find it hard to restrain a note of bitterness when assessing the efforts of their predecessors. R. F. Gould,[1] whose history of Freemasonry was among the earlier and the most important contributions to the new critical research, begins his work with references to writers 'with whom

[1]*The History of Freemasonry*, 3rd edition, edited by the Rev H. Poole, Caxton Publishing Co. Ltd., 1951.

enthusiasm supplied the place of learning' and to others who 'evinced an amount of credulity which, to say the least, was commensurate with their learning'. And another reputable Masonic historian, Bernard E. Jones, writes:

The old-fashioned Masonic books so often tell a story that is more romantic than factual, and repeat fallacies that should long ago have died a natural death.[1]

The truth is that there has been no limit to Masonic wishful thinking devoted to almost fanatical attempts to hallow the movement with ancient inspiration from gods and men. There is the amazing theory that Shakespeare created Freemasonry and all its rituals;[2] and Dr George Oliver must surely speak from the outer fringe of fantasy when he writes:

Ancient Masonic traditions (and I have good reasons for being of this opinion) say that our science existed before the creation of this terrestrial globe and was widely spread throughout the various solar systems.[3]

Some of the more mundane, if now discarded, theories of the possible origins of Freemasonry are worthy of review, if only because of the hold they still have on the minds of some members of the Craft.

Any system of rituals making extensive use of symbolism is bound to suggest points of contact with a variety of religions and philosophies, and these have been explored by generations of Masonic writers. Thousands of books have been published on Freemasonry, but for the most part Masonic speculations have merely added to the difficulty of tracing the beginnings of Freemasonry. Most of the theories put forward are tortuous structures, and what is missing all the time is any tenable link with modern Freemasonry.

[1]*Freemasons' Guide and Compendium*, Harrap and Co. Ltd., 1963 edition.
[2]*Shakespeare, Creator of Freemasonry*, Alfred Dodd, 1936.
[3]*Antiquities of Freemasonry*, London, 1823.

The more obscure the sect or group to which a part in the founding of the movement might be attributed, the more many Masonic writers seem to be pleased. It has been suggested that Freemasonry owes something to the system of Pythagoras. Another school of writers say Masonry derives from the Druids, a particularly ingenious piece of etymological guesswork being that as the May, or Maypole, was the sign of the Druids, they might have taken the name of Men of the May, or Mays-sons.

Other writers have traced Freemasonry back to the Culdees, the ancient monastic order which had settlements in Scotland and Ireland during the eighth century and was imagined to have preserved primitive Christianity free from Roman corruption. The Essenes, the Jewish sect which established monastic communities in the region of the Dead Sea, have also been credited with the inspiration of Freemasonry; so have the ancient Mystery religions of Egypt and Greece; and Mithraism, one of the last of the oriental cults to reach the West with its Indo–Iranian God of Light, Mithras.

Masonic writers in search of the Craft's pedigree point out that the Pythagoreans had secrets (a maxim of the sect was that everything was not to be told to everybody, and for common meals they met in companies of only ten), and that they were divided into three classes—*Acustici*, *Mathematici*, and *Physici*—sharing surreptitious signs of recognition. The initiated into the Mystery religions had secret signs, too; and an alleged fraternity of priests and lay architects of the fertility god who later became associated with wine, Dionysus (or Bacchus), were said to have been organised within grades possessing clandestine recognition signs; and to have used building implements in a ceremonial context in much the same way as do Freemasons. There are also suggestions that Freemasonry derives from China, at least one Chinese philosopher being said to have urged men figuratively to apply the square, compasses and level to their lives in order to find the true path of wisdom.

Other authors have preferred an omnibus solution to the enigma of Masonry's origins, postulating that all secret fraternities are successive links of one unbroken chain and the repository of ancient wisdom which has been bequeathed to modern Freemasonry. The theory is as plausible as any so far discussed, but absence of evidence prevents any of them finding a sound historical basis.

There is also no supporting evidence to link modern Free-masonry with the Roman Collegia—the religious, political and craft clubs which did possibly influence the development of English Craft Guild practice. Nor can any proof be found for the school of thought which attributes Masonry's beginnings to a company of Italian architects said to have been commissioned by the Pope to travel through Europe building churches—no Bull or diploma giving authority for such an organisation can be traced in the Papal archives. Another similarly fancied body, and more than likely part of the same legend, to attract the attention of Masonic writers had been the 'Comacine Masters', a supposed group of masons whose title is attributed to the site of their original headquarters, an island in Lake Como; but, although the Lombard builders travelled widely over western Europe, no evidence has appeared to suggest that they had an organisation offering any similarities with Freemasonry.

More fruitful ground for speculation is to be found within the craft organisations of Germany and France. The establishment of many religious orders and houses in Britain brought into the country architects and skilled workmen from Europe. English masons in their turn, but probably to a much smaller extent, travelled to France and to other parts of the Continent during a time when the Church was the great power in the Western world and gave a unity to medieval Europe.

The guild of stonecutters in Germany (the Steinmetzen) is thought to have grown out of the gradual amalgamation of church and craft builders begun in about the twelfth century, although a single society does not emerge until 1459, when the earliest known text of their guild regulations was drawn up at Regensburg. As in all other guilds, the Steinmetzen used a secret form of greeting and, possibly, a grip; but

26

not, according to available records, secret words or initiation ceremonies, and it is unlikely that they admitted honorary members.[1] The writings of Fallou,[2] published more than a century ago, did much to popularise the Steinmetzen theory and were followed uncritically by later writers. Considerable 'support' of this kind led to the theory being widely accepted, although Fallou failed to put forward any evidence to substantiate his claim and was writing about a century after Freemasonry in its present form had penetrated into Germany from England.

The histories of the French trade guilds and of the Compagnonnage, the association formed by the journeymen craftsmen of France to make life easier on their travels, might support a convincing case that France merits the most important place in the genealogy of Freemasonry. The difficulty is that French historians simply accepted popular opinion during the early eighteenth century that Freemasonry was of French origin and, even if they had attempted to examine the craft guilds of France from a Masonic point of view, it is impossible to say whether or not the claim could have been satisfactorily proven.

Historically, the French guild system is older than anything in Britain and probably developed directly from the old Roman corporations or colleges, the evolution beginning in southern France and eventually overcoming German influence in the north to provide an almost uniform municipal and guild system over the entire country by the thirteenth century. French cities around this time had a form of Republican Government, the various trade guilds providing officers who, with the priests and bishops, formed the municipal councils; but in Paris power, instead of being vested in the leaders of all the guilds, was concentrated in the officers of one great guild, the Parisian Hanse, which, under the name of Marchands de l'Eau, controlled all the city's commerce and shipping. Later this super-guild appeared under another name—the Marchands or Six Corps de Paris—and was so influential

[1] For the regulations see R. F. Gould, *The History of Freemasonry*.
[2] *Mysterien der Freimaurer*, 1848.

that in 1305 the Six Corps was able to dictate to the young Regent of France the impeachment of his ministers, the liberation of the King of Navarre and the appointment of a council to assist the Dauphin. Charles VI tried to abolish the municipality and to prohibit all trade fraternities; but the guilds did not disband and the municipality itself was restored in 1411, the provost of the merchants ultimately regaining his former authority—something that was retained until the French Revolution.

The earliest code of any French association of builders to be preserved is said to date from 1260. It relates to an organisation of masons, stonemasons, plasterers and mortarers, and its special interest is a reference to Charles Martel, the Frankish sovereign who won a decisive victory over the Saracens on the field of Poitiers in 732 and was Charlemagne's grandfather. The importance of the reference to Charles Martel is that he is also mentioned in the ancient documents, the Old Charges,[1] which were handed down from the operative masons in Great Britain and are one of the historic springs of modern Freemasonry. The words from the old code, the only link, if it is one, between British Freemasonry and the Master's Guilds of France are:

The mortarers are free of watch duty and all stonemasons since the time of Charles Martel, as the wardens (*preudomes*) have heard tell father to son.

The fact that both French and English masons both claimed Charles Martel as a patron could mean that both early craft organisations sprang from the same source, or that there was early French influence on the British craft tradition; but the fact remains that coincidence might have played a part, and the evidence, such as it is, remains too insignificant to support any conclusion.

The French guild system had the primary intention of ensuring good workers, by insisting on an apprenticeship

[1]cf. Chapter II.

and a high standard of workmanship. A master had one apprentice at a time, usually for a period of seven years, and the apprentice out of his time became a journeyman, visiting various towns to work for different masters during what he called his 'tour de France'. The Compagnonnage was instituted, it is believed, to assist the craftmen making these tours and it offers several characteristics in common with modern Freemasonry. It was organised in three large divisions styled the Sons of Solomon, the Sons of Maître Jacques and the Sons of Maître Soubise, and to one of these each trade belonged. The Compagnonnage also used initiation ceremony and had legends connected with the building of Solomon's Temple, which named Maître Jacques and Maître Soubise as master masons. Each division revered and claimed origin from a traditional chief supposed to have conferred a charge, or duty, on his followers.

It seems that the Sons of Solomon was the oldest of the three great divisions and to it belonged stone masons, joiners and locksmiths. The Sons of Maître Jacques also included craftsmen and apprentices from these trades, but, in addition, almost all the handicrafts were embraced by this division. This made it the strongest numerically, yet so intense were the heriditary feuds between the various trade groups that the Sons of Maître Jacques only united to confront the other two rival divisions. The Sons of Maître Soubise comprised carpenters, tylers, and plasterers. All three divisions were governed by senior members and consisted of two grades, companions and aspirants. The discipline among the Sons of Solomon appears to have been of a benign and paternal character. In the other two divisions, rules of protocol were so severe that aspirants were treated almost as drudges.

Until the middle of the nineteenth century the existence of the Compagnonnage was only generally known through the bloody battles waged between their three divisions with long, heavy, iron-tipped canes, bedecked with ribbons indicating the various crafts. Then, in 1841, a workman member of the society, Agricol Perdiguier, set himself the task of reconciling the feuds between the various groups and published his *Livre de Compagnonnage*, an account of the history and traditions of the society and an appeal to resolve internal conflicts. George Sand was so impressed she invited Perdiguier to visit her and financed him to journey around France and preach peace to his fellows. George Sand wrote a novel, *Le Compagnon du Tour de France*, and other writers, some of them also companions, drew attention to the Compagnonnage.

The similarities between the practices of the French journeymen's society and those of modern Freemasonry are remarkable and too numerous to detail here.[1] Many of them are typical of almost any secret society and, suggestive though they are of an ancient connection with Freemasonry, too little is known of the Compagnonnage *before* Perdiguier; his book appeared at a time when Freemasonry had been widespread for a century. Even the question particularly significant to the genealogy of Freemasonry, whether or not the Compagnonnage had a Hiramic legend before Freemasonry came to France, is bedevilled by the belatedness of accounts of the society.

All that Perdiguier has to say about the legend of the Sons of Solomon, to which he himself belonged, is that the division claimed that 'this king had given them a charge and incorporated them fraternally within the precincts of the Temple'. There was, he added, a fable current among them relating to Hiram, or Adonhiram; but he regarded it as a Masonic invention, introduced into the Compagnonnage by men initiated into both secret societies.

After Perdiguier's dismissal of Hiram, it is enough briefly to review the legendary figures of the other two divisions of the French companions. Maître Jacques was said to be one of the first masters of Solomon and was murdered by five villains, after being betrayed at prayer by a disciple's kiss; and Maître Soubise, one-time bosom friend of Maître Jacques, may have been the instigator of the crime. Practically nothing

---

[1]See R. F. Gould, *The History of Freemasonry*.

is known of the mythical Maître Soubise; but the resemblance of the Maître Jacques legend to Christ's Passion is underlined by further details. The clothes of Maître Jacques were divided among his followers (his hat to the hatters, tunic to the stonemasons, sandals to the locksmiths, cloak to the joiners, belt to the carpenters and staff to the wagonmakers); the disciple who betrayed him committed suicide; and the five wounds inflicted by the daggers of the assassins correspond with the pierced hands, feet and side of Christ. The main weakness of the theorising which links the Compagnonnage with modern Freemasonry is that the Hiramic legend finds no historically convincing ancestry within the French organisation and the contemporary verdict must be that while the companions may have influenced Masonry they did not give birth to it.

Two other popularly ascribed 'sources' of modern Freemasonry deserve examination because of the tenacious way they have survived sceptical scholarship, the Knights Templar and the Rosicrucians. Both organisations have the common appeals essential to the search for a place for Freemasonry in ancient history: they are veiled in a decent antiquity and romanticism; and they offer the necessary connections to the wisdom of the East. They also find echoes in the modern Masonic system. In Freemasonry today a man can become a 'Knight Templar', for this is the title of one of Masonry's chivalric and Christian degrees. There is, too, a Masonic and Christian Rose Croix degree, the eighteenth of a series of thirty-three Masonic degrees—the number of which corresponds with the number of years of Christ's life. Neither degree is recognised as part of ancient Masonry, and both are among a large number of 'side degrees' open to Masons with the time and money to pursue them. No doubt, however, the existence of the degree today sustains belief in historical associations with the Knights Templar and the Rosicrucians.

The Knights Templar even provide an historical bonus for the Masonic writer—an undisputed association with King Solomon's Temple, for the knights' alternative title

31

was 'Poor Knights of Christ and of the Temple of King Solomon'. One of the three great military and religious orders of knighthood founded during the course of the crusades, the Knights Templar were a fighting order, unlike the Hospitallers and the Teutonic Knights, from their beginnings in 1119. The original founders were two knights who undertook the protection of pilgrims flocking to Jerusalem after the First Crusade. Other knights soon joined in the task and they established a religious community. Later, the King of Jerusalem gave the order the Temple of Solomon for a headquarters and the knights became known as the Templars.

Out of their pious police action grew great power. The Templars won privileges and immunities from the Church, gathered wealth by acting as bankers, and established strongholds from Armenia to Ireland. For more than a hundred years they wielded considerable political influence throughout Europe and particularly in France. History yields no evidence to suggest that the rule of their order was anything other than that which would justify the confidence popes and kings placed in them; but strange stories of secret rites practised by the knights at midnight meetings gained widespread acceptance and were to prove fatal to the Templars. There was no effective protest when King Philip IV of France, acting well within the traditional behaviour pattern of tyrant and dictator, seized the Templars' leaders and confiscated their wealth. On the night of Friday, 13th October 1307, King Philip had the Grand Master at that time, Jacques de Molay, and sixty of his brethren arrested in Paris. After brutal treatment in the palace, they were handed over to the Inquisition for further torture under which thirty-six died and, among others, the last Grand Master of the Templars confessed to denying Christ and spitting on the Cross. Pope Clement issued a Bull calling upon all kings and princes to arrest the Templars, and their fate was sealed.

Historians have long been divided as to whether or not the order was innocent or guilty of the specific charges on

32

which they were condemned, but the most diligent research has failed to produce any trace of a secret rule governing the Knights Templar. Nor is there any evidence to link the knights with modern Freemasonry, although Perdiguier hazarded that at one time the Compagnonnage consisted solely of Sons of Solomon and a breakaway group arose and placed themselves under the protection of Jacques de Molay. A more fancied and fanciful theory claims that the Knights Templar were not suppressed with such ferocity in Britain, and their esoteric doctrines survived and were merged with those of the Freemasons. Finally, so far as the contemporary Knights Templar Masonic degree is concerned, there is no record of such a degree being worked before the eighteenth century; but the legend with its Masonic overtones persists.

Claims that Freemasonry has an historical association with the Rosicrucians rest mainly upon the fact that Elias Ashmole, founder of the famous museum, was initiated into Masonry in the Lodge at Warrington in 1646 and, if not actually a Rosicrucian himself, was undoubtedly greatly interested in it. Apart from the personality of Ashmole, there is also the possibility that Freemasonry's Hiramic legend may have been based on the legend of the Rosicrucians.

Historically, the earliest extant writing to refer unequivocally to a Rosicrucian order is the famous *Fama Fraternitatis*, first published in 1614, although circulated in manuscript somewhat earlier. The legend it recounts has magical elements enough for it to be dismissed as a myth, or a cleverly fabricated literary hoax.

The *Fama Fraternitatis* describes the journey of the reputed founder of the movement, Christian Rosenkreuz. He was said to have been brought up in a German monastery and to have set off for the Holy Land when he was about twenty-five years of age. Apparently, he went on a grand tour to Damascus, Damcar in Arabia, Egypt and Fez, where he was well received and able to study secret wisdom. He returned to Germany at some time during the year 1402 and chose three disciples with whom he founded a secret order. One of the articles of agreement they were alleged to have adopted was that the fraternity should remain secret for a century. In 1484, when Rosenkreuz was at least one hundred years old, he died; and a hundred and twenty years later the secret burial-place and his embalmed body were discovered by one of the then members of the order in a vault decorated with mystical devices and containing a number of documents. The vault was re-covered and—too conveniently, perhaps—its exact location remains a mystery.

There is little here to support the idea that the Hiramic legend evolved by modern Freemasonry around Hiram Abiff, the murdered principal architect of King Solomon's temple, owes anything to the extraordinary story of Christian Rosenkreuz. The discovery of a vault, however, plays an important part in the symbolism of the Royal Arch, the allied degrees of Masonry which are widely regarded as the completion of the third, or Master Mason, degree in Craft Masonry. Also, there is within the orbit of contemporary Freemasonry an offshoot called the *Societas Rosicruciana in Anglia*, formed in 1866 and now consisting of 'Colleges' in England, Australia and New Zealand. The *Societas Rosicruciana* maintains fraternal communications with similar societies in Scotland and the United States.

Certainly the members of this organisation are more Masonic than Rosicrucian, for although it is supposed by *Encyclopaedia Britannica* that there are 'Rosicrucian societies, fraternities, orders, fellowships or lodges in most countries of the modern world', the statement—without the supporting evidence, which is lacking—means little more than that there was a vogue in the eighteenth century for the secret society which led to a recrudescence of the style Rosicrucian. Significantly, perhaps, the name has been appropriated by American Theosophy, and none of the later societies, Masonic or not, can claim any historical continuity with any original groups.

Nevertheless, the Rosicrucian legend of the *Fama Fraternitatis* and those who studied it—including Elias Ashmole—may have contributed to modern Freemasonry. Rosicrucians assert that Freemasonry owes all or most of its philosophy, symbolism and secrecy to them. The Masonic writer A. E. Waite has offered the fullest account of the Rosicrucians,[1] and a highly personal view of the history of Freemasonry;[2] but more students are likely to agree with Bernard E. Jones when he writes:

It is just and proper to admit the possibility of our Craft degrees having been influenced by individual Rosicrucians, but to dismiss utterly and completely any suggestion that speculative (philosophical as opposed to ancient guild membership) freemasonry is largely a survival of the Rosicrucian cult or is the seventeenth-century invention of its adherents, organised or otherwise.[3]

For the historian and the Masonic seeker of historical status for modern Freemasonry the sad, or gay, truth about Masonry is that history has no proof to furnish of alleged links with any particular cult of Ancient Wisdom, Arabic or Egyptian tradition, medieval orders of knighthood, or primitive craft guilds. Even the widely held belief that the Masonic pedigree goes back to the British masons guilds of medieval times is suspect; but that is a question for examination in the next chapter.

[1]*Brotherhood of the Rosy Cross*, 1924.
[2]*The Secret Tradition in Freemasonry.*
[3]*Freemasons' Guide and Compendium.*

CHAPTER II

History and Fact

Few of the hundreds of thousands of men who suffer the indignities of Masonic initiation ever bother to inquire into the origins and history of the movement they join. They are content to know a smattering of ritual and ceremonial and to possess vague notions about the antiquity of the society.

The false idea of a Craft genealogy which reaches back to ancient civilisations and beyond may to some extent be encouraged by the pretension of a Masonic calendar. On a Freemason's membership certificate two dates are given: one accords with the ordinary everyday calendar, and the other with the Masonic calendar. Instead of reckoning the year from the birth of Christ, the Craft calendar uses Anno Lucis, meaning 'In the Year of Light', and abbreviated 'AL' Anno Lucis is the 'Year of Masonry' and is arrived at by adding to the calendar year the number 4,000, representing the number of years once supposed to have elapsed since the beginning of the world. The system is based on the chronology of the seventeenth-century Archbishop Usher, who calculated the Creation took place in 4004 BC. For convenience, the Masonic calendar usually ignores the odd four years, so that AD 1989 is AL 5989. The calculations might be confusing, but the implication is clear: Freemasonry is as old as the world itself; the calendar is an expression of those Masonic aspirations which would make Adam the first Freemason and confers a suggestion of credence to similarly naïve fantasies.

Masonic Knights Templar recognise a chronology based on Anno Ordinis, or 'In the Year of the Order', abbreviated 'AO'. To calculate the year AO, 1118 is subtracted from the conventional calendar year, so that 1989 becomes 871. Yet another esoteric Masonic Templar calendar is based on the historical date of the destruction of the original order and is calculated by subtracting 1314 from the calendar year.

Masonic wishful thinking is in this way sustained by an anniversary game that might assist the more gullible to accept some of the remote and spurious propositions for which Masonic authors have been responsible. These include suggestions that Masonry in Ireland owes its foundation to the prophet Jeremiah; that 27,000 Masons went with Christian princes to the Crusades; and that Martin Luther became a Freemason on Christmas night 1520, fifteen days after he had burned the Pope's Bull. There are no esoteric calendars for these particular myths, nor is there a special chronology for the most commonly accepted and most plausible theory of Masonic origin, a comparatively short, and obscure, pedigree deriving from the medieval organisation of practising masons.

Historically, present-day Freemasonry may owe something to the man who actually worked freestone with axe, mallet and chisel. The obscurity that surrounds this common sense possibility is due to the fact that there are no records available of the lodge meetings of medieval freemasons. In Scotland the earliest extant documents show the proceedings of lodges for the year 1599, as written up at the time in their minute-books. In England the oldest lodge of which the records can be traced is Alnwick Lodge, in Northumberland. Unfortunately for English Masonic writers, this lodge was apparently wholly operative and a speculative Masonic lodge did not grow from it. Also, the minutes of the old English operative lodge only date back to 1701, a mere sixteen years before the formation of the Grand Lodge of England in 1717.

It seems probable, however, that the urban craft guild was not a suitable organisation for all medieval stonemasons.[1]

---

[1]See 'The Evolution of Masonic Organisation', D. Knoop and G. P. Jones, *Transactions of the Quatuor Coronati Lodge*, London xlv.

Many of them travelled in search of employment or experience and were often conscripted for work on large buildings in remote places. For these men the essential unit was much more likely the lodge connected with the building on which they were employed. Records show that such lodges existed, for example, at York Minster in 1352, and at the Church of St Nicholas, Aberdeen, in 1483. The stonemasons who met in these lodges, which they used as canteen, rest room and store, were taught common myths about their craft. They learned that it had been expounded by Euclid at the famous mathematical school of Alexandria in Egypt and applied at the building of the Tower of Babel and the Temple of Solomon. They were also told that masons in England had been honoured by St Alban and favoured and regulated by King Athelstan.

This legendary history, together with the rules, customs and traditions of the stonemasons of the Middle Ages, are preserved in the Old Charges, known also as the Manuscript Constitutions of Masonry. About a hundred versions exist, and there is reason to believe that another fifteen have existed. The documents are the main source of information for the Masonic histories and the oldest are almost certainly the Regius Manuscript, written in verse, probably about 1390, and the Cooke Manuscript, in prose, dating from about 1400 or 1410.[1]

The legend contained in the manuscript tells of the problem of finding a source of income for the children of noblemen in early times. Euclid is consulted and suggests masonry, which, therefore, finds its genesis in Egypt, reaching England many years afterwards in Athelstan's day. King Athelstan is said to have called an assembly of the aristocracy of the time to draw up the rules and regulations of the craft. These assume the existence of the three grades normally included in a medieval craft guild: the apprentice, learning his trade; the fellow, who has learned it and works

[1]The documents are numbered in the British Museum: *Bibl.Reg.17 A I* and *Add. MS. 23,198*.

as a journeyman; and the full master, employing or at any rate ordering and supervising the journeyman on a building operation.

The legendary content includes an account of the Quatuor Coronati, the four Christian stonemason martyrs, who were buried alive in leaden coffins and cast into the River Tiber after refusing to build a statue of the heathen god Aesculapius for the Emperor Diocletian. There are also many Biblical references and a reminder to the stonemason of his religious duties, together with instructions to those who might be ignorant of the customs of polite society. Finally, there comes a brief prayer.

The later manuscript versions of the narrative contain the same major elements of a legend or history, the craft regulations, including an injunction to secrecy, and a prayer. But none of the manuscripts mentions the legendary death of Hiram, the architect of King Solomon's temple, which is central to the ritual of the third degree of present-day Freemasonry, nor is Solomon's temple given any special prominence.

It is possible that the Old Charges, or parts of them, were read out to the stonemasons assembled in the lodge, and in this way they provided the germ of contemporary Masonic ritual. At all events, modern Freemasons claim to have inherited from the medieval stonemasons an organisation characterised by three grades of members, a unit called a lodge, a legendary history of the craft, a tradition of fraternal and benevolent relations between masons, and a rule of secrecy about what was discussed in the lodge.

Another factor which almost certainly contributed to the development of Masonic ceremonial was the Mason Word. This is the secret word given to a Master Mason at his 'raising' to the third degree. The candidate at this ceremony is made to represent Hiram Abiff during a re-enactment of the legendary murder of the temple's architect. He is given the word after he has been raised from a mock grave on the Five Points of Fellowship—hand to hand, foot to foot, knee to knee, breast to breast, and hand over back.

The word is Machaben or Machbinna, although at various times several versions have appeared in print: Mahabyn (the Sloane Manuscript, *circa* 1700); Matchpin (the Trinity College Dublin Manuscript, 1711); and Mahabone and Macbenach (Richard Carlile, *Manual of Freemasonry*, 1825).

It has been fairly well established that the Mason Word originated in Scotland[1] and that there was a process of question and answer whereby a mason showed that he possessed the Word and the secret associated with it. The secret was also connected with a legend. This is recounted in the Graham Manuscript which came to light at York in 1936 and, significantly, includes reference to the Mason Word. The date of the manuscript can be read as 1672 or 1726, and the latter is generally accepted as authentic. This is the grim tale the manuscript relates:

Shem, Ham and Japheth decided to go to their father Noah's grave for to try if they could find anything about him for to lead them to the vertuable [*sic*] secret which this famous preacher had.... Now these three men had already agreed that if they did not find the very thing itself that the first thing that they found was to be to them as a secret ... so came to the grave: finding nothing save the dead body almost consumed away, taking a grip at a finger, it came away: so from joint to joint, so to the wrist, so to the elbow. So they reared up the dead body and supported it, setting foot to foot, knee to knee, breast to breast, cheek to cheek, and hand to back ... so laid down the dead body again ... not knowing what to do. So one said 'Here is yet marrow in this bone' and the second said 'But a dry bone', and the third said 'It stinketh.' So they agreed for to give it a name as is known to freemasonry to this day.... Yet it is to be believed ... that the virtue did not proceed from what they found or how it was called but from faith and prayer.[2]

[1] *The Scottish Mason and the Mason Word*, D. Knoop and G. P. Jones, Manchester, 1939.
[2] *The Early Masonic Catechisms*, D. Knoop, G. P. Jones and D. Hamer, Manchester, 1943.

An interesting comparison with the legend of the Graham Manuscript is the conclusion of the Edinburgh Register House Manuscript of 1696, which reads as follows:

Question: How many points of the fellowship are there?
Answer: Five, viz. foot to foot, knee to knee, heart to heart, hand to hand, and ear to ear. Then make the sign of fellowship and shake hand and you will be acknowledged a true mason. The words are in the I of the Kings chapter 7 verse 21 and in II Chronicles chapter 3 verse last.

Both Bible references are parts of accounts of the building of King Solomon's temple. The verses mention the two pillars in the porch of the temple and give the name of the right-hand one as Jachin and that of the left pillar as Boaz. In the Craft rituals practised by Freemasons today the word Boaz is the secret word given to the candidate during initiation to the first degree and Jachin the secret word of the second degree.

The legend contained in the Old Charges—with either Noah or Hiram as the occupant of the grave—could provide a basis for ritual and allegory, and it is certain that some ceremonial accompanied the communication of the Word, or of different Words. These, then, are the two sources from which modern speculative Freemasonry might derive: an English element, the Old Charges; and a Scottish element, the Mason Word.

There is no doubt that the old Charges penetrated into Scotland. Versions of them, written in the second half of the seventeenth century, were possessed by lodges in Aberdeen, Dumfries, Kilwinning, Melrose and Stirling.[1] Also, the Mason Word penetrated into England. The English poet, Andrew Marvel, a friend of Milton, wrote in 1672 that 'those that have the mason's word secretly discern one another'.

Even so this is flimsy evidence upon which to support a direct lineal descent from medieval operative masonry to the contemporary speculative system. The conjectures ignore

[1] *A Handlist of Masonic Documents*, D. Knoop and G. P. Jones, Manchester, 1942.

the possibility that Scottish operative masonry may have had a philosophical or mystical content of its own, which owed nothing to the English Old Charges. More important, no satisfactory explanation emerges to show what attracted to groups of operative masons men who had little or nothing to do with the building trades.

In Scotland these honorary members were admitted at least as early as 1600. In London the terms 'accepted' and 'adopted' mason were in use as early as 1620. Elias Ashmole was initiated into Masonry in the lodge at Warrington in 1646 and among other prominent men known, or supposed, to have been made Freemasons were the third Randle Holme, the Chester antiquary and genealogist, and the first Duke of Richmond. Instances from Scotland include John Boswell, laird of Auchinlech, member of an Edinburgh lodge in 1600; and Alexander Seaton, brother of the Earl of Winton, made a mason at Aitchinson's Haven Lodge in 1672.

By 1686 Dr Robert Plott was able to write in his *Natural History of Staffordshire* that 'persons of the most eminent quality did not distain to be of this Fellowship' and that the custom of admitting men into Freemasonry 'spread more or less all over the Nation.' There is no reliable historical evidence, however, to support the popular belief that Sir Christopher Wren was a Freemason. Maybe after centuries of religious strife men in this country were glad to welcome the simple morality of Freemasonry expressed in the symbolism attached to the working tools of stonemasons. Psychologically, they may have been ripened for acceptance by the rise of seventeenth-century Deism, the widespread popularity of secret societies at this time and the emergence in London of the club. Nevertheless, the spread of Freemasonry remains an unexplained social phenomenon and one almost completely ignored by historians.

The growth of modern speculative Freemasonry was a gradual process. No doubt during the seventeenth century there were three classes of lodges, those that were purely operative, those with some accepted members, and the completely speculative lodges. By the early eighteenth century, however, the speculative lodges were in the majority and predominated in London. So it seems reasonable to regard seventeenth-century Freemasonry as a phase of development preceding today's speculative Freemasonry and to accept the foundation of the Grand Lodge of England on 24th June 1717 as the official birthday of Masonry as we know it.

Unfortunately, no minutes of that Grand Lodge exist before 1723, and so for six years of important history the main source of information is Dr James Anderson,[1] the son of an Aberdeen glazier who became a Presbyterian minister and a Freemason. Anderson claims that he was invited by Grand Lodge to digest the Old Charges and to issue them in a revised and improved form. From the modern point of view, his writing are uncritical and credulous. His book, *The Constitutions of the Freemasons*, was published in 1723 with a certain measure of approval from Grand Lodge, and may, therefore, be taken as presenting the official view of the history and tenets of Freemasonry at that time. The result of Anderson's efforts is described by Bernard E. Jones:

The Old MS Charges brought masonry, or geometry, from the children of Lamech to Solomon, and by various steps finally to England. But Anderson traces the art from Adam himself, who instructed his son Cain in geometry and made it possible for him to build a city. He introduces Noah and his sons and Grand Master Moses; he derives all civilized architecture from Solomon's temple; he traces the progress of the science through Greece and Sicily to its culmination in Rome. All knowledge of the art is lost in Britain after the Romans retired, but Charles Martel of France helps England to recover the true art after the Saxon invasions. Monarchs up to Elizabeth all advanced the art to the best of their ability, while Renaissance architecture, which he claims as having been introduced into England by James I, was return to a

[1]For an account of the founding of Grand Lodge and the career of James Anderson see *The Genesis of Freemasonry*, D. Knoop and G. P. Jones, Manchester, 1947.

model from which Gothic had been merely a barbarous lapse. And so forth.[1]

Changes or additions to the spurious ideas of Masonic genesis are hardly important compared with Anderson's most striking alteration, one very much in line with the Deism of the day. The Old Charges had instructed Masons to love God and the Holy Church. The first charge in Anderson's constitutions did not require Freemasons, as such, to hold any Trinitarian or even Christian belief:

'tis now thought more expedient only to oblige them to that Religion in which all Men agree, leaving their particular Opinions to themselves.

Anderson's book first appeared only eight years after the Jacobite rising of 1715, so he may also have been influenced by sharp memories of religious and political troubles when he wrote, and Grand Lodge approved:

our Politics is merely to be honest and our Religion the Law of Nature and to love God above all things, and our Neighbour as ourself; this is the true, primitive, catholic and universal Religion, agreed to be so in all Times and Ages.

The constitutions also place emphasis on charity, making it clear that the practice of the operative lodges in assisting the unemployed or otherwise needy brethren is to be continued by the speculative Freemason. Anderson states the duty in this way:

Behaviour towards a strange Brother . . . if he is in want, you must relieve him if you can, or else direct him how he may be relieved: You must employ him some Days, or else recommend him to be employed. But you are not charged to do so beyond your Ability, only to prefer a poor Brother, that is a good Man and true, before any other poor People in the same Circumstances.

[1]*Freemasons' Guide and Compendium.*

A second edition of Anderson's *Constitutions*, published in 1738, gives his account of the founding of the Grand Lodge of England. The event took place twenty-one years earlier and it is unlikely that Anderson is writing from first-hand knowledge. He describes how four lodges which met at London taverns, the Goose and Gridiron Alehouse in St Paul's Churchyard, the Crown Alehouse, Parker's Lane, the Apple Tree Tavern, Charles Street,[1] and the Rummer and Grapes Tavern, Channel Row, Westminster, held a joint meeting at the Apple Tree, in the year 1716. At that meeting the Grand Lodge was constituted and it was decided to hold an annual assembly to choose a Grand Master.

Accordingly, on St John the Baptist's Day, 24th June 1717, the assembly and feast of the Free and Accepted Masons was held at the Goose and Gridiron Alehouse. There the Grand Lodge was officially constituted and Antony Sayer was elected the first Grand Master. Grand Lodge's jurisdiction, as late as 1724, does not seem to have extended farther than ten miles from London. Yet, four years later, its authority was recognised by lodges as far from London as Carmarthen and Salford, and by 1728 there were subordinate Provincial Grand Lodges in Cheshire and South Wales. Recognition of Grand Lodge became widespread, though not universal, as it found the means to bring old lodges under its banner and regular ways by which new lodges could be brought into existence.

It may have been that Grand Lodge believed itself acting with a precedent when it established its annual meeting and feast. The Old Charges refer to annual or triennial assemblies[2] of operative stonemasons and the Roberts Manuscript of 1722 mentions that such an assembly had taken place in December 1663. At all events, the setting

---

[1] According to the *Masonic Record*, September 1966, the street is now called Wellington street and the tavern, is probably No. 28.
[2] *The Two Earliest Masonic Manuscripts*, D. Knoop, G. P. Jones and D. Hamer, Manchester, 1938.

up of a central authority and, more particularly, the revision of the Old Charges carried out by Anderson were to be turning-points.

The speculative Freemasonry which had begun to establish itself a century before now started to attract antiquaries and other learned men in considerable numbers. Significantly, perhaps, antiquarianism was a vogue in the early eighteenth century, and the present Society of Antiquaries was founded in the same year as Grand Lodge. Even more important for the spread of Freemasonry abroad, it had begun to take root among the military. Many military lodges were established and these were allowed to hold meetings wherever the regiment might be; from the eighteenth century Freemasonry follows the flag.

The influence of Anderson's *Constitutions* was also far-reaching. Editions of the books were soon in many countries. The earliest Irish constitutions (1730) were modelled on Anderson's work, and in 1735 his book was reprinted in America.

Anderson's use of Scots terms also made a permanent impression on masonic ritual, for he used the words 'Entered Apprentice' derived from the Scots practice of entering each apprentice in the records and also the term 'Fellow Craft' or 'Fellow of Craft', which he also took from Scots operative masonry, preferring it apparently to the English term 'Fellow'. The first degree in Freemasonry today initiates a man as an 'Entered Apprentice', the the second as a 'Fellow Craft', and the third as a 'Master Mason'.

It seems certain at the time of Anderson's first book of *Constitutions* most Lodges were working only two degrees, that of Initiate or Entered Apprentice and that of Fellow; neither was the equivalent of present-day Masonic degrees. Whatever these two degrees involved, it was not until the early eighteenth century that the third degree, with its symbolic re-enactment of the death of Hiram Abiff, began to emerge as a distinct and separate Masonic degree. Like so much of Freemasonry's history, even this crucial issue is obscure. The choice is to assume either that the original two degrees contained the foundations for the third, or that the third degree, as it now is, was an invention of the early eighteenth century.

Contemporary exposures of Masonic ritual reveal the existence of a separate third degree evolved around the Hiramic legend by 1730. The most important of these exposures was published in that year. It was *Masonry Dissected*, by Samuel Prichard, who described himself as 'late Member of a constituted Lodge'. Ironically enough, his exposure may have itself been one of the most important factors in the establishing of the third degree. His book was so successful it ran through three editions in eleven days, subsequently going through scores of editions in England, Ireland, America and on the Continent. Among Prichard's readers were thousands of Masons who until then had been entirely dependent upon a ritual handed down by word of mouth, for printed rituals from Masonic publishers, designed as *aides-mémoire*, were not allowed or tolerated until about the 1840s.

Prichard's book was the first publication to give details of the third degree, including an explanation of the raising of candidates from a mock grave on the Five Points of Fellowship. According to *Masonry Dissected*, when the grave of Hiram, the murdered master mason at King Solomon's temple, had been found, by Solomon's orders he was 'raised . . . as all other Masons are, when they receive the Master's Word. . . . By the Five Points of Fellowship. . . . Hand to hand, foot to foot, cheek to cheek, knee to knee, and hand in back'.

Grand Lodge was not only embarrassed by the disclosures, it was panicked; and in order to protect the lodges from intruders it decided to transpose the secret words of the first and second degrees. The resulting acrimony among Freemasons caused by this change and over existing differences of ritual and ceremonial practice was to sustain a bitter quarrel between rival Masonic factions over sixty years.

Other factors also contributed to the continuing controversy, which by 1751 had precipitated the establishment of a rival Grand Lodge. There were the strong local traditions of provincial lodges and the resentment of Grand Lodge's patronising attitudes. The new mobility in the eighteenth century brought to London Freemasons who were unaware of the alterations or angered by them. Many of the military lodges, meeting on foreign service, knew nothing of the changes, or preferred the old traditions.

Strong leadership from Grand Lodge might have resolved all the difficulties, but at the time it was incapable of envisaging, let along responding to, the problems which were being created.

The first Grand Master, Antony Sayer, gentleman, had hardly got off to a promising start. Often in financial difficulties, he has the distinction of being the first petitioner to Grand Lodge for relief. He was also arraigned before Grand Lodge for 'irregularities' and, although cleared of the charges, given a warning.

George Payne, the second and fourth Grand Master, was in better circumstances. When he died in 1757 he was Secretary of the Tax Office. His most notable contribution to Freemasonry had been the compiling of the General Regulations incorporated in Anderson's *Constitutions*.

The third Grand Master, Dr John Theophilus Desaguliers, was the son of a French Protestant minister, who fled to Guernsey to escape the persecution of Protestants in France and then later settled in England. Educated at Christ Church, Oxford, Desaguliers took orders in 1710, but his interests were scientific rather than clerical and four years later led to his election as a Fellow of the Royal Society. The association with Grand Lodge of such a man might be expected to exert a considerable influence on the Craft and so it did

With the arrival of Desaguliers, Freemasonry took on a new and broader outlook. A visit he paid to Edinburgh in 1721 may have played a part in the introduction of speculative Masonry into Scotland. But Desaguliers is more commonly remembered as the man responsible for the initiation of the first Royal Freemasons.

In 1731 he acted as Master of an Occasional Lodge at The Hague for the initiation of the Duke of Lorraine, afterwards German Emperor, Francis I. At the Palace of Kew, in 1737, he presided as Master of a Lodge at which Fredrick Lewis, Prince of Wales, was initiated. Royalty's interest in Freemasonry was established; and Sayer, Payne and Desaguliers were the only three men to become Grand Masters not of royal or noble birth.

The choice of Lord Byron, a great-uncle of the poet, as Grand Master in 1747 at the age of twenty-five was unfortunate in view of the disagreements over ritual and ceremonial practice which were coming to a head. At this critical time Lord Byron was to hold the office for five years and during that period to attend Grand Lodge on only three of the nine occasions on which it met.

Leadership of the rival Grand Lodge, certainly for its important first twenty years, was good. Among the early Grand Masters were the Earl of Blessington, a former Grand master of Ireland, and the third and fourth Dukes of Atholl, both of whom had been Grand Masters of Scotland. The new Grand Lodge's secretary in its second year, Laurence Dermottt, was a particularly remarkable character, full of words and energy.

An Irish journeyman painter with the gift of the gab, Dermott not only drew up a set of by-laws for private lodges, he issued in 1756 the constitutions of the rival Grand Lodge. These were printed under the extraordinary title of *Ahiman Rezon*, a result of Dermott's slight knowledge of Hebrew and in kindest translation assumed to mean 'Brother, Secret' or 'The Brother's Secret Monitor'. In the dedication of his book to the Earl of Blessington he appealed to Freemasons to support the new Grand Lodge as the defender of Freemasonry's 'ancient landmarks', a phrase meaning those principles of the Craft which are fixed and unalterable, but which Freemasonry has never officially defined.

Dermott also dubbed the original Grand Lodge, 'The Moderns': the rival Grand Lodge, pledged to resist the alterations to ritual, was truly the 'Antient' one. So to the conflicts of Freemasons at this time is added a confused terminology, further complicated by the advent of a compromise group some Masonic historians are pleased to call 'Traditioners'.

The long road to the reconciliation enshrined in the twenty-one Articles of Union, set out under the heading 'In the Name of the Great Architect of the Universe' and signed in 1813, is too devious to map here. Suffice to say that out of the protracted wrangle came the Craft degrees of Masonry as they now are, and the amalgamation of the two Grand Lodges to form 'The United Grand Lodge of Antient Free and Accepted Masons of England', known more simply to English Masons today as 'The Grand Lodge.'

CHAPTER III

A Guide to the Labyrinth

Modern lodges of Freemasons are private clubs whose members are pledged to ideals of brotherhood, morality and charity, but they also exist to perform the rituals of Masonry in which the movement's ideas are expressed within a series of dramatic initiation rites. Most lodges in England are primarily concerned with the three ceremonies leading to full membership of the lodge as a Master Mason and these lodges are described as Craft lodges. The initiation rituals practised by Craft lodges are known as the degrees of Craft Masonry and they are: the first, or Entered Apprentice degree; the second, or Fellow Craft degree; and the third, or Master Mason degree. Freemasons describe only the first ceremony as an initiation. In the official language of Masonry the lodges 'make' Masons, 'pass' them to the second degree, and 'raise' them to the third. At any one time an established and active Craft Lodge will have, in addition to its officers, three grades of ordinary members: a few Apprentices and Fellow Crafts, and a majority of Master Masons.

Most Craft lodges in the provinces meet in the Masonic Halls to be seen in the High Street of almost every town and these buildings contain temples reserved for the ceremonies and formal meetings of the lodges. In London some lodges meet at Freemasons' Hall, the movement's headquarters in Great Queen Street, and many others gather in hotels and restaurants which have Masonic temples for hire. Every regularly constituted lodge in Britain holds a charter, or warrant, from a Grand Lodge in which is invested the authority to govern the craft as practised by the lodges under its control. Britain has three Grand Lodges, those of England, Scotland

and Ireland. There is no Grand Lodge of Wales. Craft lodges are also grouped into Provinces and each has a Provincial Grand Lodge.

When a man is admitted to Freemasonry in England the Master of his Craft lodge shows him the lodge's warrant and presents him with a copy of the lodge's by-laws and the book of the Constitutions of the Grand Lodge of England. Later on in the ceremony the candidate is told:

Your fidelity must be exemplified by a strict observance of the Constitutions of the Fraternity, by adhering to the ancient land-marks of the Order, by never attempting to extort or otherwise unduly obtain the secrets of a superior degree, and by refraining from recommending anyone to a participation of our secrets unless you have strong grounds to believe that by a similar fidelity he will ultimately reflect honour on your choice. Your obedience must be proved by a strict observance of our laws and regulations, by prompt attention to all signs and summonses, by modest and cor-rect demeanour in the Lodge, by abstaining from every topic of political or religious discussion, by a ready acquiescence in all votes and resolutions duly passed by a majority of the brethren, and by perfect submission to the Master and his Wardens whilst acting in the discharge of their respective offices.

The phrase 'the ancient landmarks of the Order' is a confusing one to the Freemason as well as to the outsider. Briefly, it means those beliefs and practices which are essen-tial to the true character of the movement. For example, the stipulation made by British Freemasonry that only candidates are acceptable whose religious beliefs, while not perhaps embracing Christianity, extend at least to the acknowledge-ment of a Supreme Being. All British Freemasons profess adherence to these basic beliefs and practices called land-marks and the Constitutions of the English Grand Lodge state:

The Grand Lodge possesses the supreme superintending authority, and alone has the inherent power of enacting laws and regulations for the government of the Craft, and of altering, repealing, and abrogating them, always taking care that the ancient landmarks of the Order be preserved.

The problem is that the landmarks have never been defined officially and the only thing that can be said with surety is that, by negative definition, a landmark is any aspect of Masonry which Grand Lodge cannot change. In fact, experienced Masons differ about what is or is not a landmark, and the uncertainty surrounding this important question is such that the most trivial suggestions for changes within Masonry are liable to prompt the charge that the landmarks are in danger.

While the Constitutions of the Grand Lodge of England virtually ignore this matter, they set out in considerable detail the powers of the Grand Master and how the lodges under the authority of Grand Lodge will be conducted. To carry out the business of Masonry in England, Grand Lodge meets four times a year and reports of its proceedings and resulting instructions are sent to the secretaries of member lodges. At these quarterly meetings, however, Grand Lodge may not discuss any resolution the Grand Master judges contrary to the landmarks.

Government of the Craft is conservative. The supreme figure in national Masonic jurisdictions is the Grand Master of his country's Grand Lodge and the only time his authority has ever been challenged has been on those occasions when division among Masons has been so acute as to lead to the establishment of rival Grand Lodges. The Grand Master is addressed with the prefix Most Worshipful; ordinary lodge Masters are merely Worshipful Master. No regulations exist to deal with a Grand Master who abuses his extensive authority, the Constitutions provide that these can be made should it be found necessary. The rule adds that 'the Ancient Fraternity have had no reason to provide for an event which they have presumed would never happen'.

The Grand Master is nominated in December each year and elected at the next quarterly meeting of Grand Lodge in March, but often the annual election is a mere formality.

Lengthy tenures of this high office are the rule rather than the exception in England, and English Freemasons are disposed to look for their leader among men of the Royal Family or from those aristocratic families with which the Crown is closely associated. The list of English Grand Masters elected in this century begins with Prince Arthur, Duke of Connaught and Strathearn, who resigned in 1939 after holding office for thirty-eight years.[1] The next three Grand Masters held office until their deaths: Prince George, Duke of Kent, 1939–42; the sixth Earl of Harewood, 1942–7; and the tenth Duke of Devonshire, 1947–50. The eleventh Earl of Scarbrough was installed in 1951 and stepped aside sixteen years later when the Duke of Kent became the tenth Grand Master since the formation of the United Grand Lodge in 1813.

The installation of the Grand Master takes place at the annual Grand Festival, usually held on the first Wednesday following St George's Day.[2] The customary setting for the ceremony is the Grand Temple in Freemasons' Hall, where a dais provides accommodation for some 500 Grand Officers and there is also seating for about 1,500 members. (Freemasons' Hall is conveniently close to one of London's largest banqueting suites, appropriately styled The Connaught Rooms.) Once in the Chair, the Grand Master appoints the following Grand Officers:

Deputy Grand Master
Assistant Grand Master (or Masters)
Two Grand Wardens
Two Grand Chaplains
Grand Registrar

---

[1] A record reign over the English Grand Lodge, but the third Duke of Leinster was Ireland's Grand master for over 60 years, 1813–74.
[2] The old crafts and guilds had their patron saints and many ancient lodges held their summer festival on St John the Baptist's Day and their winter festival on St John the Evangelist's Day. The United Grand Lodge of England held its first meeting on St John the Evangelist's Day 1813, but subsequently adopted St George's Day, 23rd April, or a date conveniently near to it. Scotland's Freemasons install their Grand Master on St Andrew's Day, 30th November.

Deputy Grand Registrar
President of the Board of General Purposes
President of the Board of Benevolence
Grand Director of Ceremonies
Twelve Grand Deacons
Grand Sword Bearer
Deputy Grand Directors of Ceremonies
Two Assistant Grand Chaplains
Two Assistant Grand Registrars
Grand Superintendent of Works
Two Assistant Grand Superintendents of Works
Twelve Assistant Grand Directors of Ceremonies
Deputy Grand Sword Bearer
Two Assistant Grand Sword Bearers
Two Grand Standard Bearers
Six Assistant Grand Standard Bearers
Grand Organist
Grand Pursuivant
Four Assistant Grand Pursuivants
Nineteen Grand Stewards[1]

Provision is also made in the Constitutions for the Grand Master, if a Prince of the Blood Royal, to nominate a Pro Grand Master, who must be a Peer of the Realm. The Grand Secretary is appointed by the Grand Master to continue in office until retirement, so long as he pleases Grand Lodge; but the Grand Treasurer is elected annually. It is also open to the Grand Master to appoint additional Assistant Grand Masters, a Deputy Grand Secretary, an Assistant Grand Secretary, a Deputy Grand Organist and an Assistant Grand Secretary for Foreign Correspondence.

Conferment of the rank of Past Grand Officer is within the Grand Master's authority and he may also appoint to London

---

[1]They are nominated annually by each of nineteen London lodges, known as 'Red Apron Lodges'. Their main job is to organise the Grand Festival at which the Grand Master is installed, a privilege for which they pay. The Grand Officers contribute the balance, for the Constitutions say that no expense for the Festival shall fall on Grand Lodge.

Grand Rank past Masters of London lodges, those lodges that meet within ten miles of Freemasons' Hall. So there is an elaborate pecking order of rank and precedence among members of Grand Lodge covering some seventy grades of current and past office-holders and at the end of the list come the Masters, Past Masters and Wardens of lodges under the Grand Lodge. The personal power of the Grand Master to patronise and control is not confined within Grand Lodge. He may designate any area of England a Masonic Province and appoint Provincial Grand Masters to serve 'during his pleasure'. These nominees exercise power of appointment within the Provincial Grand Lodge where the membership consists of present and past officers, the Masters, Wardens and Past Masters of lodges included in the Province.

New Craft lodges may be founded only after petition to the Grand Master supported by an established lodge and, where required, approval must be obtained from the Provincial Grand Lodge. Precedence among lodges is determined by the order of their numbers as registered by the Grand Lodge and the name or title of private lodges may not be altered without approvals from the Grand Master and Provincial Grand Master. Lodge warrants are the property of the Grand Master and are to be produced at every lodge meeting. The Master of a lodge is not permitted to hold a meeting without the warrant[1] and, if it is lost, must suspend all meetings until a new authority is forthcoming from the Grand Master.

Regular officers under a lodge Master in order of precedence are: Senior Warden, Junior Warden, Treasurer, Secretary, Senior Deacon, Junior Deacon, Inner Guard, and Tyler (outer guard). The Master and the Treasurer are elected each year and so may be the Tyler. The other offices are within the patronage of the Master. The lodge Master may also appoint as additional officers a Chaplain, a Director of Ceremonies, an Assistant Director of Ceremonies, an Almoner, an Organist,

[1] With the exception of two lodges operating under 'immemorial constitutions'—the Lodge of Antiquity, No. 2, and the Royal Somerset House and Inverness Lodge, No. 4.

an Assistant Secretary, and a Steward or Stewards.

No Mason can become the Master of his lodge unless he has already served either as Senior or Junior warden, and, before he is placed in the Chair, he solemnly promises to preserve the landmarks and to observe 'the ancient usages and established customs'. A lodge Master, unlike the Grand Master, may hold office for two consecutive years only; but can be elected again after being out of office for one year.

The Tyler, or outer guard, must be a Master Mason, though not necessarily a member of the lodge, and it is this provision which enables many hotels and restaurants to hire a temple and the services of a Tyler to Freemasons. The Constitutions also permit lodges to initiate men as 'serving brothers'. Such men are excused fees, can be raised to Master Mason, and are frequently employed as Tyler; but they can only become full lodge members after election and by paying the same fees as initiates.

Discontent arises from time to time over the appointment of officers to Grand Lodges and within the private lodges. Freemasonry's paid officials are said by some Masons to be overpaid and to have an inflated view of their own importance—despite the wide powers given them by the Constitutions. The most relevant objection appears to be the fact that the Constitutions can place the lodge Master in some difficulty if he puts the greater interest of his lodge above the risk of becoming unpopular with a few members whom he declines to appoint to office. In fact, although no advancement can be claimed as a matter of right, it is customary in lodges for the longest-serving brother not yet in office to be made a steward and for each officer to be promoted to the next senior office.

The system, aptly described as the taxi-rank principle, means that dissension and suspicion of favouritism are avoided and a tradition observed. American Freemasons are less traditionally minded and a report to the Grand Lodge of Tennessee said:

This insidiously detrimental custom has prevented the membership of lodges from electing any of their officers. Any institution, religious, commercial or fraternal, thus governed is heading for trouble. In our opinion this has been the greatest factor in causing a lack of good leadership in our Lodges, which is resulting in poor interest and in poor attendances, simply because such leaders fail to furnish their Lodges with the inspiration of an active, wide-awake programme.

Reactions to the suggestion from America varied. The English *Masonic Record* in July 1964 commented:

We are not in favour of substituting the election by lodges of all officers for the discretion now exercised by the Master. In general, the system works reasonably well and there could be dangers in replacing it by election.

Unfortunately, the leader writer of the magazine did not go on to comment on what might be the English interpretation of an 'active, wide-awake' Masonic programme. The *Masonic Journal of South Africa* favoured the American report:

If the practice of automatic ladder promotion of officers must be discarded in order to obtain the kind of leadership we should have, then by all means let us discard the foolish custom. There is nothing in the winning of an endurance contest, in itself, that qualifies a man to be Master of his Lodge. If the so-called 'line' of officers must be shortened to enable men of ability to serve their Lodges without devoting six or seven years to minor offices, then what are we waiting for? Why not shorten the line?

In practice, the promotion problem for ordinary Masons is an important factor in the founding of new lodges. When a lodge has grown to seventy or eighty members it can be a long time before the younger Master Masons get a chance to take part in the ceremonies themselves, and in these circumstances a number of Past Masters usually take the initiative and found a new lodge.

Lodges provide central funds for Masonry by meeting the Grand Lodge registration and capitation fees; but Craft lodges fix their own membership subscriptions and fees for initiation.

Appointment to office or rank within the Grand Lodge or any of the provincial Grand Lodges involves the payment of fees to the Fund of Benevolence.

To become a Freemason a man is required to be twenty-one years of age and in reputable circumstances. A younger man may be admitted if the Grand Master or provincial Grand Master agrees. Lodge members must ballot to decide whether or not to initiate a man as a Mason. Each lodge member is given a black and a white ball with which to vote and files past a ballot box in which there is a hole large enough for him to thrust through a hand and to drop a ball onto a tray. When all the members have voted the tray is pulled out to reveal the result. Membership is refused the candidate if three black balls appear against him or, if so stipulated in the lodge by-laws, two black balls, or one black ball. Lodge by-laws may also allow the possibility at a future date of re-application and another ballot. English lodges are not permitted to initiate more than two candidates at a time and may carry out only one of the three initiation rituals with the same candidates on the same day. Given special authority, however, important people can always be hustled to the top as Master of a Craft lodge, or even to the leadership as Grand Master. The fourth Duke of Atholl of the Antient Grand Lodge, the rival organisation to the English Grand Lodge of the eighteenth century, had such a swift ascent to power. He was initiated, passed, raised, installed Master of Grand Master's Lodge, and elected Grand Master all within four days. Normally, there is at least a month's delay between a candidate's initiation and passing to the second degree and a further month until he is raised to Master Mason.

The Constitutions do not stipulate whether lounge suits or evening dress will be worn in the lodge. Dark suits are now customary and the wearing of white gloves widely favoured. Grand Lodge, however, does lay down every detail of dimension, colour and decoration of the aprons worn by Masons. These must be made of plain white lambskin and during the ceremony of initiation the candidate receives his first Masonic apron from the Senior Warden. It is presented with the words:

'I invest you with the distinguishing badge of a Mason. It is more ancient than the Golden Fleece or Roman Eagle, more honorable than the Garter or any other Order in existence, being the badge of innocence and the bond of friendship.' As he progresses in Masonry, the Freemason's collection of aprons grows by the addition of a different one for each grade of membership within the Craft lodge and, possibly, for elevation to the ranks of Master and Past Master of the lodge. Further adornments and aprons indicate past or present Grand ranks.

Similarly comprehensive regulations from Grand Lodge govern the jewels, chains, collars and gauntlets of office and rank, also the protocol concerning the occasions on which they are to be worn. Once Masonic parades through the streets were fairly commonplace, but today Masonic dress may not be worn in public without a dispensation from the Grand Master.

A Freemason is at liberty to resign from his lodge at any time. He may do so in writing, or simply state his intention at a regular meeting of the lodge; and, if he does not pay his subscription for three years, he is automatically lapsed. Lodges with fewer than five subscribing members may be wound up by the Grand Master and so may those lodges whose members fail to meet for one year. Masons who break any of the regulations laid down in the Constitutions may be admonished or suspended; Grand Lodge alone has the power to expel Masons and to erase lodges.

No figures are available to the outsider, or to most Free-masons, about the number of men in the movement. The Grand Lodge of England publishes a *Year Book*, which it circulates to lodge secretaries and members may see it on application; but this merely lists the lodges which acknowledge the authority of Grand Lodge. Unfortunately, the size of Masonry's membership cannot be calculated from the total number of lodges in existence, for each lodge has a varying number of members and any Freemason may join as many lodges as he can afford and as will accept him.

A monthly magazine for Freemasons in England, the *Masonic Record*, reported in May 1964 that during the past ten years the number of lodges on the register of the Grand Lodge rose from 6,640 to 7,110; and that individual membership certificates issued in 1954 totalled 21,000, compared with the average for the following years up to 1963 of approximately 20,000. The figures clearly suggest that more men are becoming Freemasons, but whether or not they are joining lodges in England is another question. Grand Lodge has upon its register about 800 lodges in countries overseas.

In the absence of detailed figures from Britain's Grand Lodges, the statistics published in America by *The Fraternal Monitor* may seem exaggerated, but they are the only ones available. In 1951 *The Fraternal Monitor* gave the number of Freemasons in England and Wales as 550,000; Scotland, 400,000; Ireland, 47,000; Canada, 218,000; Australasia, 300,000; the United States, 3,597,810; and total world membership, 5,200,000. These figures have been widely quoted during the past few years, but usually with modifications of the membership figure for Scotland, as this seems unbelievably high. The *Sunday Express*[1] in a report on Freemasonry compiled by four writers said that 'in England and Wales there are more than 500,000 Freemasons; in Scotland more than 250,000.' An American magazine, the *Empire State Mason*[2] said that there were 300,000 Freemasons in Scotland.

The evidence of the *Fraternal Monitor* and of the Masonic press favours the conclusion that world membership of Freemasonry is increasing. The *Fraternal Monitor*'s figures for the years 1964 and 1965 were the same as follows: United States, 4,000,000; Canada, 250,000; Latin America, 50,000; Australasia, 375,000; Philippines, 10,500; England and Wales, 550,000; Scotland, 400,000; Ireland, 47,000; Continental Europe, 65,000; and total world membership, 6,000,000.

These figures have gone into the cuttings libraries of the media and have been widely quoted even since this book was first published. Sometimes they form the basis of revised statistics

[1] 25th October 1964.
[2] March/April 1963.

which are estimates made on the assumption that the number of Freemasons has been steadily increasing in Britain.[1] Stephen Knight in his book, *The Brotherhood*,[2] says that in the United Kingdom there are some 700,000 Freemasons; 600,000 in England and Wales, a further 100,000 in Scotland and between 50,000 and 70,000 in Ireland. The figure for England and Wales is attributed to 'official Masonic estimates'.

Strangely, since 1966 membership figures have disappeared from the Masonic press[3] and the latest reliable information about the numbers of Freemasons and their lodges in England and Wales was given by the United Grand Lodge of England to a working group of the General Synod of the Church of England. The group was told that in 1985 there was 8,253 lodges and some 320,000 members, and that statistics of membership needed to be handled with some care since individual Freemasons may be members of more than one lodge. The other source of statistics is a leaflet published by the Grand Lodge of Free & Accepted Masons of the State of New York which has 136,000 members in over 800 lodges. The leaflet in use in 1989 revealed that there were three million members in 14,000 lodges in the United States and about four million Masons and more than a hundred Grand Lodges worldwide.

Although numbers have declined dramatically there can be no doubt that Freemasonry continues to exert an important influence across the world and not least upon a great many men in England. Here the movement has drawn to it many men of power and influence in business and the professions, and the favourable attentions of the Royal Family. English Freemasonry's connection with the Royal Family dates back to 1737, when Prince Frederick, father of George III and then Prince of Wales, was initiated. The Act of Union between

[1] One notable exception, the *Economist*, 2 July 1988, gave the number of Britain's Freemasons as well over 200,000.
[2] Granada Publishing, 1984. The author died in 1985 from cancer, aged 33.
[3] Apart from those given by the Earl of Scarbrough at the Installation of the Duke of Kent as Grand Master of the United Grand Lodge of England in 1967. In his address the Earl said that there were more than five million Freemasons in all parts of the world and 'Our Brethren exceed 600,000 men'.

England's two rival Grand Lodges was achieved, in 1813, under Royal leadership and it founded the present United Grand Lodge of England. Down the centuries Masonry in England has had Royal patronage and, more recently, leadership. Among the Grand Masters of the past are:

Grand Lodge of England 1717–1813

1782–1790	H R H Henry Frederick, Duke of Cumberland
1790–1813	H R H The Prince of Wales (later George IV)
1813	H R H Augustus Frederick, Duke of Sussex

Atholl, or Antient Grand Lodge 1753–1813

1813	H R H Edward, Duke of Kent

United Grand Lodge of England

1813	H R H the Duke of Sussex
1874–1901	H R H the Prince of Wales (afterwards King Edward VII)
1901–1939	H R H the Duke of Connaught and Strathearn
1939–1942	H R H the Duke of Kent

The rank of Past Grand Master is sometimes conferred honorarily, but so far only upon Royalty.

Past Grand Masters

1869	H R H the Prince of Wales (afterwards King Edward VII)
1888	H M King Oscar II of Sweden
1891	H R H the Duke of Connaught and Strathearn
1897	H R H the Crown Prince (afterwards King Frederick VIII) of Denmark
1936	H M King Edward VIII (later H R H the Duke of Windsor)
1937	H M King George VI
1946	H M King Christian X of Denmark
1947	H M King Gustaf V of Sweden

The latest Royal recruit is the Duke of Kent, who in 1967 succeeded the Earl of Scarbrough as Grand Master of the United Grand Lodge of England. Some doubt exists about the lodge in which the Duke of Kent was initiated into Freemasonry. The *Sunday Telegraph*[1] reported:

He has joined the Grand Master's Lodge, No.1. whose Master is the Earl of Scarbrough, Grand Master of the United Grand Lodge of England and until last year Lord Chamberlain of the Queen's Household. It is significant that the Duke, at present serving in Germany as adjutant of the Royal Scots Greys, should be a member of a lodge consisting largely of Masonic grandees.

The *Daily Telegraph*[2] said that the Duke 'has joined the Royal Alpha Lodge, No. 16, which was founded in Iver and has links with the Royal Family stretching back for many years'. According to Masonic historian Norman Knight the *Daily Telegraph* was right: 'The Duke was initiated in the Royal Alpha Lodge on 16th December, 1963; passed to second degree 30th January, 1964 and raised to third degree 4th May, 1964.' Since 1843 candidates for admission to this lodge have needed the approval of the Grand Master. While Prince of Wales and Grand Master, Edward VII initiated his son Albert Victor in the lodge (1885) and Prince Arthur of Connaught was initiated in 1911.

No doubt, the involvement of Royalty has greatly assisted Freemasonry to recruit among the aristocracy, the Armed Forces, the legal and medical professions, churchmen and businessmen.

Apart from the secrecy which surrounds Freemasonry in England, for no outsider is permitted to watch the ceremonies of a Craft lodge, it would seem that an important attraction

[1] 16th August 1964.
[2] 17 August 1964.

of the movement is its eminent, and eminently respectable, leadership. The less-privileged man joining Masonry may be disappointed if he expects to hobnob with the leaders and distinguished members of the order. This is possible, particularly as Freemasons may visit each other's lodges and visiting is one of the popular aspects of membership with some Freemasons; on the other hand, to be accepted into the higher ranks and lodges of the Craft requires influential friends, and money.

The initiation of the present Duke of Kent illustrated that the Craft lodges of England are of differing status. Alpha Lodge, one that the Duke is reported to have joined, has traditional associations with the Royal Family. It was founded only five years after the establishment of the first Grand Lodge and most members are of the Masonic hierarchy. There are other lodges of special antiquity or standing; one consists largely of former Lord Mayors of London. Even particular communities of interest are represented. There are university lodges and military lodges. Masons who are Methodists can join the Epworth lodges, named after John Wesley's birthplace, Epworth Rectory. For historians the leading lodge of Masonic research is Quatuor Coronati Lodge.

It is freely admitted that progress in Masonry depends upon money. In answer to the question: 'How far should I go in Freemasonry?' the *Masonic Record* advised readers:[1]

Every brother is entitled to, and must, make his own decision and in the light of his own circumstances. He must consider how much time he can devote to Freemasonry without detriment to family, business and his other commitments. The more he progresses in Freemasonry the greater will be the demands on his pocket and he must decide whether he can meet these extra financial obligations.

The additional money is needed for further initiation fees, subscriptions, and charity donations.

If Masonry is regarded purely as a charitable club, its organisation is fantastically wasteful. If it is simply a society

[1]June 1964.

of men interested in preservation and performance of rituals, its membership is remarkably large. No doubt both charity and ritual are important aspects of modern Freemansonry; but they do not seem sufficient to comprise the whole purposes of a movement attracting such a variety of men in such large numbers.

CHAPTER IV

Inside the Temple

The essentials of a Masonic temple are not difficult to provide. Early English Craft Freemasons met in tavern rooms and their lodge properties were few. A pedestal for the Master was flanked by two candles rising from candlesticks placed upon the floor. The lodge Bible lay open on the Master's pedestal and members stood while candidates were initiated. Later, during the lectures to the candidates, which today still account for a lot of ceremonial time, they sat around a table with candles on it. Sometimes they smoked and ate and drank during the ceremonies.

During each of the three contemporary Craft initiation ceremonies a formal lecture is related to a picture composed of Masonic symbols and called a tracing board. There is a different tracing-board lecture for each degree; the appropriate tracing board is laid on the lodge floor for each degree being worked. Early English Masons frequently called upon their Tyler to draw these illustrations in chalk or charcoal on the floor and, after the ceremony, the candidate was presented with a mop and bucket to wipe off the marks.

None of this easy informality remains in lodge procedure today, and the Masonic temple now expresses traditions. The layout and furnishings of the Masonic temples of Craft lodges are described in some detail by the first tracing-board lecture, sometimes given to the candidate at the end of the initiation ceremony, and for further information I have relied upon the photographs to be found in Masonic books and journals.

Like churches, Masonic temples are supposed to face east and west and where this is not possible it is assumed that the Master's chair and pedestal are in the 'east' and the other sides of the room referred to by the relative compass points. The lodge's Past Masters and the Senior Deacon also sit in the east. The immediate past Master is on the left of the Master and the Senior Deacon on the Master's right. Alongside the Master's pedestal is a candlestick and his candle must be burning when the lodge is open. In front of the pedestal is a kneeling stool for candidates taking the Masonic oaths of secrecy. The Master's chair and pedestal are designed to suggest the Ionic order of architecture and the front of the pedestal bears the Master's emblem, the square. Upon the pedestal, resting upon a cushion, is an open Bible, known to Masons as 'the Volume of the Sacred Law'. Alongside it are other items, including a square and compasses, a gavel and an Ionic column.

The other lodge members sit along the north, south and west sides of the room. Most of the floor is covered by a large carpet of black and white chequer-board pattern, referred to as 'the Mosaic pavement'. Around the chequered pattern is an indented, or tessellated, border, sometimes with tassels in the corners. The variegated design of the pavement is said to allude both to the uncertainty of all things on earth and to the variety of Creation, in this way speaking to the Freemason of the need for humility, unity and brotherly love.

Either in the centre of the floor or on the ceiling is a 'blazing star' and, hanging from or above the star, the letter 'G', denoting Great Architect of the Universe and the Grand Geometrician of the Universe. The star is emblematic of the sun and the tessellated border of the pavement of the planets which revolve around it.

In the west, opposite the Grand Master, sits the Senior Warden, whose chair and pedestal are Doric. His emblem of office upon the front of the pedestal is the level. In front of him he has a gavel and a Doric column, which is vertical when the lodge is open and horizontal when it is closed. Alongside the Senior Warden's pedestal is a candlestick and, either set before or on the pedestal, the perfect ashlar, a smooth cube of stone hung from a triangular support. The Senior Warden, with the Junior Deacon on his right, is close by the door into the temple. This is always set in the north-west corner and opens from an ante-room. By the door stands the Inner Guard, and the Tyler, or outer guard, remains in the ante-room.

The Junior Warden sits in the south and his chair and pedestal are Corinthian. He, too, has a candlestick and his emblem of office is the plumb-rule. He also has a gavel and a Corinthian column which is placed on its side when the lodge is open and left upright when it has closed. In front of the Junior Warden is the rough ashlar, an unevenly surfaced block of stone usually supported on a column.

The lodge secretary sits in the north with a table in front of him, and on this may be the broken column, a Masonic version of the collection plate. Many lodges embellish their ceremonies with music and an organ is usually placed either in the north-west or the south-west corner.

There is Masonic terminology for the paraphernalia of the temple. The Bible is the 'Volume of the Sacred Law'; the square and compasses are known as 'the central ornaments of the lodge' and are also described in the initiation ceremony as 'the three great, though emblematical, lights in Freemasonry'. In the words used by the Master during the first degree ceremony: 'The Sacred Writings are to govern our faith, the Square to regulate our actions, and the Compasses to keep us in due bounds with all mankind, particularly our brethren in Freemasonry.' Later on in the tracing-board lecture, if it is given, he declares: 'The Sacred Volume is derived from God to man in general, the Compasses belong to the Grand Master in particular, and the Square to the whole Craft.'

The jewels of office of the Master, the Senior Warden, and the Junior Warden, are miniature replicas of the square, the level and the plumb-rule, and are officially referred to as 'the movable jewels', being transferred on installation days. The tracing board, and the rough and perfect ashlars, are termed 'the immovable jewels'.

The rough ashlar represents the natural man, rough and uneducated, and is for the Entered Apprentice Mason to work on with the chisel, emblematic tool of discipline and education. The perfect ashlar, smooth and die square ready to form part of a sound wall, symbolises the mature, cultured and educated man. The method of supporting the perfect ashlar provides another piece of Masonic symbolism, for inserted into the top of the stone is a lewis, a form of grapnel, by which a hoisting chain is conveniently attached to a stone block. The lewis is said to represent the son of a Freemason and is a symbol of strength. A morbid interpretation of the perfect ashlar is the worthy Mason being lowered to rest by his son at the close of a well-spent life.

The lecture relating to the first tracing board says a lot about the temple which is at the centre of Masonic symbolism and at one time contained many other ornaments: beehives representing thrift and industry; the sickle, mortality; and Jacob's ladder, faith, hope and charity. The speech weaves a fantastic web of historical associations and near-mystical exhortations around the comparatively simple room and its furnishings.

'The usages and customs among Freemasons have ever borne a near affinity to those of the ancient Egyptians. Their philosophers, unwilling to expose their mysteries to vulgar eyes, couched their systems of learning and polity under signs and hieroglyphical figures, which were communicated to their chief priest or Magi alone, who were bound by solemn oath to conceal them. The system of Pythagoras was founded on a similar principle, as well as many others of more recent date. Masonry, however, is not only the most ancient but the most honourable society that ever existed, as there is not a character or emblem here depicted but serves to inculcate the principles of piety and virtue among all its genuine professors.

'Let me first call your attention to the form of the Lodge, which is a parallelopipedon, in length from East to West, in breadth between North and South, in depth from the surface of the earth to the centre, and even as high as the heavens. The reason a Freemasons' Lodge is described of this vast extent is to show the universality of the science; likewise a Mason's charity should know no bounds save those of prudence.

'Our Lodges stand on holy ground, because the first Lodge was consecrated on account of three grand offerings thereon made, which met with Divine approbation. First, the ready compliance of Abraham with the will of God in not refusing to offer up his son Issac as a burnt sacrifice, when it pleased the Almighty to substitute a more agreeable victim in his stead. Secondly, the many pious prayers and ejaculations of King David, which actually appeased the wrath of God and stayed a pestilence which then raged among his people, owing to his inadvertently having them numbered. Thirdly, the many thanksgivings, oblations, burnt sacrifices, and costly offerings, which Solomon, King of Israel, made at the completion, dedication, and consecration of the Temple at Jerusalem to God's service. Those three did then, do now, and I trust ever will, render the ground of Freemasonry holy.

'Our Lodges are situated due East and West, because all places of Divine worship as well as Masons' regular, well formed, constituted Lodges are, or ought to be, so situated: for which we assign three Masonic reasons: first, the Sun, the Glory of the Lord, rises in the East and sets in the West; second, learning originated in the East and thence spread its benign influence to the West; the third, last and grand reason, which is too long to be entered upon now, is explained in the course of our Lectures, which I hope you will have many opportunities of hearing.

'Our Lodges are supported by three great pillars. They are called Wisdom, Strength, and Beauty: Wisdom to contrive, Strength to support, and Beauty to adorn: Wisdom to conduct us in all our undertakings, Strength to support us under all our difficulties, and Beauty to adorn the inward man. The Universe is the Temple of the Deity whom we serve; Wisdom, Strength and Beauty are about His throne as pillars of His works, for His Wisdom is infinite, His Strength omnipotent, and Beauty shines through the whole

71

of the creation in symmetry and order. The Heavens He has stretched forth as a canopy; the earth He has planted as a footstool; He crowns His Temple with Stars as with a Diadem and with His hand He extends the Power and Glory. The Sun and Moon are messengers of His Will, and all His Law is concord. The three great pillars supporting a Freemasons' Lodge are emblematic of those Divine attributes and further represent Solomon King of Israel, Hiram King of Tyre, and Hiram Abiff. Solomon King of Israel for his Wisdom in building, completing and dedicating the Temple at Jerusalem to God's service; Hiram King of Tyre for his Strength in supporting him with men and materials; and Hiram Abiff for his curious and masterly workmanship in beautifying and adorning the same. But as we have no noble orders of Architecture known by the names of Wisdom, Strength, and Beauty, we refer them to the three most celebrated, which are the Ionic, Doric and Corinthian.

'The covering of a Freemasons' Lodge is a celestial canopy of divers colours, even the Heavens. The way by which we, as Masons, hope to arrive there is by the assistance of a ladder, in Scripture called Jacob's ladder. It is composed of many staves or rounds, which point out as many moral virtues, but three principal ones, which are Faith, Hope, and Charity: Faith in the Great Architect of the Universe, Hope in salvation, and to be in Charity with all men. It reaches to the Heavens, and rests on the Volume of the Sacred Law, because, by the doctrines contained in that Holy Book, we are taught to believe in the dispensations of Divine Providence, which belief strengthens our faith, and enables us to ascend the first step; this Faith naturally creates in us a Hope of becoming partakers of the blessed promises therein recorded, which Hope enables us to ascend the second step; but the third and last, being Charity, comprehends the whole, and the Mason who is possessed of this virtue in its most ample sense may justly be deemed to have attained the summit of his profession; figuratively speaking, an Ethereal Mansion, veiled from mortal eyes by the starry firmament, emblematically depicted here by

72

seven stars, which have an allusion to as many regularly made Masons, without which number no Lodge is perfect, neither can any Candidate be legally initiated into the Order.

'The interior of a Freemasons' Lodge is composed of Ornaments, Furniture and Jewels. The Ornaments of the Lodge are the Mosaic pavement, the Blazing Star and the Indented or Tessellated border; the Mosaic pavement is the beautiful flooring of the Lodge, the Blazing Star the Glory in the centre and the indented or Tessellated Border, the skirtwork round the same. The Mosaic pavement may justly be deemed the beautiful flooring of a Freemasons' Lodge, by reason of it being variegated and chequered. This points out the diversity of objects which decorate and adorn the creation, the animate as well as the inanimate parts thereof. The Blazing Star, or Glory in the centre, refers us to the Sun, which enlightens the earth, and by its benign influence dispenses its blessings to mankind in general. The indented or Tessellated Border refers us to the Planets, which in their various revolutions form a beautiful border or skirtwork round that Grand Luminary, the Sun, as the other does round that of a Freemasons' Lodge. The Furniture of the Lodge consists of the Volume of the Sacred Law, the Compasses and Square; the Sacred Writings are to rule and govern our faith, on them we obligate our Candidates for Freemasonry; so are the Compasses and Square, when united to regulate our lives and actions. The Sacred Volume is derived from God to man in general, the Compasses belong to the Grand Master in particular, and the Square to the whole Craft.

'The jewels of the Lodge are three movable and three immovable. The movable Jewels are the Square, Level and Plumb Rule. Among operative Masons the Square is to try and adjust rectangular corners of buildings, and assist in bringing rude matter into due form; the Level to lay levels and prove horizontals; and the Plumb Rule to try and adjust uprights while fixing them on their proper bases.

Among Free and Accepted Masons, the Square teaches morality, the Level equality, and the Plumb Rule justness and uprightness of life and actions. They are called Movable Jewels, because they are worn by the Master and his Warden, and are transferable to their successors on nights of Installation. The Master is distinguished by the Square, the Senior Warden by the Level, and the Junior Warden by the Plumb Rule. The Immovable Jewels are the Tracing Board, and the Rough and Perfect Ashlars. The Tracing Board is for the Master to lay lines and draw designs on; the Rough Ashlar for the Entered Apprentice to work, mark, and indent on; and the Perfect Ashlar for the experienced Craftsman to try and adjust his jewels on. They are called Immovable Jewels, because they lie open and immovable in the Lodge for the Brethren to moralise on.

'As the Tracing Board is for the Master to lay lines and draw designs on, the better to enable the Brethren to carry on the intended structure with regularity and propriety, so the Volume of the Sacred Law may justly be deemed the Spiritual Tracing Board of the Great Architect of the Universe, in which are laid down such Divine Laws and Moral Plans, that were we conversant therein, and adherent thereto, would bring us to an Ethereal Mansion not made with hands, eternal in the Heavens. The Rough Ashlar is a stone, rough and unhewn as taken from the quarry, until by the industry and ingenuity of the workman it is modelled, wrought into due form and rendered fit for the intended structure; this represents man in his infant or primitive state, rough and unpolished as that stone, until by the kind care and attention of his parents or guardians, in giving him a liberal and virtuous education, his mind becomes cultivated, and he is thereby rendered a fit member of civilised society. The Perfect Ashlar is a stone of true die or square fit only to be tried by the Square and Compasses; this represents man in the decline of years, after a regular well-spent life in acts of piety and virtue, which can not otherwise be tried and approved than by the Square of

God's Word and the Compass of his own self-convincing conscience.

'In all regular, well-formed, constituted Lodges, there is a point within a circle round which Brethren cannot err; this circle is bounded between North and South by two grand parallel lines, one representing Moses, and the other King Solomon; on the upper part of this circle rests the Volume of the Sacred Law, supporting Jacob's Ladder, the top of which reaches to the Heavens; and were we as conversant in that Holy Book, and as adherent to the doctrines therein contained as those parallels were, it would bring us to Him who would not deceive us, neither will He suffer deception. In going round this circle, we must necessarily touch on both those parallel lines, likewise on the Sacred Volume, and while a Mason keeps himself thus circumscribed, he cannot err.

'The word Lewis denotes strength, and is here depicted by certain pieces of metal dovetailed into a stone, forming a cramp, and when in combination with some of the mechanical powers, such as a system of pulleys, it enables the operative Mason to raise great weights to certain heights with little encumbrance, and to fix them on their proper bases. Lewis likewise denotes the son of a Mason; his duty to his parents is to bear the heat and burden of the day, which they, by reason of their age, ought to be exempt from; to assist them in time of need, and thereby render the close of their days happy and comfortable; his privilege for so doing is that of being made a Mason before any other person, however dignified.

'Pendant to the corners of the Lodge are four tassels, meant to remind us of the four cardinal virtues, namely: Temperance, Fortitude, Prudence, and Justice, the whole of which, tradition informs us, were constantly practised by a great majority of our ancient Brethren. The distinguishing characteristics of a good Freemason are Virtue, Honour and Mercy, and may they ever be found in a Freemason's breast.'

It is also not uncommon for lodges to have two large pillars topped by spheres placed just within the entrance to the temple or on each side of the Master's chair. Reference to the symbolism of these is made in the tracing-board lecture of the second degree:

'When the Temple at Jerusalem was completed by King Solomon its costliness and splendour became objects of admiration to the surrounding nations, and its fame spread to the remotest parts of the then known world. There was nothing, however, in connection with this magnificent structure more remarkable, or that more particularly struck the attention, than the two great pillars which were placed at the porchway or entrance. That on the left was called BOAZ, which denotes in strength; that on the right, JACHIN, which denotes to establish; and when conjoined, stability, for God said: In strength I will establish this Mine house to stand firm for ever. The height of those pillars was seventeen cubits and a half each, their circumference twelve, their diameter four; they were formed hollow, the better to serve as archives to Masonry, for therein were deposited the constitutional rolls. Being formed hollow, the outer rim or shell was four inches or a hand's breadth in thickness. They were made of molten brass, and were cast in the plain of Jordan, in the clay ground between Succoth and Zeredathah, where King Solomon ordered those and all his holy vessels to be cast. The superintendent of the casting was Hiram Abiff. Those pillars were adorned with two chapiters, each five cubits high; the chapiters were enriched with network, lily-work, and pomegranates. Network, from the connection of its meshes, denotes unity; lily-work, from its whiteness, peace; and pomegranates, from the exuberance of their seed, denote plenty. There were two rows of pomegranates on each chapiter, one hundred in a row. Those pillars were further adorned with two spherical balls, on which were delineated maps of the celestial and terrestrial globes, pointing out Masonry universal. They were considered finished when the network or canopy was thrown over them. They were set up as a memorial to the children of Israel of that miraculous pillar of fire and cloud, which had two wonderful effects: the fire gave light to the Israelites during their escape from their Egyptian bondage, and the cloud proved darkness to Pharaoh and his followers when they attempted to overtake them. King Solomon ordered them to be placed at the entrance of the Temple as the most proper and conspicuous situation for the children of Israel to have the happy deliverance of their forefathers continually before their eyes, in going to and returning from Divine worship.

'At the building of King Solomon's Temple an immense number of Masons were employed; they consisted of Entered Apprentices and Fellow-Crafts; the Entered Apprentices received a weekly allowance of corn, wine, and oil; the Fellow-Crafts were paid their wages in specie, which they went to receive in the middle chamber of the Temple. They got there by the porchway or entrance on the south side. After our ancient Brethren had entered the porch they arrived at the foot of the winding staircase, which led to the middle chamber. Their ascent was opposed by the Junior Warden, who demanded of them the pass grip and the pass word leading from the first to the second degree.

'The pass grip you are all in possession of, and the pass word, I dare say you recollect, is Shibboleth; Shibboleth denotes plenty, and is here depicted by an ear of corn near to a fall of water. The word Shibboleth dates its origin from the time that an army of Ephraimites crossed the river Jordan in a hostile manner against Jephtha, the renowned Gileaditish general; the reason they assigned for this unfriendly visit was that they had not been called out to partake of the honours of the Ammonitish war; but their true aim was to partake of the rich spoils with which, in consequence of that war, Jephtha and his army were then laden. The Ephraimites had always been considered a clamorous and turbulent people, but then broke out into open violence, and after many severe taunts to the Gileadites in general threatened to destroy their victorious commander and his house with fire. Jephtha, on his part, tried all lenient means to appease them, but finding these ineffectual had recourse to rigorous ones; he therefore drew out his army, gave the Ephraimites battle, defeated and put them to flight; and to render his victory decisive and to secure himself from like molestation in future, he sent detachments of his army to secure the passages of the river Jordan, over which he knew the insurgents must of necessity attempt to go in order to regain their own country, giving strict orders to his guards that if a fugitive came that way, owning himself an Ephraimite, he should immediately be slain; but if he prevaricated, or said nay, a test word was to be put to him to pronounce, the word Shibboleth. They, from a defect in aspiration peculiar to their dialect, could not pronounce it properly, but called it Sibboleth, which small variation discovered their country and cost them their lives. And Scripture informs us that there fell on that day, on the field of battle and on the banks of the Jordan, forty and two thousand Ephraimites. And as Shibboleth was then a test word to distinguish friend from foe, King Solomon afterwards caused it to be adopted as a pass word in a Fellow-Craft's Lodge to prevent any unqualified person ascending the winding staircase which led to the middle chamber of the Temple.

'After our ancient Brethren had given those conclusive proofs to the Junior Warden he said Pass, Shibboleth. They then passed up the winding staircase, consisting of three, five, seven, or more steps. Three rule a Lodge, five hold a Lodge, seven or more make it perfect. The three who rule a Lodge are the Master and his two Wardens; the five who hold a Lodge are the Master, two Wardens, and two Fellow-Crafts; the seven who make it perfect are two Entered Apprentices added to the former five. Three rule a Lodge because there were but three Grand Masters who bore sway at the building of the first Temple at Jerusalem, namely, Solomon King of Israel, Hiram King of Tyre, and Hiram Abiff. Five hold a Lodge, an allusion to the five noble orders of Architecture, namely, the Tuscan, Doric, Ionic, Corinthian and Composite. Seven or more make a perfect Lodge, because King Solomon was seven years and upwards in building, completing, and dedicating the Temple at Jerusalem to God's service. They have likewise a further allusion to the seven liberal Arts and Sciences, namely, Grammar, Rhetoric, Logic, Arithmetic, Geometry, Music and Astronomy.

'After our ancient Brethren had gained the summit of the winding staircase, they arrived at the door of the middle chamber, which they found open, but properly tyled against all under the Degree of a Fellow-Craft by the Senior Warden, who demanded of them the sign, token, and word of a Fellow-Craft. After they had given him those convincing proofs he said Pass, Jachin. They then passed into the middle chamber of the Temple where they went to receive their wages, which they did without scruple or diffidence; without scruple, well knowing that they were justly entitled to them, and without diffidence, from the great reliance they placed on the integrity of their employers in those days.

'When our ancient Brethren were in the middle chamber of the Temple their attention was peculiarly drawn to certain Hebrew characters which are here depicted by the letter G—*the immediate Past Master gives a single knock, followed by the Wardens*—denoting God—*all stand to order with the sign of Reverence*—the Grand Geometrician of the Universe, to whom we must all submit, and whom we ought humbly to adore.'

When the Freemason arrives at his lodge in answer to a notice of meeting (a 'summons' to Masons) he is wearing a dark lounge suit and tie, and carrying apron, white gloves and any jewel, collar and gauntlets of office in a regalia case. He is about to enjoy a pleasant mixture of morally purposeful business and pleasure, for lodge meetings are by custom followed by a dinner. The Masonic season is a short one, as lodges usually close during May, June, July and August, and not many candidates are required to keep the lodge busy at initiation rituals between its annual ceremonies for the installation of officers.

The Tyler at the door of the temple ensures that only those members initiated to the degree in which the lodge is working are admitted. Once inside there is always some ceremonial, for there are short set rituals for opening and closing the lodge in the various degrees.[1] Then there is the lodge business: the reading of any communication from Grand Lodge; the almoner's report about sick or needy members; ballots for new members; and, if there is no initiation ceremony to be performed, a lecture on some aspect of Masonry.

Lodge membership fees are related to the scale of the entertainment after the meeting, which may be held in the Masonic Hall or in a near-by restaurant. Most subscriptions include the cost of dinners and of the Tyler, who must continue guard duties while dining at a separate table, a service for which he is frequently rewarded beyond his fee by members' tips. The Mason who spends much of his time in silence in the lodge as a spectator is now invited to enjoy toasts and speeches. Masonic toasts are usually drunk in heavy 'firing' glass and accompanied by 'fire', the banging down on the table of hands or glasses to suggest gunfire and to demonstrate that there has been no heel-tapping. Both the drinking and the speech-making can be extensive.

In his autobiography,[2] Lionel Fraser, a prominent London businessman, recalls:

I joined the brotherhood soon after the end of the first world war. It was all too matey, too forced. The ritual failed to appeal to me, and shutting oneself up in a tightly closed room for hours on end whilst the same old ceremonial was droned out, all dressed up in evening clothes at three o'clock in the afternoon with a little apron on, was too much for me. I know the Masonic movement performs wonders in charitable acts, and in their schools and hospitals. But I am afraid I became desperately impatient of the insincerity and adolescent behaviour of some of the brethren, especially after the

[1]See Appendix 3.
[2]*All to the Good*, Heinemann, 1963.

dinners which followed the proceedings in the afternoon when they toasted one another to such an extent that the speeches became little more than incoherent and platitudinous drivel.

Many Freemasons are ritualists, others more interested in the practical aspects of the charitable work of the movement, and to both sorts of men membership offers the rewards of fellowship. The appeal to the ritualist is, however, particularly strong and made the more attractive because of the esoteric nature of the Craft. Talking to the Council of Public Schools' Lodges in 1962,[1] Mr J. H. M. Dulley declared:

The explanation of the first tracing board, which is, unfortunately, too seldom given in our lodges, tells us something of the nature and ancient origin of Freemasonry. How much may have been lost or added during the centuries we cannot tell. But it may be that we Freemasons of the twentieth century are the modern representatives of the ancient Magi, or Wise Men of the East, though sadly shrunken in stature from those great and gifted men. The secrets and mysteries which they knew and understood have become for us a formula of words, of which the inner, esoteric meaning is seldom even suspected. But our need is as great as theirs. The object of our search is the same. Freemasonry resembles the ladder of Jacob—that emblem of man's power of inner development, which enables those who wish to move away from the material and the intellectual towards the spiritual. It is like the veil of the temple, which hides its inner meaning from us and at the same time shows us where to search.

There is a real danger that some Masons find in the lodge temple a substitute for religion and the Church. The Rev Leonard Griffith, a Canadian who joined Freemasonry in 1945 after graduating from university and later became the Minister at the City Temple in London, told me in a television interview:

[1]Printed *Masonic Record*, August 1964.

It is true that many Freemasons do make Masonry a substitute for the Church . . . but it is my experience that most good Masons are also good Churchmen.

Another Freemason and a Minister of the Church of Scotland, Dr William J. Baxter, commented before the camera:

Some of the very best elders in the Kirk, ministers, moderators, even; and missionaries are Freemasons. I can't understand how any man who takes his Freemasonry seriously would make it a substitute.

Both Mr Griffith and Dr Baxter, a Freemason since 1918 and a past Grand Chaplain of the Grand Lodge of Scotland, agreed that there are, not surprisingly, Freemasons who do not live up to the ideals of the Craft. Some men, said Mr Griffith, found very superficial needs satisfied by membership, 'it may give him nothing more than a night out with the boys, a kind of ordinary fellowship with other men; it may even give his little life a sense of significance that it lacks in his home life or his daily work.' On the same theme, Dr Baxter said in an interview:

I think it supplies a need that people have for the dramatic. There's a touch of drama in Freemasonry which I think appeals to a great many men. But I think the great thing is fellowship, a rich abounding fellowship, which you can get almost nowhere else.

The Grand Lodge of England made it quite clear in a statement in 1962 that in no way is Freemasonry to be regarded by members as a substitute religion: its teaching is to be complementary to religion. The basic principles of Freemasonry are given in the *Year Book* and state that a belief in the Grand Architect of the Universe and His revealed will shall be an essential qualification for membership; that the three Great Lights of Freemasonry, the Volume of the Sacred Law, the Square and the Compasses, shall always be exhibited in the lodges, the chief of these being the Volume of the Sacred Law; and that the discussion of religion and politics within the lodge shall be strictly prohibited.

Grand Lodge and the vast majority of Freemasons are also sensitive to suggestions that their ritualistic and charitable lodges should be considered something more sinister, élite clubs whose members are prepared to allow their shared interests to overflow into the world outside the lodge to the detriment of social justice. The Grand Lodge notes about points of procedure ask all Masons to do all they possibly can to prevent the use of any form of advertisement indicating connection with the Craft, and go on:

It is felt to be in the highest degree undesirable that endeavour should be made in this way or by circular, personal solicitation or newspaper advertisement, to secure professional, commercial or sectional advantage. All attempts to associate Freemasonry with or for business development are deeply deplored.

In matters of religion and ethics, however, it is comparatively simple to legislate, but impossible to exercise effective government. Clearly, there is much in the symbolism of the lodge temple and the ceremonies carried out in it that is of a religious nature and appeals to the spiritual yearnings of many men. It is quite obvious also that a movement which has groups meeting in secret throughout the country is open to abuses by misguided and self-seeking men and that some possibilities of misuse are beyond the safeguard of a majority of right-thinking members whose dedication to the high ideals of the organisation is above question.

CHAPTER V

The Breakaways

I will strive to live with love and care
Upon the level, by the square.

Those words and the date 1517 are inscribed upon a brass square found at the rebuilding of Baal's Bridge over the River Shannon near Limerick in Ireland. The inscription suggests that Irish masons were early to establish an ethical symbolism around the working tools of their craft; but there is insufficient information for scholars to date the emergence of speculative Freemasonry in Ireland. It was well established by the eighteenth century; the *Constitutions*, which Dr James Anderson has said he was invited to write for the English Grand Lodge and published in 1723, enjoyed good sales in Dublin and Cork.

Two years after the publication of Anderson's *Constitutions* appears the first record of the Irish Grand Lodge, which can now claim to be the second oldest in the world. The widely accepted date for its establishment is 1725, and the source is an issue of the *Dublin Weekly Journal* of 26th June of that year. This contains a report of a Grand Lodge meeting two days before at which the Earl of Rosse was elected new Grand Master. As the word 'new' implies, he may not have been the first holder of the office. The fact is that the date of the founding of the Irish Grand Lodge is unknown, since none of its official records exist before 1760, which makes the absence of any minutes for the first six years of the existence of England's Grand Lodge seem trifling, if none the less remarkable.

The Earl of Rosse was twenty-nine when elected Grand Master and reputed to be one of the leading spirits in the Dublin Hell Fire Club and a close friend of the Duke of Wharton. He is said to have inherited nearly a million pounds from his grandmother, and to have been well known for his wit and wild habits. Whether or not he was Grand Master until his death in 1741 is uncertain; but in 1725, he was not the only Freemason in Ireland with the title Grand Master.

The earliest official documents relating to Freemasonry in Ireland are the Munster Records and these chronicle the proceedings of a Grand Lodge and a private lodge, No. 1 of Cork, both dating from the year 1726. The first entry records the election of James O'Brien as Munster Grand Master and it seems obvious that the Grand Lodge was in existence before then, The Munster Grand Lodge continued until 1733, but its end was foreshadowed two years earlier by the installation of the 'Establishment' figure, Lord Kingston, as Grand Master. Lord Kingston was already Grand Master of Ireland and, in 1729, had been Grand Master of England.

Another challenge to the authority of the Irish Grand Lodge came in 1807 with the foundation of a rival Grand Lodge in Dublin. This was the work of one man, Alexander Seton. In the previous year he had been dismissed as Deputy Grand Secretary of the Irish Grand Lodge after allegations about misappropriated funds. At all events, Seton made personal property of Grand Lodge's register of lodges, its seal, the plate for printing certificates, and a number of dormant warrants. For a time he was even able to carry on his rival Grand Lodge from Irish Grand Lodge premises. The confusion created by the existence of two Grand Lodges in Dublin seemed over after a reconciliation between Seton and Irish Grand Lodge in 1808; but within months Seton had established another rebel headquarters. This was the Grand Lodge of Ulster, and the considerable support it received showed that many Ulster, Freemasons were ripe for resistance to authority from Dublin.

The Ulster Grand Lodge met at Dungannon, Co. Tyrone, for three years and then moved to Belfast. The peak of support had passed before the move. By 1810 lodges were falling away and returning to the Irish Grand Lodge. A Chancery Court action started five years earlier for the return of Grand Lodge property ended in 1813 with a judgement against Seton. The result effectively ended the revolt and dissident lodges scampered back to the aegis of the Irish Grand Lodge. Its rival in Belfast lasted until 1814.

Lord Donoughmore had been Grand Master of the Irish Grand Lodge from 1789 to 1813 and, in the year of the Union of the two English Grand Lodges, was succeeded by the Duke of Leinster, who was to rule for sixty-one years, during which the fortunes of the Freemasonry in Ireland fluctuated considerably. The biggest setback for the movement was the Unlawful Oaths in Ireland Act of 1823. This was designed to strike at a large number of clandestine organisations, such as the Orangemen and Ribbonmen. These societies had become part of the fabric of Irish life and, although predominantly religious, their members practised rituals and took oaths of secrecy. Freemasonry was not exempt from the provisions of the Act and the Irish Grand Lodge suspended all meetings of Freemasons. A petition was presented to Parliament, but it was ten months before an official announcement that the Government in framing the Act had not contemplated Freemasonry. The Masonic historian R.F. Gould comments:

Though the incident provided a test for the loyalty of the Irish lodges and one in which they did not fail, the cost was a heavy one, both directly and indirectly; directly, because many lodges in country districts, having ceased to meet, never resumed their working; indirectly, more especially because it was from about the date of the Secret Societies Act that the growing hostility of the Roman Church made Freemasonry virtually impossible for its members. Hitherto no rigid ban on membership of the Craft had been imposed by the Roman Church: and it is a remarkable fact that Freemasonry was the only ground on which Catholic and Protestant met in amity.[1]

[1] *The History of Freemasonry.*

The number of lodges on the register of the Irish Grand Lodge fell by more than half to well below 500; and the decline of Freemasonry in Ireland was protracted not only by the hostility of the Catholic Church but also by the economic depressions of the mid-century and the consequent flow of emigrants abroad, especially to America. In recent years the *Fraternal Monitor* of America has put the number of Free-masons in Ireland at 47,000.

The embarrassing early difficulties and challenges offered to the British Grand Lodges testify to the understand-able, if obdurate, attachment of Freemasons to traditions and status, and it is not surprising that a dispute over the relative antiquity of two of Scotland's lodges should figure prominently in the history of Masonry there. The two concerned are Mother Kilwinning Lodge and Lodge of Edinburgh No. 1, and let it be said at the outset, there is not enough evidence available today to settle the dispute authoritatively.

Freemasons like to trace their decent from the builders of abbeys and cathedrals, so Kilwinning has for them a special sound to it and something of the appeal of Mecca. Situated three miles north of Irving, near the Irish Sea, it was the site of the Abbey of Kilwinning founded in 1140 and dedicated to St Winning. The antiquity of the Abbey's foundation made Kilwinning a name to conjure with, and by the eighteenth century some Masonic mythmakers had included among early legendary lodge Masters of Kilwinning, Robert the Bruce.

Today Kilwinning holds pride of place at the top of the register of the Grand Lodge of Scotland, but Edinburgh's (Mary's Chapel) No. 1 has a proven claim to seniority. To understand the position it is necessary to look a little more closely at the development of Freemasonry in Scotland and to remember that the Grand Lodge has ruled merely upon precedency and not antiquity.

Edinburgh's case rests primarily upon a minute dated 1599, a piece of evidence establishing the existence of its medieval lodge forty-three years before any date which can be similarly authenticated by Kilwinning. But it is not quite as simple as that. Whether in Scotland city incorporations, a form of guild, of stonemasons or stonemasons' lodges came first is not known. Mary's Chapel claims origins going back to the city's company of Masons and Wrights incorporated in 1475 and there is mention of the lodge of Edinburgh in 1491. In England, the London Masons' Company may have existed as early as 1356 and there was a grant of arms for it in 1472. A few other English cities also had incorporations, but there is no English history of operative lodges comparable with that of Scotland, where lodges were answerable to supervising lodges and these in turn to the King's master of work.

The Schaw Statutes, drawn up in 1598 and 1599 by William Schaw, master of work to the Crown of Scotland, laid down a comprehensive code of organisation for stonemasons. The Statute of 1599 also proclaims the Edinburgh lodge as the first and principal lodge of Scotland, and Kilwinning as the second. This does not seem to have been challenged until towards the end of the seventeenth century, when there was a rapid expansion of lodges in Scotland, rather like the growth of Freemasonry in England, which followed the foundation of the first Grand Lodge in London.

For two hundred years the lodge of Edinburgh had exercised control in and around the city, but in 1677 a new lodge was founded in the Canongate which proclaimed itself a branch of Kilwinning. Then, in 1688, a Canongate and Leith lodge was established without authority from Edinburgh or Kilwinning.

Within Edinburgh itself restrictive practices on the part of employers were the justification put forward for the formation of the Lodge of Journeymen Masons. Elsewhere the tendency for groups of masons to meet and informally and irregularly to found a lodge, usually incorporating the word Kilwinning into the title, was not uncommon. The lodge of Holyroodhouse came into being this way in 1734, two years before the formation of the Grand Lodge of Scotland.

It was Canongate Kilwinning lodge which took the initiative in 1735 by appointing a committee to discuss with other lodges the choice of a Grand Master for Scotland. The lodge itself had a very strong candidate. Canongate Kilwinning had initiated William St Clair, a descendant of the St Clairs of Roslin, whose claim to an inherited right to govern the mason craft in Scotland is put forward in the St Clair Charters of 1601 and 1628.

The first regulations for Scotland's Grand Lodge were agreed in October 1736 at a meeting of four old lodges, Canongate Kilwinning, the lodge of Edinburgh (Mary's Chapel) No. 1, Kilwinning Scots Arms, and Leith Kilwinning. A few weeks later more than thirty out of the hundred or so lodges in Scotland sent their masters and wardens to elect a Grand Master.

There is reason to believe that many of them had intended to vote for the Earl of Home, but William St Clair of Roslin produced a written resignation of any claims which his family might have had to the Grand Mastership. It is difficult to imagine what relationship these claims could conceivably have had to speculative Freemasonry and yet the gesture so affected the assembly that they elected William St Clair.

When the Grand Lodge arrived at the difficult task of determining the precedence of lodges, it gave Edinburgh premier place. The decision rankled and in 1743 Kilwinning resumed its independence and maintained it for the next seventy years. Reconciliation with Grand Lodge followed a compromise. Kilwinning was placed, with Grand Lodge, at the head of the list of lodges without a number and the documented claims of Edinburgh were put aside for the sake of unity.

The Masonic magic in the name Kilwinning had some influence, too, on Scotland's greatest poet, Robert Burns. He was initiated in St David's Lodge, Tarbolton, in 1781, but a year later he was among brethren who withdrew to form a new lodge, the lodge of Tarbolton Kilwinning, St James. David Daiches says in a biography of Burns:

89

He became a Freemason . . . partly for the insurance that membership automatically brought (for the prime purpose of such local Scottish lodges was assistance to distressed members) but also for social reasons. He liked an audience, and he continued to seek it wherever he could find it. . . .

His greatest Masonic triumph had occurred when at a meeting of the Grand Lodge of Scotland he heard the Grand Master give the toast, Caledonia, and Caledonia's Bard, Brother Burns.[1]

In England, an historically older and, therefore, deeper Masonic romance surrounds the ancient city of York, where Freemasons, inspired by local traditions, staged one of the revolts against the Grand Lodge of England. In fact, this country has had six Grand Lodges, four of them operating at the same time. One of these, the Grand Lodge of All England, came into being at York in 1725, when perhaps, local lodge members concerned with precedency took too seriously an apocryphal account suggesting that an assembly of masons was summoned at York in 926 by Prince Edwin. If this could be established, it would make York a centre of such Masonic antiquity that, in theory, it could dispute any claim to superiority from London.

Historically, the repercussions were slight. The Grand Lodge of All England did nothing from 1740 until 1861, when it began to warrant dependent lodges. There were only about a dozen of these and, after a rather ineffectual existence, the All England lodge faded away in 1792. But York's Masonic history, a mixture of fantasy and fact derived from the building of York Minster, has made a deep psychological impression on Freemasonry. To this day, particularly in America, the expressions 'York rite' and 'York Masonry' are associated with the preservation of the oldest and best aspects of the Craft.

In 1779 the All England lodge at York authorised 'The Grand Lodge of England, South of the River Trent'. Founded in London, this Grand lodge sprang from the

[1]*Robert Burns*, Bell, 1952.

Lodge of Antiquity[1] whose Master at the time was William Preston, the Masonic historian. He had been Assistant Grand Secretary to the Grand Lodge of England until he resigned when the job of writing a new edition of the *Book of Constitutions* was taken away from him. Preston's decision to found another Grand Lodge split the members of the lodge of Antiquity; but the Master and his supporters took the lodge furniture one night and set up in the grand manner in fresh rooms.

The Grand Lodge of England, South of the River Trent continued in its dubious glory for ten years, during which time it constituted two lodges in London, one of them the Mitre Tavern, Fleet Street. Then, in 1789, Preston and his fellow rebels made their peace with the Grand Lodge of England. They were restored to their former Masonic standing and the Lodge of Antiquity was reunited.

Even the union between the Moderns and Antients in 1813 failed to stop the free-lance founding of Grand Lodges. Ten years later four of the lodges erased by the United Grand Lodge founded 'The Grand Lodge of Free and Accepted Masons of England according to the Old Institutions'. All the erased lodges were in Lancashire and the new Grand Lodge had its headquarters at Wigan. From there it issued warrants to six lodges of which only one remains, Wigan's Lodge Sincerity. This lodge's independent existence ended in 1913 when it accepted a new warrant from the United Grand Lodge and by that time the Lancashire Grand Lodge had faded away.

In effect, the present-day pattern of Masonic organisation in Britain with its three-tier system of Craft Lodges, Provincial Grand Lodges and supreme Grand Lodges had been firmly established when the Grand Lodges of England, Scotland and Ireland met in 1814 to sign an

[1]Formerly the lodge meeting at the Goose and Gridiron Alehouse in St Paul's Churchyard and a founder lodge of the Grand Lodge of 1717.

International Compact. The new United Grand Lodge of England was admitted to 'the full fraternal reciprocity of Grand Lodges' and it was agreed that there was conformity among the three organisations concerning ritual and perfect unison 'on matters that can neither be written nor described'.

CHAPTER VI

International Masonry

Freemasonry has followed the flag, and the rich, across the world. It has been adapted to the needs and purposes of a variety of men of differing nationalities and, abroad, many Masons have found in the secrecy surrounding the lodges the privacy essential for conspiracies against the Church and State. Ever since the eighteenth century the struggle to keep British Masonry in all the countries where it thrives aloof from politics and religion—and faithful to tradition—has been one of the preoccupations of Masonic leaders. It remains so today and limits the international aspect of the movement by curtailing slightly the number of Masonic organisations which the British Grand Lodges are prepared to recognise.

The most feared rivals of the British concept of Free-masonry, because they were political, anti-clerical and open to atheists, developed on the Continent, notably in France among lodges controlled by an organisation called the Grand Orient. These foreign forms of Freemasonry, like the British strain, were carried abroad, and now it is not unusual for some countries to have Freemasons' lodges owing allegiance to a Grand Lodge within their own borders or to a Grand Lodge in another country.

France has three Grand Lodges, the Grand Orient of France, the United Grand Lodge of France, and the *Grande Loge Nationale Française.* Only the last of these is recognised by the United Grand Lodge of England, which broke off relations with the Grand Orient in 1877, when French members of the order removed from their Constitutions the affirmation of the existence of the Grand Architect of the Universe.

Another example of these international complications is provided by South Africa, where, in 1961, lodges formerly under the Masonic jurisdiction of the Grand Lodge of the Netherlands established the Grand Lodge of Southern Africa in its place. Other lodges in South Africa still acknowledge the authority of one of the British Grand Lodges, all three having some jurisdiction there. Surprisingly, perhaps, the colonising efforts of the three British Grand Lodges continued unco-ordinated even after the International Compact between them in 1814. So to this day in almost every British, or formerly British, possession there are lodges with loyalties shared often between two of Britain's Grand Lodges, sometimes amongst the three.

The Grand Lodge of England recognises foreign Grand Lodges only if they conform to a set of basic principles. The Grand Lodge seeking acceptance must be legally established by a recognised Grand Lodge or by three, or more, regularly constituted lodges. Members must believe in the Grand Architect of the Universe and His revealed will. Initiates must take their oaths on, or in full view of, the open Volume of the Sacred Law—'by which is meant the revelation from above which is binding on the conscience of the particular individual who is being initiated'. The Grand Lodge and lodges under its authority must be composed exclusively of men and permit no 'Masonic intercourse' with mixed lodges or organisations that admit women members. The Grand Lodge shall have supreme and undivided authority over the Craft degrees, and its lodges while at work exhibit the Volume of the Sacred Law, the Square and the Compasses. No discussion of religion and politics within the lodges is to be allowed and the landmarks, customs and usages of the Craft are to be strictly observed. Under these conditions the United Grand Lodge of England, in fact, recognises a great many Grand Lodges in addition to those of Ireland and Scotland.

In Europe: Austria, Belgium, Denmark, Finland, France (Grande Loge Française), Germany, Greece, Iceland,

Ireland[1], Italy (Grand Orient), Luxembourg, Netherlands, Norway, Scotland, Sweden, Switzerland, Turkey.

Commonwealth:
Alberta, British Columbia, Canada (Ontario), India, Manitoba, New Brunswick, New South Wales, New Zealand, Nova Scotia, Prince Edward Island, Quebec, Queensland, Saskatchewan, South Australia, Tasmania, Victoria, West Australia.

Also: South Africa, Israel, Philippine Islands, forty-nine in USA, eleven in South America, five in Central America and two in West Indies.

It is most surprising that the list of foreign Grand Lodges recognised by the United Grand Lodge of England includes the Grand Orient of Italy. With its history of anti-clericalism and continuing involvement in politics Freemasonry in Italy was eschewed by British Masons until 1972 when the United Grand Lodge accorded recognition. A report from the Board of General Purposes pointed out that the earliest lodges in Italy had obtained their warrants from England and the present-day Freemasons were in direct Masonic descent from those lodges and from other equally regular parent bodies. The report went on:

There appear to have been sufficient survivors from the period of suppression of Freemasonry under the Fascist regime for organised activity to start again almost at once. Unfortunately it started haphazard under a considerable number of authorities which constantly regrouped themselves and gave little evidence of either permanence, stability or sovereignty. Furthermore, shortly after the best established and most widespread had sought recognition from England, what appeared to be good evidence came to light that its

[1]Includes the Republic of Ireland and Northern Ireland.

leaders had sought to apply pressure on their members to vote in a particular direction at a General Election. The Board at that point declined to recommend recognition, feeling that the Italian situation was obscure and unsatisfactory.

The whole matter has, however, been kept under review and continuous scrutiny: interviews have taken place with the leaders of various facets of Italian Masonry as well as conversations with the Grand Lodges of Ireland and Scotland, and with other Masonic authorities inside and outside Europe which have been able to give first-hand information. From all this, four main points have emerged:

(i)   The Grand Orient of Italy is now indisputably the predominant organisation in the whole of Italy: while splinter groups exist in the light of the fissile nature of Italian affairs (for it should be remembered that Italy as a nation is a bare century old), they are only splinter groups unrecognised outside Italy and unable inside Italy seriously to contest the Grand Orient's claim to Masonic sovereignty.

(ii) The Grand Orient has been meticulous in the last two decades in avoiding any imputation of political interference and has removed from the questionnaire put to candidates for initiation any reference to political affiliations.

(iii) The Grand Orient does not, since the restoration of relations between the United Grand Lodge of England and the Grand Lodge Alpina of Switzerland, have relations with any Grand Lodge which England considers to be irregular or does not recognise.

(iv) The Grand Orient's principles correspond closely with those of other recognised Lodges, and are such as the United Grand Lodge of England can accept as satisfactory.

The decision to recognise Italy's Grand Orient Masons caused embarrassment in 1981 following the exposure of a secret Masonic lodge in Italy. The publication of a list of members, nearly a thousand names in all, of men so powerful and influential as to constitute a real threat that they might become a state within the state, brought down the Christian Democrat Government of Arnaldo Forlani. Under the headline, 'Dismay among the British brothers', the *Sunday Telegraph*, 31 May 1981, reported 'a high-ranking Mason' as saying:

Fraternal relations were resumed because they had met our requirements. They agreed to keep the Bible open during meetings and to swear their oaths on it. Politics were also to be played down. Now we are deeply shocked and offended. We feel as if we have a renegade brother who has not lived up to family standards.

To all recognised foreign Grand Lodges the United Grand Lodge of England has appointed representatives and they in turn are represented at the English Lodge. It would be a mistake, however, to suppose that the Grand Lodges which recognise each other all concur fully with the principles laid down by the Grand Lodge of England. According to Mr Ward B. Arbury[1]—a Past Grand Master of the Grand Lodge of New York—the United Grand Lodge of France, which is not recognised by English Masons, is accepted by at least ten Grand Lodges in the United States.

The Grand Lodge of Israel, founded in 1953 under the auspices of the Grand Lodge of Scotland, was reported by another American Freemason, Mr Samuel Kaltman,[2] to maintain fraternal relations with more than a hundred Grand Lodges: forty-nine in USA, ten in Europe, eight in Canada, seven in Australia and New Zealand, thirteen in Central America, fifteen in South America and two in Asia.

In time of war, of course, the fraternal relations between Grand Lodges which in peace recognise each other are suspended; feelings ran so high in the First World War that the Grand Lodge of England ruled that Freemasons in this country of German, Austrian, or Turkish birth should not attend any Masonic lodge meetings.

Between the two World Wars considerable attention was paid to international Freemasonry and its possible influence. Reports of a Masonic Congress in Paris in 1917 attracted much attention and, although referred to in the memoirs of

[1]*Empire State Mason*, January/February 1963.
[2]*Empire State Mason*, June 1962.

Kaiser William II,[1] stem mainly from a single contemporary newspaper account. This appeared in *The Tablet* of 21st July 1917, and stated that Masonic delegates from the allied and neutral powers attended the Paris Congress at the invitation of the French Grand Orient and passed resolutions regarding postwar settlements with particular reference to claims by France and Italy. Reports of this Congress are documented among sources in a book by the Rev E. Cahill,[2] who also quotes an extract from the official Vatican organ, the *Osservatore Romano*, referring to another Masonic Congress at Amsterdam in 1929 called by the International Masonic League. Father Cahill says the League was founded in 1925 and also mentions an International Masonic Association, founded in 1921 with its headquarters at Geneva.

The International Masonic Association (or 'Union', as Father Cahill calls it elsewhere) is said to have been modelled on the League of Nations. Father Cahill further claims in his book:

The League of Nations is of Judaeo–Masonic parentage; and the Judaeo–Masonic forces place great hopes on it for the realisation of their anti-Christian programme.

There is an extensive literature on the theme of Freemasonry's internationalism, its relationship with the Jews, and its alleged influences upon world events. Suffice to say here that many authors have written from standpoints reflecting deep prejudices and much of their work is now rightly regarded with a healthy scepticism.

Perhaps the most controversial documents in the history of Freemasonry and allegations concerning international plotting are the *Protocols of the Sages of Sion*, first published in Russia in 1901 and translated since into most languages

---

[1]*My Memoirs*, 1878–1918, London, 1922.
[2]*Freemasonry and the Anti-Christian Movement*, M.H. Gill & Son Ltd., 5th impression, Dublin,1959.

of the world.[1] Briefly, the *Protocols* purport to be notes for putting into action a world-Jewish-Bolshevik plot and are said to have been gathered by secret agents of the Czarist Government from the archives of a French Jewish Masonic lodge. It is enough for present purposes to say that many investigators have concluded that the documents are forged and spurious.

The possibility of such an extravagantly conceived master plan for world government without direct resort to arms intrigues most of us and is an entertaining theme of fiction; but it preys upon the minds of some as a serious threat.

Undeniably, there are international Masonic organisations; but the British Grand Lodges have been emphatic about their consistent refusal to have any connection with the Grand Orient movement and its associated bodies until United Grand Lodge of England's recognition in 1972 of the Grand Orient Lodge of Italy. In 1965 the Grand Lodge of England declared that members who continued to associate with the Universal League of Freemasons, an international body founded in 1905, would be suspended or expelled, because the League's membership included many Masons owing allegiance to Grand Lodges not recognised.

There is justification for fears about an organisation which has attracted a world membership of about four million and whose adherents meet in private and are sworn to secrecy about their proceedings. On the other hand, it is extremely unlikely that Freemasonry represents any danger to the State and Government in Britain or anywhere else where its leaders are also men whose respectability is unimpeachable. The traditional connection with Freemasonry of the Royal Family in England has already been mentioned and America has had fourteen Masonic Presidents.

Freemasonry abroad often has been taken up by free-thinkers and revolutionaries, and in this respect Grand

[1]A short bibliography to the extensive literature on the Protocols is given in *Freemasonry and the Anti-Christian Movement*, Rev R. Cahill, p. 112. See also *A History of the Jewish People*, James Parkes, Penguin Books, 1964.

Orient lodges can be considered Masonically to have a bad record; but, it must be said, time changes historical judgements. Now, of course, it is a matter of pride for Masons to recall that among the past members of the order were many revolutionaries who at this distance are regarded as liberators: Simon Bolivar, Giuseppe Garibaldi, Lajos Kossuth, the Marquis de La Fayette, Giuseppe Mazzini, Paul Revere and George Washington—to mention but a few.

The present leadership of the movement both in Britain and in America is a guarantee against sinister Masonic conspiracies. Nevertheless, Masonry is international and, because of the colonising activities of the Grand Lodges, can be said to give many men a loyalty beyond the bounds of their own country. Also, between the various Grand Lodges there are sufficiently good communications for each to be in close touch with every variety of Freemasonry wherever it exists.

It should also be said that the additional degrees of Freemasonry beyond these practised in the Craft lodges provide ancillary international relationships. The Royal Arch degrees, for example, are considered by the Grand Lodge of England as the completion of the Master Mason's degree and it was Freemasons from England who established Royal Arch Masonry in Switzerland during the years 1961 to 1964. Also in recent years the National Grand Lodge of Finland, established under the auspices of the Grand Lodge of New York, turned to England for help to establish their Royal Arch Chapter.

The respectability and worthiness of Masonic aims as well as its leadership must also be taken into account when considering the character of international Freemasonry. The British Grand Lodges recognise this and from time to time since 1938 have published a statement entitled 'Aims and Relationships of the Craft'.[1] This again emphasises that Freemasons acceptable to the British Constitutions must

[1]Full text, Appendix 69.

believe in a God, display the Volume of the Sacred Law in the lodges and ensure that oaths of membership are taken upon it. The statement goes on:

Everyone who enters Freemasonry is, at the outset, strictly forbidden to countenance any act which may have a tendency to subvert the peace and good order of society; he must pay due obedience to the law of any State in which he resides or which may afford him protection, and he must never be remiss in the allegiance due to the Sovereign of his native land.

While English Freemasonry thus inculcates in each of its members the duties of loyalty and citizenship, it reserves to the individual the right to hold his own opinion with regard to public affairs. But neither in any Lodge, nor at any time in his capacity as a Freemason, is he permitted to discuss or to advance his views on theological or political questions.

The Grand Lodge has always consistently refused to express any opinion on questions of foreign or domestic State policy either at home or abroad, and it will not allow its name to be associated with any action, however humanitarian it may appear to be, which infringes its unalterable policy of standing aloof from every question affecting the relations between one government and another, or between political parties, or questions as to rival theories of government.

By sheltering in this way from any threat of political controversy, and adhering to theism, the British Freemason believes he is contributing to a bland movement for world peace by membership of an international club for gentlemen. Dr Baxter said of South Africa:

I am glad to know we've got at least eighty lodges in the Transvaal and Orange Free State connected with the Scottish Institution alone. That's bound, in my opinion, to make for peace and harmony, maybe slowly but it's a great force to achieve that end.

Judge D. H. Botha, who conducted the commission of inquiry into secret organisations in South Africa, reported:

Attempts made by Italian, German and American negro organisations to institute lodges in South Africa have hitherto been prevented by the local Masonic organisations. All the lodges and their members in South Africa accept, and co-operate according to, the same fundamental principles and are subject to similar rules.

Many British Freemasons because they are churchmen or clergymen also see in the movement powerful support to ecumenical ambitions. Dr Baxter again:

At the General Assembly [of the Church of Scotland, 1964] one elder from India told what a great thing it had been for him because of his religion, to meet with men of other faiths, as he never would have done in any other connection. And this has a very great value; it is one of the great forces for peace in the world, I think. I, myself, have sat in a lodge in King Solomon's quarries in Jerusalem where there were Arab, Jew and Christian and there was perfect peace and harmony—and I don't know any other institution that could achieve that.

In America there is identification of Freemasonry with the fight against Communism. Masons there are also less inhibited about Masonic pronouncements than British Freemasons. Mr M. W. H. Lloyd Jones, a Past Grand Master of New York's Grand Lodge, was able to speak publicly about the mission of Freemasonry and told the Men's League of the Marble Collegiate Church, New York, on 10th October 1961:

As citizens and Masons, there are two challenges in particular which concern us very deeply, and they relate to our youth and to communism. . . . As to communism, this probably presents the greatest challenge of our times; and concerns not only Masons and non-Masons in our country alike, but the peoples of the free countries throughout the world. Foremost in the hearts of God-fearing people is the yearning for Peace on earth, Goodwill among all men. But the greatest obstacle to the achievement of this Peace comes from those who would inflict a godless communism on the world.

Repeatedly, the Director of the F.B.I., Mr J. Edgar Hoover, himself a distinguished member of the Masonic Fraternity, has come out strongly, warning the American people that the danger of communism in our country is very real; he has also said that the apathy shown by many Americans is alarming and shameful.

These considerations, together with the fact that Americans have raised extrovert qualities to the level of a national characteristic, explain why American Freemasonry reaches out through a multitude of parallel organisations for mother, son and daughter. One of the movements for women which flourishes in America, the Order of the Eastern Star, has a following in Britain. The Order is ignored by the United Grand Lodge of England in spite of the fact that it has its own legends and ceremonies and these do not give an insight into the men's Freemasonry.

The basic principles for Grand Lodge recognition laid down by the Grand Lodge of England and quoted earlier say that English lodges are only for men and there is to be no Mansonic intercourse with mixed lodges or organisations that admit women members. The Constitutions of the Grand Lodge also provide that no man may be initiated into a Craft lodge if he has in any way been connected with quasi-Masonic organisations, or those imitative of it. A Mason who forms, and continues with, such associations after admission will be expelled.

British Freemasons I have spoken to enjoy the movement's exclusive masculinity, particularly clergymen members. Dr Baxter, Church of Scotland, remarked:

I thought it was a good thing for me to have an all-male society amongst all my other things. A minister is compelled to do a lot of duties that bring him in touch with women only.

The Minister at London's City Temple, the Rev Leonard Griffith, said:

I think there is a man's world and I think every man needs to get into that world occasionally and Masonry is perhaps one expression of this. Certainly in the Churches I've always been depressed by the fact that there seemed to be a much larger proportion of women there than men. I like to be with men and perhaps that's one reason why I enjoy attending a meeting of a Masonic lodge.

Other Freemasons who think differently are not officially recognised as Masons by the British Grand Lodges, but International Co-Freemasonry, or mixed Masonry, has wide support. It was founded in France in 1893 by Mlle Maria Desraines with help from a French Freemason, Dr Georges Martin, and is now truly international. As one might expect, Mlle Desraines was a strong advocate for women's rights and Dr Martin a sympathiser. The movement is still sometimes referred to as *Le Droit Humain*, after the name of the original lodge in Paris, and its development in England, where the first lodge was founded in London in 1902, is associated with Theosophy. Mrs Annie Besant, at one time an assistant of a well-known atheist and secularist of the nineteenth century, Charles Bradlaugh, later became a prominent disciple of both Theosophy and International Co-Freemasonry.

The movement now exists in many parts of the world such as Canada, New Zealand, Australia, South Africa, the United States of America, South America and India. The Supreme Council of the organisation consists mainly of women, still has its headquarters in Paris, and exercises a limited degree of control over the lodges spread throughout the world. During his inquiries into Freemasonry in South Africa, Judge Botha paid some attention to International Co-Freemasonry and comments in his report:

Under the Supreme Council (which performs functions similar to those of a grand lodge of ordinary Freemasonry), there are, in the various countries where the organisation operates, so-called Federations which handle the affairs of the lodges in their respective countries. At the moment the lodges in the Republic still fall under the British Federation, but their affairs are conducted mainly by a local Advisory Council. Under the British Federation fall not only the lodges in South Africa and the United Kingdom but also those in Canada and Panama.

The basic principles of the organisation and its ritual in the Craft degrees correspond in the main to those of the Masonic bodies under the English, Scottish, Irish and Southern African constitutions, but principally because the organisation, contrary to the fundamental principle of Freemasonry, admits women to membership, it is not recognised as a Masonic order, and they have no dealings with one another.

It is contended, in fact, that the organisation is not entitled to the use of the name Freemason. Whatever the case may be, it is apparent that, except for the fact that the organisation has a more international character because of its control from Paris and that it also does more to recruit members, its constitutional rules, its ritual in the Craft's degrees, and its principles, aims and activities do not differ materially from those of ordinary Freemasonry.

Judge Botha adds that International Co-Freemasonry is

Open to men and women, without distinction of race or religion, who are free, of good report, and of sound mind and strict morals. It imposes no restrictions on the free search for Truth, and, to secure that freedom, expects tolerance from all its members. It pledges its members to obedience to the laws of the country, loyalty to the Sovereign, silence with regard to Masonic secrets, a high standard of honour and a ceaseless endeavour to promote the welfare of humanity.

The first woman ever admitted to Masonry was possibly Elizabeth St Leger, a cousin of the man who instituted the famous St Leger horse race. The initiation took place in about 1710, when the lady was only seventeen. The facts of the story, now generally accepted and well documented by R. F. Gould, are that she spied upon a lodge meeting at

105

her father's house in Ireland and was caught by the butler. When the lodge members found out they decided the only thing to do was to make Elizabeth a Freemason. Elizabeth eventually became the Hon Mrs Aldworthy and was made a patroness of the Craft. Her Masonic apron exists today.

There are other instances of women having been admitted into Freemasonry and women have so successfully penetrated the movement that, in addition to International Co-Freemasonry, there are the Order of Women Freemasons, founded in 1908, and the Honourable Fraternity of Ancient Freemasons, which cannot claim the antiquity of the men's movement as it was established in 1913.

CHAPTER VII

Following the Flag

Freemasonry has flourished in the armed forces and is still prevalent among servicemen of all nations which permit Masonry to exist. Military lodges spread Freemasonry across the world in the eighteenth century and in more recent times many men have turned to Masonry, seeking either a civilian expression and embodiment of the comradeship of arms or the confirmation of status achieved during war service.

The number of English lodges rose sharply after both the Crimean and the Boer Wars and dramatically following the World Wars. This was the pattern of expansion at the end of the First World War: fifty-three new lodges in 1918, 121 in 1919, and 183 in 1920. In the twenties there was a decline and from 1926 to 1939 the annual figure was always below a hundred, and three times fell below fifty. The pattern was repeated at the end of the Second World War: 198 new lodges in 1945, 191 in 1946, 187 in 1947, and 201 in 1948. Then numbers fell again and from 1950 to 1960 fewer than a hundred new lodges were founded each year and in four years the number was below fifty.

As far as the two World Wars are concerned, a social motive may well have been at work: men who obtained commissions, but did not come from the traditional officer class, certainly hung on to their new status when they returned to civilian life and may have found in Freemasonry a help towards maintaining it. The same thought is suggested by the fact that after the Second World War quite a number of lesser public school lodges were founded, to take their place alongside the older and more eminent ones. Very few 'Old Boys' lodges existed before 1914.

The earliest recorded Masonic initiation on English soil is that of Sir Robert Moray, Quartermaster-General to the Army of Scotland. At the time, 1641, the Scots army was about to enter Newcastle, but members of the Chapel lodge of Edinburgh found the opportunity for a lodge meeting at which Robert Moray was admitted. Military men were also prominent from the early days of English Free-masonry. When Elias Ashmole was initiated at Warrington in 1646 among those present was his father-in-law, Colonel Mainwaring. The fifth Grand Master of the Grand Lodge of England, the Duke of Montagu, was Master-General of the Ordnance.

The earliest purely military lodge of which there is evidence was founded in Gibraltar in 1728 and, unlike most of the military lodges that were to follow, it was stationary. Later military warrants allowed military lodges to meet anywhere. The Grand Lodge of Ireland first warranted military lodges in this way and the Grand Lodges of Scotland and England followed suit. Military lodges were also established in Belgium, France, Germany, Holland, Russia and Sweden.

Grand Orient Freemasonry is the oldest Masonic system in France and owes much to the symbolic lodges established in the country by English and Scottish servicemen and other British groups. French prisoners of war captured during the Seven Years War of 1756 to 1763 were allowed on parole to visit lodges in this country and in some cases to establish their own Grand Orient lodges. By 1787 there were seventy-six French military lodges; but expansion stopped with the Revolution of 1789, and by 1821 French military lodges had gone out of existence.

Both within and without the army, the Grand Orient probably gained its greatest influence in France towards the end of the eighteenth century. According to one account,[1] the Grand Orient existed in 1725 and was prohibited by the police on 14th September 1737, having aroused the

[1]*Le Grand Orient de France, Paris, 1936.*

misgivings of the Government. It appealed to various currents of opinion, including several shades of Protestantism, some mainly anti-Roman, some more political; as well as to people with progressive ideas about society, among them devotees of concepts of the 'noble savage' and the 'return to nature'.

In 1743 Freemasonry became acceptable through the election as Grand Master of the regular lodges of the Comte de Clermont, a prince of the royal blood. Degrees and titles within the order proliferated. So did scandals and dissensions. After Clermont's death a cousin of the King, Louis-Philippe d'Orléans, Duc de Chartres, became the Grand Master. The organisation was re-formed under a new constitution, but continued to attract the dissentient and subversive. In 1778 Voltaire was initiated a member of a lodge called 'les Neuf Soeurs'. During his long stay in France, Benjamin Franklin, one of the founders of American Freemasonry, was a prominent member of this lodge. It was the rendezvous of the encyclopaedists, physicists and philosophers who were working out the ideas of a new society which played an influential part in preparing men's mind for the Revolution.[1] Danton and Robespierre were both Masons.

Napoleon subjected the Grand Orient to his orders, 'Obey or disappear'. His brother Joseph was appointed Grand Master from 1804 to 1814, and many of the top officials of the Empire were Masons—Masséna, Murat, Kellerman, Lacépède, Lefebvre, Gambacères. Indeed, the question was sometimes asked whether Napoleon was boss or dupe of the Grand Orient.

During the political changes that followed, French Freemasonry was entirely opportunist. It became Bourbonienne with Louis XVIII, acclaimed Charles X, adopted the Revolution of July 1830 and again that of 1848. The Assembly of

---

[1] Banknotes of the French Revolution, 1791, had Masonic symbols in two of the corners. Masonic symbols also appear on some modern American notes and were incorporated in the designs of the twopence-halfpenny and threepenny Victory stamps after the Second World War.

1848 was believed to be virtually a branch of the Grand Orient. There were renewed attacks on Freemasonry and Louis-Napoleon, an old Carbonari[1] who understood secret organisations, made his cousin the Prince Murat head of the Grand Orient in 1852. When Prince Murat resigned in 1861, he named Marshal Magnan as Grand Master. Most French Masons were bourgeois and Bonapartist, but the evolution of Grand Orient was ultimately towards democracy and rationalism. Freemasons were prominent in the attempted revolution of 1871 and mounted the barricades of the Commune. It was in 1871 that the office of Grand Master was abolished and replaced with that of President, and in 1875 Grand Orient removed from its constitutions the affirmation of the existence of the Great Architect of the Universe. Two years later the United Grand Lodge of England withdrew recognition and so did many other lodges.

At the beginning of the century half of the French Council of Ministers were Freemasons and eighty per cent of high positions in the Republic were filled by Masons.

The effect of the Grand Orient upon political life during the early years of the Third Republic has been described by D. W. Brogan:

In all sections of the new political class, there was at work the secret, unifying, bewildering force of Masonry, above all the militantly atheistic Masonry of the Grand Orient. Deputies otherwise obscure . . . were potent in the Chamber, since they directed the Masonic vote, and that was powerful in all parties but those of the extreme Right. The decisions of the 'convent' of the Grand Orient were often more important than those of party congresses or of the open debates and votes of the Chamber. And in the lodges, rich and not so rich, Jew and Gentile, met in a fraternity that made public

---

[1]The Carbonari were members of secret revolutionary societies active in the nineteenth century in France and Italy; in Southern Italy, 1808–15, they were protected by Murat.

doctrinal differences unimportant. . . . And because the power was real, was great, it was exaggerated in the popular imagination and so increased.[1]

One of the most sensational revelations of the abuses which this preponderance of Freemasons in the national executive created is the 'Affaire des Fiches'. Following upon the transfer of the responsibility for promotions from the Army Commission to the Minister of War, the Grand Orient was used to spy upon officers thought to have religious convictions. The historian Alistair Horne comments:

Promotion became more a matter of an officer's political views, and particularly to which church, and how often, he went on Sundays, than of merit. Thus, as late as 1917, the newly-appointed and respectably Protestant Commander-in-Chief, General Nivelle, could fly into a temper on discovering that his Headquarters had once been a Catholic Priests' seminary. Officers like Foch, whose brother was a Jesuit, and de Castelnau, who was accompanied to the wars by his own private chaplain, would always be at a disadvantage, and it was no coincidence that in 1911 the office of the new Chief of the General Staff, fell to a general who ostentatiously ate meat on Good Friday.[2]

The findings are identical with those of D. W. Brogan:

The purge was entrusted to that coy body, the Freemasons of the Grand Orient. Their headquarters in the Rue Cadet replaced the notorious Jesuit school in the Rue des Postes. Officers of all ranks were encouraged to inform on their comrades: that one went to mass; that other sent his children to a Church school; that other made irreverent remarks about the Ministers of the Republic. These titbits were collected and collated and sent to Paris. The informants ranged from the commander of an army corps to lieutenants. And very Republican officer knew that the elimination of Catholic officers lightened the promotion lists.[3]

[1]*The French Nation*, Hamish Hamilton Ltd.
[2]*The Price of Glory*, Macmillan & Co., 1962.
[3]*The French Nation*, Hamish Hamilton Ltd.

Today, Grand Orient is said to work very little ritual, possibly their members are more concerned with continuing the
French tradition of discussions about religion and politics
within the lodges. But Grand Orient, although still the most
influential of French Masonic systems, is not without rivals.
There are two other active systems; the more important
is the United Grand Lodge of France, established under
the auspices of a Supreme Council of the Scottish Rite which
originated in America early in the eighteenth century. Its
lodges work a good deal of ritual similar to that found in
England, but like Grand Orient the lodges include atheists
among the members. There are also very close links between
United Grand Lodge members and Grand Orient. In many
parts of France lodges of the two systems meet in the same
rooms and members of both groups frequently visit each
others' lodges.

A third group of French Freemasons was established
under the Grande Loge Nationale Française, founded in
Paris in 1914. This is the smallest of the three systems and is
recognised by the United Grand Lodge of England and many
other lodges. Its ceremonies closely resemble the workings
in England and a belief in God is essential. Religious and
political discussion is forbidden within the lodges.

Inspired at least in part by a desire to leave the old European controversies behind them, British colonists took Freemasonry to America and military lodges spread the movement across the continent. Freemasonry, with its emphasis
on brotherhood, attracted many leading Americans, who saw
how it could be used to establish groups of men devoted to
the principles of liberty and equality. They made American
Freemasonry patriotic and political.

Some historians, and most of today's American Freemasons, believe that Paul Revere with other members of
the St Andrews Lodge of Boston were responsible for
the Boston Tea Party. Lodge members were seen going
into their meeting-place, the Green Dragon Tavern, on
16th December 1773. Later 'Indians' boarded ships in

the harbour and threw into the sea chests of tea worth £18,000.

George Washington was made a Freemason in the lodge at Fredericksburg, Virginia, in 1752 and became a Master Mason the following year. During the Revolutionary War he favoured the creation of military lodges for soldiers and many of his generals were Freemasons. Most of the signatories of the Declaration of Independence were Masons and, according to one American Masonic magazine,[1] the war was financed by Haym Solomon, 'noted financier and a great Mason'.

A convention of delegates from military lodges in 1780 wanted to found a single Grand Lodge for America and had they succeeded George Washington would have become national Grand Master. But Massachusetts Masons were not in favour and the idea died.

The Revolutionary War produced many incidents illustrating Masonic chivalry during battle. They mostly concern the capture and return of lodge emblems and treasures, but among them is a report involving an Indian Freemason. An American army captain, McKisty, was about to be burnt at the stake by Indian allies of the British when a Mohawk Chief intervened and saved his life. The chief, Joseph Brant, had been initiated in London in 1776 and recognised McKisty's Masonic appeal for help. Later McKisty was handed over to some English Freemasons, who returned him uninjured to the American lines.

When the war ended and the British evacuated New York City on 25th November 1783, the British members of the Provincial Grand Lodge of New York gave the grand warrant to the few American members who remained, leaving lodges and their records to the American Masons against whom they had fought.

American Freemasonry seized independence, too. It had been organised under a system of provincial Grand Lodges

---

[1] *The Empire State Mason*, May/June 1963.

with masters appointed or authorised by the Ancient or Modern Grand Lodges of England or by the Grand Lodges of Scotland or Ireland. Now, these provincial Grand Lodges set themselves up as independent Grand Lodges with territories corresponding to state boundaries.

When the Civil War began in 1861, American Free-masonry had 200,000 members[1] and the movement was firmly established in all of the states, North and South. There were attempts to use Freemasonry to prevent and then to end the war. Sometimes, the special circumstances of civil war made Masonry a bond stronger than uniform and military expediency. The experiences of L. J. Williams,[2] who fought for the North and was taken prisoner at Savannah, illustrate the hold the movement had upon members in both armies. At the time of his capture Williams had taken only the first two degrees of Masonry, Entered Apprentice and Fellow Craft. He was anxious to go on to the third degree and, although in a Southern prison, he contacted friends in the North and his own lodge in New York arranged for a lodge in Savannah to carry out the ceremony. Williams was smuggled out of prison to the lodge and raised to the third degree in the presence of Confederate Army officers and men. Later that night he was taken into no-man's-land and freed to make his way to his own lines.

The struggle over four years produced more than a hundred new military lodges and these contributed to the rapid growth of the movement. By 1900 its membership was 800,000.

Efforts to found a single Grand Lodge of America continued without success, and to this day the Grand Lodges of the states remain sovereign in Masonic matters within their territories. A permanent association of twenty-seven Grand Lodges was formed in 1911 to launch the project for a national Masonic memorial to George Washington at Alexandria, Virginia. This led to annual meetings there

[1] *Life Magazine*, 8th October 1956.
[2] cf. *Empire State Mason*, July/August 1961.

of the Grand Masters of the Masons in all states, but the conferences have no authority over any Grand Lodge.

Americans in their newly found independence and unity were so preoccupied as to be content to ignore developments in Europe. The possibility that the 'incident' which was the trigger for the First World War might have been a Masonic plot concerned few people, Masons or non-Masons, apart from the jury at the trial of the Sarajevo assassins. Questions were put about possible connections the accused might have had with Freemasonry and their answers were guarded. It seems that the men who killed the heir to the Austrian throne on 28th June 1914, at Sarajevo in Bosnia, did not know much about the people who promoted the assassination and whether or not they were Masons.

What is quite clear, however, is that a few British Masons took arms in the First World War with a confidence fed by the accounts of Masonic chivalry generated and circulated among the military lodges. They were the members of Ailwyn Lodge, No. 3535, who went to war with a card of introduction for use abroad printed in English, French, Italian, German and Arabic. Many other soldier Masons may have had similar hopes of Masonic privileges: only Ailwyn Lodge members had so tangible an expression of them.

In the early days of the war German lodges may have been anxious to demonstrate their loyalty to the fraternal principles of the craft. Certainly, German Masons sometimes joined their conquered brethren for lodge meetings. One group allowed itself to be photographed in uniform alongside civilian brothers at a lodge in Belgium. Another was pleased to be pictured at a Masonic banquet shared with subject Freemasons.

The special comradeship of Freemasonry was frequently obvious behind both front lines as Mason troops found opportunities to meet and to perform the ceremonies of their movement. Dr William Baxter, a Past Master of a Glasgow lodge and a Past Grand Chaplain of the Masons of Scotland, was a young man on active service at Poperinghe, near Ypres, when he discovered Masons going to a field lodge meeting.

This surprised him; and so did the fact that officers and men were attending together regardless of rank:[1]

I said: 'You mean to say that the brass hats and the jocks are going to the same meeting?' They said: 'Oh yes: it's the Freemasons.' 'Well,' I said, 'I don't know any institutions that can do that except the Kirk and it doesn't always succeed. If I live to come out of this tramash, I'll join the Freemasons'.

At home Freemasons donated considerable sums to war-time charities, including a special fund to help interned brethren in enemy countries. Three nursing homes were maintained at different times for wounded soldiers and these, though primarily for Freemasons, were open to non-Masons.

After the war, Freemasons' Hall, the headquarters of the United Grand Lodge of England, was built in Great Queen Street, London, as a Masonic Peace Memorial. It was originally estimated to cost one million pounds, but the actual figure must have considerably exceeded that and has never been given.

The growing public belief in the wealth behind the Masonic movement, even if greatly exaggerated in terms of the total amount, was already a powerful part of Masonry's folklore by the twenties. One of Hitler's early followers, Richard Frank, gave his party leader a glimpse of the power behind the legend. Recalling the incident in February 1942, Hitler said:

Richard Frank is one of the greatest idealists I've known. Since we needed a headquarters, he made efforts to procure the money

[1]According to Walton Hannah (*Christian by Degrees*, Britons Publishing Co., 1954, footnote p. 34): 'It is usually a by-law of Naval and Military lodges that no sailor below the rank of Petty Officer, or no soldier below the rank of Sergeant, is eligible for initiation in this universal Brotherhood.'

116

for us. With this object he introduced me, in Munich, to a certain Dr Kuhlo. On Frank's initiative, this Kuhlo had formed a syndicate to buy the Hotel Eden, situated near the station. It was obviously out of the question to make this purchase with the Party's money. This was in 1923, and the sellers demanded payment in Swiss Francs. When all was ready, the syndicate met, with Kuhlo in the chair. The latter rose to his feet and announced that the hotel would be put at the Party's disposal for a modest rental. He suggested, in passing, that perhaps the Party might suppress the article in its programme concerning Freemasonry. I got up and said good-bye to these kindly philanthropists. I'd fallen unawares into a nest of Freemasons.[1]

In the same year, 1923, a decree of the Grand Fascist Council of Italy offered Masons in that country a choice of membership of Craft or Party. Masonic temples were closed, looted and wrecked. Mussolini shared Hitler's hatred and fear of the Freemasonry movement and in Italy Free-masons were dismissed from office, frequently to face trial and imprisonment or execution.

Spain also had a dictatorship in 1923. General Primo de Rivera was appointed to run the country by King Alfonso XIII and held power until 1930. In the following year the monarchy was overthrown and a Republican Government succeeded it. Five of the members of the new Government were Freemasons[2] and, there-fore, regarded by the right wing as partners in some kind of international Masonic plot designed to estab-lish atheistic Communism. An extreme view, but one reflecting the fact that on the Continent Masonry had proved a magnet for the liberal-minded and lodge mem-bers often tended to be anti-religious as well as merely anti-clerical.

Freemasonry had been introduced into Spain by the Duke of Wharton, a Past Grand Master, who was in Madrid in 1728, and its spread was considerably assisted by the Napoleonic Wars. Its popularity among Army men was

[1]*Hitler's Table Talk 1941-44*, Weidenfeld and Nicolson, 1953.
[2]*The Spanish Civil War*, Hugh Thomas, Eyre and Spottiswoode, 1961.

enduring and at the time of the 1931 Republican Government the Spanish Army was riddled with Masonic lodges. Hugh Thomas writes:

Some generals, such as Goded, Gueipo de Llano, Fanjul and Cabanellas, who later took prominent roles against the Republic, were believed to belong to a military lodge, many of whose members were, however, fervent Republicans.

The conflict of opinion was to find bitter and violent reflection in the three years of civil war. A general election in February 1936 put into power a left-wing coalition of 'the Popular Front'. In July, Spanish generals led by Francisco Franco declared war on the Government and marched on Madrid. Franco speedily took possession of several important provinces and in Nationalist Spain the only groups permitted were the Falange and the Carlists. By the end of the war Freemasons had been persecuted as vigorously as trade unionists and Communists. Both sides had shown an appalling ferocity and deep appetites for murder and execution. Freemasonry had gone full circle and today the movement in Spain is once again underground, anticlerical and political. As such it is eschewed by the United Grand Lodge of England.

Masonic influence is not always as successful as some bitter opponents of the movement claim. An example of failure to manipulate events in post-war Italy is the more interesting because it involved not only Freemasons but American Army officers and the Mafia. Norman Lewis in his account of the Mafia[1] says that the American gangster Nick Gentile was asked by US Army Colonel Max Brod to enlist the support of the Mafia for the cause of King Umberto II. Lewis continues:

---

[1] *The Honoured Society*, Collins, 1964.

Gentile agreed and suggested that the Freemasons be roped in, and in due course he and and his friend the Grand Master were received in audience by Umberto. The King asked Gentile for the Mafia's support 'for a last glorious victory for the scutcheon of the House of Savoy' . . . Yet, despite the power of the Mafia, and the secret labours of the service chiefs and the Freemasons, the House of Savoy was to founder . . . and Umberto was sent packing.

Hitler's detestation of Masonry was as thoroughgoing as Mussolini's. Looted articles of furniture, regalia and jewellery from German Masonic lodges were used to fill a museum in Nuremburg. A lavishly illustrated catalogue reproduced the photographs of German Masons in the First World War who had fraternised with conquered Freemasons in Belgium and complained that Belgian citizens who took part in the officers' field lodge ceremonies were able to overhear discussions about military affairs. The writer of this flagrantly anti-Masonic propaganda also claimed that when a field lodge was founded by German soldiers at St Quentin, 'the place which became the grave for millions of German soldiers', these military Freemasons did not hesitate to accept an offer of help from their French brothers on the other side of no-man's-land. The text of the museum's catalogue also condemned the work of the bureau of Freemasons in Geneva to assist prisoners of war.

They only cared for their brothers and did not bother about any other prisoner, who had been their comrade during the fighting.

The broader basis of the Nazi antipathy towards Freemasonry found full and frequent expression in the German Press. These extracts will suffice to illustrate the themes.

In the last two centuries the secret organisation of Freemasonry has tried again and again to obtain control over the political leadership of all European states and over the shaping of the life of the people within; Great Britain alone, the Mother of Freemasonry, was spared. The reason was that English Freemasonry, serving always none but a small British–Jewish leading set, was at all times active for English interests only. By transplanting the secret organisation into other countries British support for political purposes was created and it became possible at the same time to decompose to the advantage of England the national and public units of the rest of the world. . . . (*Völkischer Beobachter*, 12th March 1941).

There are more than 43,000 Jews among 300,000 British Freemasons (*Brüsseler Zeitung*, 15th March 1941).

So Freemasonry in Germany went underground and there it stayed until the end of the war and the arrival of the Allied armies and the Control Commission, when German Freemasons emerged to ask for permission to hold lodge meetings once again. The head of the Control Commissions' Religious Affairs Branch at the time, the Rev Edwin Robertson, told me:

The dilemma was that there were so many Freemasons among the senior officers of the British occupying forces, as there were also among the American forces, and they felt obliged to do the quite sensible thing of continuing the ban on all secret societies. Therefore, the Freemasons themselves, the German Freemasons, naturally approached their fellow Masons and it was soon put to various departments of the Control Commission.

In fact, it was bumped about from tray to tray until at last it came into my tray. As soon as I looked into this, and many with me too, we recognised that we were not dealing just with one movement, namely the Freemasons as we knew them in Britain, we were dealing also with another variety, a sort of Reformation within Freemasonry which had been caused in the nineteenth century in France by the breakaway from the fundamental principle of a belief in Almighty God.

The Grand Lodge of the Orient, which was not in any way connected after that with British Freemasonry, was represented pretty strongly among the Freemasons in Germany. We also knew that the Grand Lodge had a pretty bad record in the underground movement, not only under Hitler, but in many other places too, in Russia and in France—at the time of the Revolution in Russia as well as earlier at the time of the Revolution in France. We knew

120

that its record was not always a clearly simple and harmless one: it had had political implications.

The dilemma was there, the first that the Freemasons naturally wished, with their strong feeling of brotherhood, to help the German Freemasons to re-establish themselves, but also they knew that this could not be done if we were going to occupy Germany effectively. But they salved their conscience, I think, by recognising there was a difference between the Grand Lodge of the Orient and British Freemasonry. It was banned therefore, and for several years after the war.

No lodges, as far as we knew, met. It is probable they did meet in secret. Most of the societies that we banned in Germany after the war managed to keep together. As gradually power went over from the occupying forces to the Germans, then, like many other movements, Freemasonry became free and operative again, as it is today.

In fact, a United Grand Lodge was re-established in Western Germany in 1949, but in the Russian zone Free-masonry remained proscribed.

As in the First World War, British and American Free-masons raised large sums for wartime charities. In the United States the Grand Lodges opened War and Victory chests for servicemen whether Masons or not, but special provisions were made to help returning Masonic servicemen to find employment and educational opportunities. The Grand Lodge of New York alone collected a million and a half dollars for these funds. There was an American Masonic Service Association to administer the welfare work and thousands of Masons in the forces of the United States were able to visit recognised lodges in Britain and abroad. A return gesture for the hospitality was made by a Degree Team which demonstrated the American working of Craft ceremonies to English lodges.

In London the Royal Masonic Hospital opened its doors to wounded servicemen in 1940 and from then until 1948 treated 8,600 military patients free of charge and without distinction. Special gifts to the Treasury for the relief of distress included a sum of more than £28,000, the proceeds of melting down jewels surrendered by Masons under the jurisdiction of United Grand Lodge.

After the war New York Masons honoured Generals Marshall and Wainwright with their Medal for Distinguished Achievement. Another war, the one in Korea, prompted them to give the same token of appreciation to General Douglas MacArthur in 1963. He had become a Mason in 1936 and received the 33rd degree in Tokyo eleven years later. A hand-out from the Grand Lodge's public relations officer recalled:

During the war while he was Supreme Commander of the Allied Forces in the Southwest Pacific, the Masons of New York through their war chest sent the General thousands of books, harmonicas, tennis racquets, playing cards and other recreational and educational material to be distributed to the armed forces under his command.

The Second World War also produced an unusual example of Freemasonry's appeal to men in the adversity of war. British and Australian prisoners of war incarcerated at Changi after the fall of Singapore kept lodge meetings going in the form of ritual rehearsals and lectures, made Masonic working tools, and preserved written records in spite of the Japanese guards. The 'lodge' simply became a prayer meeting or a social event if the alarm was raised. In some other Japanese prisoner-of-war camps Masons also found comfort in meeting to rehearse the words of their rituals.

Freemasonry's most successful penetration of Asia was in India. Elsewhere its roots never went deep and such growth as was in the offing ended during the Second World War. A footnote to postwar prospects is provided by the communication of United Grand Lodge of December 1963. This recorded a change in the title of the District Grand Lodge of Hong Kong and South China. It was altered to the District Grand Lodge of Hong Kong and the Far East and remained somewhat pretentious, as the new form of words was to recognise the fact that of the thirteen lodges in the District twelve met in Hong Kong and the remaining one in Kobe, Japan. The Communist fear of Freemasonry was also reflected less obliquely on the other side of the world in Cuba, where lodge officers were arrested and the movement outlawed.

In spite of such setbacks, Freemasonry, however, continues to retain its popularity with the servicemen of many nations. At a large masonic suppliers in London's Great Queen Street I was told that much of the prosperity of the business rested upon export orders for aprons and other regalia received from NATO troops in Europe.

CHAPTER VIII

The Workings

Ideally, Freemasonry induces a group feeling strong enough to make each lodge a place where a variety of men of different faiths and from many walks of life meet socially and find a common bond within ritualism. The central and most important Masonic rituals are the three Craft degrees, 'the workings', and they owe something to three sources: the manuscripts, or Old Charges, relating to the organisation and legends widely accepted by operative masons in England; the Scottish Mason's word together with the catechisms by which it was imparted; and the invention of speculative Freemasons.

Speculative Freemasons were originally honorary members accepted into lodges of men employed as masons and it is possible only to theorise about the way these lodges of masons and honorary members grew into the movement we know as Freemasonry. It is certain, however, that by the seventeenth century lodges existed consisting entirely of speculative Masons and these lodges are the most likely source of present-day Masonic rituals.

By the eighteenth century the elaboration of symbolism around the working tools of the building craft and its system of graded workers and their legendary beliefs had produced among the majoribzty of Freemasons' lodges two degrees: Initiate, or Entered Apprentice; and Fellow Craft. The second degree at that time was full qualification for office as Master of the lodge or higher rank.

Much of the Masonic legend and the further sophistication of symbolism now expressed in the third, or Master Mason's, degree was probably incorporated in the two earlier degrees. The contemporary Fellow Craft degree is emaciated of content and drama by comparison with the first and third. The third degree, built around the legendary murder of Hiram Abiff, principal architect of King Solomon's temple, was established by 1730; but it is not known exactly when the degree first appeared. Obviously, some lodges were working the degree at this time, for early exposures of Freemasonry, notably Samuel Prichard's *Masonry Dissected* (1730) and Dr James Anderson's second edition of *Grand Lodge Constitutions* (1738), recognise the three-degree system. Some lodges, however, went on for a long time with the two-degree workings and frequently put candidates through both ceremonies in the same evening.

Within Freemasonry there have always existed local variations, and indeed these differences of ritual were an important obstacle in the way of the first attempts of Grand Lodge to weld English Freemasonry into a single movement. The attachment of Freemasons to their own ways of doing things and to so-called 'landmarks' was the basic cause of the conflict leading to the establishments of the rival Grand Lodge of the Antients and to the protracted struggle before English Freemasons accepted a single supreme authority for the Craft.

The Articles of Union agreed between England's two rival Grand Lodges in 1813 established the Lodge of Reconciliation, which had as its specific task the resolution of difficulties between the two fraternities arising over aspects of ritual. The Lodge of Reconciliation consisted of nine members from each of the Grand Lodges and the two Grand Secretaries. The Rev Samuel Hemming was appointed to the onerous office of lodge Master.

The reconstructed rituals eventually agreed upon by the lodge were not written down and circulated to the lodges; no written or printed ritual has ever been approved by Grand Lodge. The Lodge of Reconciliation simply demonstrated its revised ritual; and members, and the visitors, went throughout the country to teach the lodges the agreed workings from memory.

The method could not hope to achieve uniformity, but it was politic. It permitted many variations of unimportant detail to survive without renewed conflict and preserved the tradition that workings of Freemasonry are of such secrecy as to require purely oral transmission. When Grand Lodge, in 1816, approved the rituals demonstrated by the Lodge of Reconciliation and that lodge went out of existence, its work fulfilled, its triumph was the peaceful achievement of a wide measure of conformity rather than uniformity. Differing systems of workings continued to emerge.

Two of the earliest rivals were Stability, derived from the Stability Lodge of Instruction founded in 1817; and Emulation, named after Emulation Lodge of Improvement, founded in 1823. For both systems it is claimed they most faithfully represent the workings established following the Union of 1813. Emulation appears to have the larger following of the two; but today many Freemasons practise neither and use different workings known as West End, Oxford, Logic, Taylor's and Universal.

The multiplicity of workings and local variations provides the Mason visiting another lodge with a great deal of interest. Even if he is a guest in a lodge using a working with which he is closely familiar, he can enjoy the critical exercise of determining whether any minor variations are due to time-honoured local customs or merely to lapses of memory on the part of lodge officers. Committees control the content of the workings, almost each recognised system having its ruling authority; but, of course, quality of performance depends wholly on those taking part. Some officers may gabble, others speak too softly to be heard, and a few read from printed rituals produced as cribs small enough to conceal in the hand.

The use of cribs is frowned upon and officers may learn their parts in lodges of instruction. At minimum, they are expected to work in private to commit their words to memory; but, occasionally, a lodge Master finds his ceremonial burden too heavy and divides it up among other lodge members. Whatever the working and the quality of its performance, the fundamental aim of the ritual is to teach and illustrate the principles of Freemasonry to candidates.

Candidates must be men of at least twenty-one years of age who believe in God and have sought admission to the lodge of their own free will. They must also be 'well and worthily recommended, regularly proposed and approved in open lodge'. Much of the ceremonial and of the candidate's preparation for it derives from guild and trade practices and some of it is the kind of tomfoolery still associated with the ceremonies of modern coopers who roll in a barrel the young craftsman just out of apprenticeship. The common features of most initiation ceremonies are physical discomfort, sometimes pain, and the use of spectacle and drama to impress upon the initiate the moral codes and observances of the group.

The candidate for Masonry is prepared by the Tyler in the anteroom outside the lodge, where he strips to shirt and trousers. The shirt is opened to expose the left breast and the right sleeve rolled up above the elbow. The left trouser leg is rolled up above the knee and on his right foot he wears a slipper instead of a shoe. He is blindfold and around his neck is a noose. In the anteroom he leaves not only his dignity, but anything of metal—tie pin, cuff links, watch and money—for he must enter the lodge in symbolic poverty. Depriving the candidate of metals sometimes causes difficulties because of the attachments of braces, so some lodges provide the candidate with pyjama trousers.

Apart from the object of producing a feeling of humility, the traditional explanations of the candidate's dress are that it also ensured he was not concealing any weapons and the bared left breast guaranteed no woman was ever admitted. Another theory concerning the uncovering of the chest is more symbolic than practical and says that the heart, traditionally associated with the soul, is uncovered to suggest the candidate's fervency and sincerity. Another consideration is that medieval operative masons sought apprentices of perfect physique.

A blindfold is a prerequisite for almost any initiation into a secret society. Masons refer to the one used in the lodges as a 'hoodwink' and its removal during the initiation ceremony illustrates the candidate's entry into the light of new knowledge. Less pretentiously it may be said that the use of a blindfold in many ritual and play situations adds greatly to the fun and even drama of the spectacle. It is commonly acknowledged also that an individual's suggestibility is increased by being kept in darkness.

The wearing of a rope noose (in Masonic terms, a 'cabletow') around the neck is ages old as a sign of the hostage, a display of the willingness to be led into bondage and the impossibility of resistance. The concept of holy ground may find some reflection in the slipper the candidate is given to wear, for going slip-shod, or with bare feet, has deep associations with reverence. The giving of a shoe is also a pledge of fidelity, or confirmation of a contract by Jewish tradition (Ruth 4:7–9). The three knocks given on the door of the lodge prior to the candidate's entry are thought by some to be inherited from the Christian operative lodges and to allude to the Holy Trinity or to be meant to recall Revelation 3:20; or Matthew 7:8 and Luke 11:10. At all events, the Masonic ceremonial aims to make the first moment of entry into the place where its secrets are communicated as dramatic and memorable as possible, and the final trial for the candidate at the door is the touch of a dagger upon his bared left breast.

Taking an oath of secrecy was something that the medieval craft apprentice expected to do and there was, perhaps, a special emphasis upon this among the operative masons, for whom the secret passwords and signs were the means of marking themselves out from among casual workmen. The earliest of the Old Charges, the Regius Poem, contains the lines:

> To be true to the Ordinances
> A good true oath he must there swear
> To the Masters and Fellows that be there.

Nowadays Freemasons call upon candidates to take an obligation, the word being defined as a binding agreement, rather than a solemn appeal to God in witness that a promise will be kept. Nevertheless, the wording of the Masonic obligation is, to my mind, so suggestive of an oath as to make the distinction in this case pettifogging, particularly as the candidate makes his promise of secrecy kneeling and with one hand on the Bible, or the sacred book of his religion. The barbarous penalties[1] contained in the obligations of Freemasons also derive from the medieval lodges and reflect the harsher spirit of former times in matters of this kind.

The charitable activities of the medieval operative lodges find reflection in the ceremonials of today. In the first degree ritual the candidate's symbolic poverty by the deprivation of metals is related to it. At one stage in the ceremony he is presented with an alms dish and has, of course, to say he is without money. The ceremony is meant to demonstrate his willingness to give and to impress upon his mind for future vivid recollection when he is asked to help a brother Mason that at the time of his reception into the lodge he was himself 'poor and penniless'.

It hardly seems necessary to point out that the word 'brother' has been used within guild and trade organisations for centuries and is preserved by the modern trade-union movement. It implies a brotherhood created by hard experiences and this is at the heart of the rituals of the lodge. The single part of the rituals, actually described as a 'charge', and so recalling the old manuscripts which medieval masons probably read at initiation ceremonies, is given at the end of the first-degree ceremony. It may be delivered by the lodge Master, a past Master, or by a Warden.

'Brother A.B. as you have passed through the ceremony of your initiation, let me congratulate you on being admitted a

---

[1]In 1986 United Grand Lodge of England ordered that all references to physical penalties should be omitted from the oaths sworn by candidates in the three Degrees and by a Master Elect at his installation, but retained elsewhere in the ceremonies.

member of our ancient and honourable institution. Ancient, no doubt it is, as having subsisted from time immemorial, and honourable it must be acknowledged to be, as by a natural tendency it conduces to make those so who are obedient to its precepts. Indeed no institution can boast a more solid foundation than that on which Freemasonry rests, the practice of every moral and social virtue. And to so high an eminence has its credit been advanced that in every age monarchs themselves have been promoters of the art; have not thought it derogatory to their dignity to exchange the sceptre for the trowel; have patronised our mysteries and joined in our assemblies.

'As a Freemason, let me recommend to your most serious contemplation the Volume of the Sacred Law, charging you to consider it as the unerring standard of truth and justice, and to regulate your actions by the divine precepts it contains. Therein you will be taught the important duties you owe to God, to your neighbour, and to yourself. To God, by never mentioning His name but with that awe and reverence which are due from the creature to his Creator, by imploring His aid in all your lawful undertakings, and by looking up to Him in every emergency for comfort and support. To your neighbour, by acting with him on the square, by rendering him every kind office which justice or mercy may require, by relieving his necessities and soothing his afflictions, and by doing to him as in similar cases you would wish he would do to you. And to yourself, by such a prudent and well-regulated course of discipline as may best conduce to the preservation of your corporeal and mental faculties in their fullest energy, thereby enabling you to exert those talents wherewith God has blessed you, as well to His glory as the welfare of your fellow creatures.

'As a citizen of the world, I am to enjoin you to be exemplary in the discharge of your civil duties by never proposing or at all countenancing any act that may have a tendency to subvert the peace and good order of society; by paying due obedience to the laws of any State which may for a time become the place of your residence or afford you its protection and above all, by never losing sight of the allegiance due to the Sovereign of your native land, ever remembering that nature has implanted in your breast a sacred and indissoluble attachment towards that country whence you derived your birth and infant nurture.

'As an individual, let me recommend the practice of every domestic as well as public virtue: let Prudence direct you, Temperance chasten you, Fortitude support you, and Justice be the guide of all your actions. Be especially careful to maintain in their fullest splendour those truly Masonic ornaments which have already been amply illustrated, Benevolence and Charity.

'Still as a Freemason there are other excellences of character to which your attention may be peculiarly and forcibly directed. Amongst the foremost of these are secrecy, fidelity, and obedience. Secrecy consists in an inviolable adherence to the Obligation you have entered into, never improperly to disclose any of those Masonic secrets which have now been, or may, at any future period, be entrusted to your keeping, and cautiously to avoid all occasions which may inadvertently lead you so to do. Your fidelity must be exemplified by a strict observance of the Constitutions of the Fraternity, by adhering to the ancient landmarks of the Order, by never attempting to extort or otherwise unduly obtain the secrets of a superior degree, and by refraining from recommending anyone to a participation of our secrets unless you have strong grounds to believe that by a similar fidelity he will ultimately reflect honour on your choice. Your obedience must be proved by a strict observance of our laws and regulations, by prompt attention to all signs and summonses, by modest and correct demeanour in the Lodge, by abstaining from every topic of political or religious discussion, by a ready acquiescence in all votes and resolutions fully passed by a majority of the brethren, and by perfect submission to the Master and his Wardens whilst acting in the discharge of their respective offices.

'And as a last general recommendation, let me exhort you to dedicate yourself to such pursuits as may at once enable you to be respectable in life, useful to mankind, and an ornament to the society of which you have this day become a member. To study more especially such of the liberal arts and sciences as may lie within the compass of your attainment, and without neglecting the ordinary duties of your station, to endeavour to make a daily advancement in Masonic knowledge.

'From the very commendable attention you appear to have given to this charge, I am led to hope you will duly appreciate the value of Freemasonry, and indelibly imprint on your heart the sacred dictates of Truth, of Honour, and of Virtue.'

In addition to his new apron, and as tangible reminders of his first initiation, the candidate is presented with the working tools of an Entered Apprentice Freemason. These are: 24-inch gauge, symbolic of the twenty-four hours of the day and the need to spend them wisely; a gavel, representing the force of conscience; and a chisel, emblem of the advantages of education. It should be remembered, however, that there is no evidence to prove that medieval operative masons associated this symbolism with the craft tools.

The word degree literally means a step; and American lodges are said to open 'on a step', as in England they open 'in a degree'. When presented to the lodge prepared to take his second step towards becoming a Master Mason, the candidate no longer wears the blindfold and noose. His left breast is bared as for the first degree (in some lodges it is the right); but now his left arm and right knee are bared instead of vice versa, and the slipper has been moved from the right to the left foot. The changes seem to emphasise the intermediate character of the contemporary second-degree ceremony, for to be raised to the third degree the candidate appears with both arms, both breasts, and both knees bared; and has slippers upon both feet. The most intriguing new piece of symbolism, from a spectator viewpoint, to emerge in the second degree is the way in which the candidate is brought before the Master's pedestal for his second obligation.

The Senior Deacon demonstrates the moves and then accompanies the candidate in a form of goose-stepping.

Five high-stepping movements, 'as if ascending a winding staircase', are made through a quarter circle, bringing them both before the lodge Master. The tracing-board lecture of the degree explains that Fellow Craft masons at work on King Solomon's temple were paid their wages in the middle chamber of the temple reached by a winding staircase.

There is a reference to the middle chamber in I Kings 6:8; but one allegory drawn from this part of the ceremony is that the winding stairs depict mystery, hiding what is to be reached at the top, and the middle chamber represents the unknown future. If a suggestion from an American source[1] is accepted, the overtones are of a test of courage, frequently incorporated within initiation ceremonies; but other writers have associated the winding staircase with the movement of the sun, and, therefore, a symbol related to ancient religions.

The two-degree Masonic system, widely favoured before the Union of the two rival Grand Lodges of England, has left a permanent mark upon the contemporary ritual of initiation as a Fellow Craft Mason. The tools presented are those of the greatest importance to speculative Freemasonry and their replicas are the jewels of the lodge Master and his two Wardens. Here is an echo of the former position that a two-degree English Freemason was once fully qualified for high office. The tools are: the square, to teach morality; the level, equality; and the plumbrule, justness and uprightness of life and actions. When handing them to the candidate the Master says: 'By square conduct, level steps and upright intentions we hope to ascend to those immoral mansions whence all goodness emanates.'

The drama of the third initiation ceremony is the most powerful of the Craft degrees. The candidate is made to represent the hero figure of Masonry, the principal architect of King Solomon's temple, Hiram Abiff. After being symbolically slain by a blow with a maul, the candidate is lowered into a mock grave and later 'raised' from it by the lodge

[1]Carl H. Claudy, *Introduction to Freemasonry*, Macey, New York, 1932.

Master. The Masonic legend does not, however, include the resurrection theme: the story says merely that Hiram Abiff's body was disinterred for a more honourable burial. The allegorical instruction of the third degree drama is that all Master Masons are raised from a 'figurative death' to a new way of life.

Before examining this aspect of the degree more fully, it should be said again that the entry of the Hiramic legend into Freemasonry cannot be traced. Hiram is mentioned in Old Testament accounts of the building of King Solomon's temple (I Kings 5 and 7 and II Chronicles 2, 3, and 4). Both accounts, however, tell of Hiram a metal-worker; although the name Hiram becomes Huram in Chronicles. So there is no Biblical source for Hiram, the principal architect of the temple; nor, of course, for his murder after refusal to part with the secrets of a master mason.

Consequently, many ideas to account for the rise of the Legend have been suggested. Among the favoured sources are both medieval operative masons and speculative Freemasons who could have brought to the craft a Rosicrucian influence. The Graham Manuscript is evidence that medieval masons had a similar legend concerning Noah's death and the attempts of his sons to lift their father's body from its grave in the hope of discovering secrets; and the Rosicrucian legend embraces the discovery of the tomb of Rosenkreuz,[1] a tomb decorated with secret signs and containing documents.

Whatever the origin, or origins, of the Hiramic legend it belongs to those expressing the life-death cycle of the sun which in many ancient religions finds expression in a hero-figure whose noble death is followed by miraculous resurrection. Here the Masonic ritual shows how incomplete it is by comparison with that of religion. Hiram Abiff is not a figure who triumphs physically over death, nor does he belong to a Holy Family which, in the Christian religions, fulfils the deepest spiritual and psychological needs. The

[1]See Chapter I, p. 34.

Masonic degree achieves, however, the central symbolism of rebirth for the Master Mason candidate, and, because of the circumstances of Hiram's legendary death (a direct result of his tight-lipped steadfastness) it hammers home an important part of the philosophy of any secret society: better death than betrayal and dishonour.

There are embellishments upon the third-degree ceremony in Scotland and America which extend the play-acting of the Hiramic legend. In English lodges, after the candidate has been raised from his mock grave, instructed in the secret signs and word of the degree, and presented with his Master Mason's apron, the background to the murder of Hiram Abiff is explained to him. He is told that Hiram is first missed because plans and designs fail to appear. King Solomon orders a general muster of workmen and finds three are missing. Twelve other craftsmen who had been involved in the conspiracy but withdrew confess their part in the plot and King Solomon sends fifteen Fellow Crafts to search for Hiram. The Fellow Crafts find the grave and mark the spot with a sprig of acacia at its head.

Much of this part of the legend is enacted in some Scottish lodges where the ritual requires the candidate to retire before his mock death. When he returns to the lodge, sometimes blindfolded, the candidate is asked in turn by the Wardens and the Master for the secrets of a Master Mason. He refuses and is 'slain', his body being lowered on to a sheet upon the lodge floor and covered. Once the candidate is in his mock grave, the lodge members act out the search for Hiram, the discovery of the 'grave' and the capture of the three murderers. Only then is the candidate 'raised'.

The American third-degree working offers similar dramatic elaboration, and more. Several candidates are taken together for the first part of the ceremony, then they all retire and return individually, in ignorance, of course, of the ceremony which is still to follow. When the candidate comes back into the lodge he is wearing a Master Mason's apron with a Junior Warden's collar (the collar being an

135

allusion to Hiram Abiff, who was Junior Warden to King Solomon), and he is told that although he wears the uniform of a Master Mason the ceremony has not been completed. He is taken to the altar, which in American lodges is usually in the centre of the floor, and invited to pray, saying 'Amen' when he has finished. On the word 'Amen', the lodge members sing 'Nearer My God to thee', and he is blindfolded. Three lodge members play the parts of the murderers and are called Jubela, Jubelo and Jubelum. They ask the candidate for the secrets of a Master Mason and when he resists them, ill-treat him during a knock-about scene. Finally, he is 'murdered' in the traditional manner. There is the same play-acting of the roll call of workmen orderd by King Solomon, the search by fifteen Fellow Crafts and the eventual discovery of the 'body' and the 'killers'. Jubela, Jubelo and Jubelum are 'executed' in accordance with the Masonic penalties and with suitable cries from them.

After he has been 'raised', the candidate is read a charge and a lecture and can then take a rest while he watches the ceremony repeated with the remaining candidates. All American candidates for the degree must know the obligations of the earlier degrees and are examined in them. They are also called upon to demonstrate the secret signs of their degrees before being presented with the membership certificate of a Master Mason.

The candles of the Master and his Wardens are referred to by Masons as 'the three lesser lights' of the lodge, the three 'great though emblematical lights in Freemasonry' being the Volume of the Sacred Law, the square and the compasses. In English lodges the third-degree ceremony is carried out by the light of the Master's candle only and when the candidate is lowered into the mock grave a clock may strike twelve or the hour be sounded on a gong. Often the Dead March from *Saul* is played upon the organ and the last chapter of Ecclesiastes ('Remember now thy Creator. . . .') is recited. Some Scottish lodges offer a funeral prayer over the mock grave and in the American ritual the lodge members walk around it three times, singing a funeral hymn.

All ritual owes much to play-acting. The first plays were performed as part of religious services and often the actors were members of trade guilds simply projecting themselves and their work. The use of drama helps to achieve the aim of ritual, which is to impress. If the amount of play-acting is reduced, so is the impact of the ritual, because long speeches of description and instruction are needed to replace dialogue and action. In this way, not only is the ritual often made less effective, but it can speak only to the highly literate, for it is a common experience that as speeches become longer and more formal so do both the words and the language.

The loss of colour and theatrical elements from religious rituals appears to have left many Protestant men with a deep, if often unrecognised, sense of deprivation. Dr David Steel, a Minister of the Church of Scotland who became a Free-mason during 1952 while in East Africa, said in a television interview:

The Church in Scotland, I think largely through the Puritan influ-ence of the eighteenth century, has become somewhat barren of imagery, somewhat suspicious of ritual. . . . I think myself that this subconsciously is one of the attractions of Freemasonry to men in Scotland. They find in it this richness of symbol and imagery which articulates deep feelings which they may have, not in any rational sense, but in an imaginative way.

The basic effect on the individual of the drama and ceremonial of the three Craft degrees is, nevertheless, that sought by all initiation rites—the closest possible identifica-tion of the new-comer with the group. Freemasonry spreads this process over three ceremonies, each separated by a minimum of a month's waiting, and throughout the ceremo-nial it is emphasised that within the lodge the initiate can slowly progress to higher ranks.

The dark suits and ties, aprons, the passwords and secret signs, all speak of a special and closed group, but rank is declared by the uniform of Masonry. The apron and other regalia denote various levels of authority within it. The apron is a garment particularly appropriate to Masonry not only for its association with working craftsmen but also because it was worn by candidates seeking admission to some of the ancient mysteries. Once Freemasons enjoyed considerable freedom about the decoration, shape and size of aprons. Today the Grand Lodges have their rules about Masonic clothing.

The initiate is presented with a plain white apron of lamb-skin from fourteen to sixteen inches wide, twelve to fourteen inches deep, rectangular and with a pointed flap, bib, or fall. The strings are white. The apron of the Fellow Craft is the same, with the addition only of two sky-blue rosettes at the lower corners. The Master Mason's apron is the same size, but with sky-blue lining and edging of the same colour not more than two inches wide around apron and flap; also in the centre of the flap is placed a third sky-blue rosette and from beneath the flap extend two bands, or strings, of the same colour, attached to silver tassels.

The Master and past Masters wear, in place of the three rosettes on the Master Mason's apron, perpendicular lines upon horizontal lines, thereby forming three sets of two right angles, the length of the horizontal lines to be two inches and a half each and of the perpendicular lines one inch each. These emblems which replace the sky-blue rosettes are to be of silver or of sky-blue ribbon. The collars of the lodge officers are of light blue ribbon four inches broad and from them hang the jewels of office. A past Master's collar incorporates a central band of silver braid a quarter of an inch wide.

In many American lodges only a white apron is worn by all ranks, but grades are denoted by the way in which it is worn. An Entered Apprentice has the flap of his apron pointing upwards, the Fellow Craft one of the lower corners tucked under his belt, and the Master Mason both corners tucked up. It is still customary for the Master Mason's apron to have a narrow edging of blue.

White is the colour of purity, but the source and possible associations of the blue of the Master Mason's apron continue to cause speculation. It has been suggested that the sky-blue was adopted from the ribbon of the Order of the Garter. This was a light blue upon the Order's institution by Edward III in 1348 and remained so until the early eighteenth century when the present darker shade was adopted. The suggestion finds support in the fact that England's Grand Lodge officers wear regalia of garter blue, with the exception of the Grand Stewards, whose regalia is red—the colour of the ribbon of the Order of the Bath. Scotland's Grand Lodge officers have adopted the green of the ribbon of the Order of the Thistle and the Irish Grand Lodge the light blue of the Order of St Patrick. Another explanation for the blue edging of the Master Mason's apron may be suggested by Numbers 15:37–39:

And the Lord spake unto Moses, saying, 'Speak unto the children of Israel, and bid them that they make them fringes in the borders of their garments throughout their generation, and that they put upon the fringe of the borders a ribband of blue: And it shall be unto you for a fringe, that ye may look upon it, and remember all the commandments of the Lord, and do them; and that ye seek not after your own heart and your eyes, after which ye used to go a whoring'.

The initiation ceremonies instruct the candidate in the roles of the principal lodge officers and bring him into physical contact with them as he is accompanied on perambulations around the lodge and exchanges hand grips. No satisfying explanation can be found for the derivation of the title of the first officer he meets, the Tyler; the medieval lodges of working masons had Wardens and, in Scotland, Deacons. The use of both titles is made the more reminiscent of church officers by the wands the Deacons carry as symbols of office.

Freemasonry's initiation ceremonies conspire in their ritual to satisfy deep longings for drama and brotherhood by using the trappings of religion. They achieve their purposes, for the majority of Masons take membership seriously and have a loyalty strong enough to protect the secrecy of the movement. There remain the dangers associated with almost any ritual: it may cease to speak to men in terms that they can understand or relate to contemporary experiences; and its practice may become an end in itself more important than the ideas it seeks to express.

CHAPTER IX

The Open Secret

Much of the public interest in Freemasonry is due to the misconception that it really is a 'secret' society; but present-day Masons have nothing in common with the clandestine political organisations of the nineteenth century, the criminal ambitions of the Mafia, or the racial fanaticism of the Ku Klux Klan. It is an important distinction between Freemasonry and many other secret societies that men are free to leave. Also, Masonry is not a society with a secret membership: there are Freemasons who advertise the fact with trinkets on their watch-chains and Masonic membership is often mentioned in obituaries and occasionally in Debrett. Nor can Masonry be said to be a society existing in secret. Most towns in Britain have a building where Masons meet and the words 'Masonic Hall' are over the doorway.

It is the ceremonies carried out behind the closed doors of Masonic Halls which create the mystery and inspire much of the public speculation about Freemasonry. A folklore has been woven around the movement because it is in secret that selected candidates are initiated and swear never to divulge the business of the lodge. Amid all the speculation about Freemason's activities it is not widely known that the potential dangers of the movement are recognised by legislation.

In Britain the Unlawful Societies Act of 1799, designed to suppress seditious societies at a time when the wars of the French Revolution were at their height, makes illegal all societies whose members are required to take an oath not authorised by law.[1] Freemasons' lodges, however, were exempted from the scope of the Act after intervention by the 4th Duke of Atholl (Grand Master of the Antients at the time) and the Earl of Moira[2] (Acting Grand Master of the Moderns). The same setback to the movement in Ireland caused by the Unlawful Oaths in Ireland Act of 1823[3] might have occurred in English Freemasonry if they had been unsuccessful.

It has long been supposed that each lodge secretary has to make an annual return to the local Clerk of the Peace of the names, addresses and occupations of lodge members, but that the requirement, a consequence of the 1799 Act, was seldom met. This was confirmed in December 1985 when the Home Secretary told the House of Commons that justices' clerks kept no records of persons in their area known to be Freemasons.

Freemasons welcome difficulties placed in the way of outsiders who want to investigate their movement. They argue they are a legally constituted group of men who carry out ancient ceremonies and charitable activities in private and, as such, should not be subjected to the prying of the curious. This point of view has been accepted in official quarters for some time, for Freemasons have ignored the Promissory Oaths Act since it was passed in 1868. This Act says any society requiring members to take an Oath when they join shall substitute a declaration for the oath. The practices of Masonry are now widely assumed, however, to have the protection afforded by ancient custom.

Until 1987 upon initiation a candidate joining an English lodge could still be asked to swear to keep the secrets of Masonry 'under no less a penalty on the violation of any of them than that of having my throat cut across, my tongue

---

[1] It was for administering illegal oaths that the Tolpuddle Martyrs were transported in 1834 and thereafter Robert Owen and his friends in the growing trade-union movement dropped initiation oaths and ceremonies.
[2] Appointed Governor-General of India, 1812.
[3] cf. Chapter IV.

torn out by the root and buried in the sand of the sea at low water mark, etc.' In fact, it was not until 1964 that English lodges had authority from Grand Lodge to alter the wording of the oaths by deleting the words 'under no less a penalty' and substituting 'ever bearing in mind the ancient penalty'.

The permissive alternative form was not widely adopted and in response to growing concern about the oaths Grand Lodge wrote to the lodges in 1986 instructing that the penalties should be removed from the oaths of the three degrees and the installation ceremony of the Worshipful Master not later than June 1987. Yet the Grand Lodge of Ireland decided as long ago as 1893 that lodges should revise the wording of the oaths to make it clear to candidates that the penalties were symbolic and the real punishment for failure to keep the vows is to be branded as false and faithless. More recently, the Grand Lodge of New York decided in 1931 that the penalties, if taken literally, might make the whole organisation illegal; and in 1962 the Grand Lodge of Quebec adopted the Irish practice. English lodges now also bring themselves in line with similar modifications made years ago in Denmark, Holland, Scotland, South Africa and Switzerland.

With or without the sensible modifications, a real purpose for the oaths nowadays is difficult to imagine. When practising masons, who were qualified craftsmen, travelled extensively to build castles and cathedrals, it was important that they should be easily distinguishable from unskilled applicants for work. The secret grips and signs of the initiated served as a kind of 'union card', and oaths had a valid use in preserving this secrecy. Today one can only speculate about possible secrets of lodge business which make oaths necessary.

Freemasons rightly deny they are a secret society, but continue to describe themselves as a society with secrets in spite of the fact that the principles, purposes, laws and rituals of Freemasonry have all been disclosed. Obviously, no organisation embracing about 4,000,000 men can remain secret. Members leave by the thousands every year; and copies of the ceremonies, printed so that new generations of Masons can learn their parts, can be found in bookshops and libraries. There are Masonic periodicals, commentaries, ceremonial guides and histories to provide confirmation for those who want to crack the simple code in which the printers of the rituals hide key phrases. The Rev Walton Hannah, author of *Darkness Visible*, wrote to me:

What I did not print was that I myself have visited Masonic lodges, have witnessed the conferring of all three degrees, plus the Royal Arch . . . and so successfully had I decoded the secrets that I have never been caught as a gatecrashing non-Mason.

Officially, of course, a visitor to a Masonic lodge should be personally known to one of the lodge members present, or be given 'due examination' and asked to produce his Grand Lodge Certificate of membership and proof of good standing in his own lodge or lodges. A visitor from a lodge overseas not owing allegiance to any of the British Grand Lodges may also be called upon to prove that his initiation into Masonry was 'according to the ancient rites and ceremonies' and that his own lodge is under the jurisdiction of a recognised Grand Lodge. In practice, a visitor to lodges in the past has seldom been asked to produce a membership certificate, the 'passport' in Masonry; but there has been a considerable tightening of lodge security.

It is too late now, however, for Masons to renew their precautions to protect the rituals from exposure. They continue to justify the attempt by arguing that their ceremonies teach by allegory and symbolism, and so deeper meanings are not revealed by merely reading them, but by subjective experience. The same point could equally well be put forward about the rituals of religion, yet these are on view to the public.

Of course, it is easy to make ritual appear absurd, even in this country, where the entire nation is accustomed to a wide variety of fancy-dress shows—from the State opening of Parliament to Helston Furry Day—as an everyday part of its national life. It may also be inconvenient, even embarrassing, for Freemasons to find their time-honoured practices and attitudes, good though they may be, the subject of public debate. On the other hand, if what Masons say of themselves is the whole truth, why should they fear the verdict of a public forum?

Many critics of Masonry resent its exclusiveness, they fear that important social and economic advantages may attach to membership. Freemasonry answers these fears by pointing to the declaration all candidates sign before initiation:

'I being a free man, and of the full age of twenty-one years, do declare that, unbiased by the improper solicitation of friends, and uninfluenced by mercenary or other unworthy motive, I do freely and voluntarily offer myself a candidate for the mysteries of Masonry; that I am prompted by a favourable opinion conceived of the institution, and a desire of knowledge; and that I will cheerfully conform to all the ancient usages and the established customs of the Order.[1]

The declaration is almost meaningless, because the worthless secrecy surrounding Freemasonry is such that most candidates imagine they must enter the movement knowing little or nothing about it. In the circumstances it is difficult to see how they can possibly be 'prompted by a favourable opinion conceived of the institution'. They may be influenced by admiration of the character of men they know to be Masons; but it is more likely they are prompted to seek membership by the folklore which attaches to Freemasonry and is sustained by its secrecy.

An important part of this folklore is the belief that Freemasonry is a powerful and wealthy club which provides its members with comprehensive social security and enhanced prospect of advancement. To be honest and to admit that this is what the majority of non-Masons think is not to cast a slur upon every man who becomes a Mason, but to emphasise that motives for joining might be greatly clarified if the movement in this country was prepared to publicise more widely its aims, objects and activities. The preconceived ideas with which candidates approach Masonry may be modified by knowledge

[1]United Grand Lodge of England Constitutions.

of men who are Masons and later by experience in the lodge; but part of the price of Masonic secrecy is that ignorance and misunderstanding attracts men whose motives are unworthy of the best in the movement.

Some protection against abuse is provided by the screening of applicants, yet this is sometimes circumvented because men are invited to become lodge members (although this is strictly against Masonic regulations) and sometimes briefed on how to reply to questions when interviewed by the lodge committee. A leaflet giving guidance on admission into Freemasonry begins:

It has been noted that in many instances the only introduction applicants for admission into Freemasonry have received has consisted of an interview by a lodge committee. This is often conducted on stereotyped lines. In some cases the applicants have been warned and given expected replies to set questions. Others come to the interview without any knowledge of the institution they are aspiring to join, sometimes not even knowing the time or the cost involved. In general, the principles of Freemasonry are seldom adequately explained and there is insufficient emphasis on Freemasonry being in no sense a benevolent institution and that it must not be used for the furtherance of private ends.[1]

A candidate, of course, must be approved by all, or nearly all, of the lodge members. He may be proposed and seconded for initiation at a regular meeting; and, if the ballot is not so taken, the proposal lapses. Both proposer and seconder must know the candidate personally and be able to say he is 'a man of good reputation and well fitted to become a member of the lodge'. In theory this should mean that the sponsors can guarantee that their candidate is a man they know well in business, social and domestic life; that he believes in a Supreme Being; is of reasonable financial standing; has no criminal convictions or involvement in unsavoury court proceedings; and is not seeking to join Masonry for financial advantage.

[1]Published by London Grand Rank Association and reprinted in full in the *Masonic Record*, March 1966.

The screening and rules of election help to ensure the acceptability of new candidates, but how carefully are men prepared for admission into Freemasonry? The answer is: not very throughly. Norman Knight, a barrister and Masonic historian, says:

I had an embarrassing experience in my Mother lodge when a candidate whom I had proposed was duly initiated but, then, a fortnight or so later, resigned because, he said, he had no idea what terrible things he was going to be told to swear on the Bible.[1]

Many men who feel this way do not resign and become 'country members' instead, having no more connection with Freemasonry than the payment of subscriptions. One such Mason told me during a filmed interview that he was invited to join his lodge.

I had no thought at that time of becoming a Mason. But I was flattered; I was curious. And in the end I accepted. I went along after some months, to be initiated as a Mason, and I had a vague idea of what was going to happen, but I couldn't believe that my friend, and his friends, would indulge in this sort of spurious ceremony that I'd heard about. Well, in fact, they did.

It is still not permitted to show the candidate a copy of the oath he is expected to take before his initiation, although this is done in Holland, and it seems only reasonable that a candidate should be given a chance to study solemnly binding obligations before he accepts them.

The price Masons pay for insisting that the wording of the oaths is kept secret is that some men who might be particularly valuable members are kept away because they are not prepared to make another person, however respected a friend he may be, the temporary guardian of their conscience. A Christian may find it difficult to commit himself by oaths to a

[1]*Masonic Record,* August 1964.

147

course of action the nature of which is not revealed in advance. He may find himself involved in vows and practices which are in his view out of accord with the teaching of Christ; and he can hardly feel that his decision to join a 'sub-Christian' society is in itself a justification for taking such a risk.

Candidates are told in advance, and during the initiation ceremony, 'in these vows there is nothing incompatible with your civil, moral, or religious duties'; but the assurance comes from Masonry and demands of the candidate that he makes another man, who may not be a Christian, the custodian of his conscience. The Panel on Doctrine of the Church of Scotland which reported on Freemasonry and the taking of oaths in 1965 described this dilemma as 'blank cheque action' and said that where individuals were in doubt about its wisdom they ought to refrain from it. The report went on:

On the other hand it is difficult to believe that individuals apply for membership of a Masonic Lodge in total ignorance of the nature of its activities. There is a certain degree of more or less common knowledge; there is a fairly substantial literature widely available, and, the Panel heard with interest, it is now the practice in some Masonic Lodges to issue a booklet giving some information to candidates on receipt of their formal application. Into the bargain it is likely that candidates are influenced in some measure by the example of others whom they know to be Masons, whom they trust and respect, and whose society they wish to join. Thus the decision is not a completely blind one.

Moreover, the Masonic movement does not solicit new members, nor does it intend its members to do so, and those who of their own free will do join are likewise free to withdraw at any time, subject to the observance of the vow of secrecy. It remains a fact, however, that Masonry does not intend its rituals to be known prior to joining; and there will always be those to whom the Masonic movement has no appeal or who will find themselves for reasons of conscience decisively inhibited at this initial stage.

Because it is strictly secretive, English Freemasonry is compelled to hold out as a guarantee of its worthiness an eminently respectable leadership, and perhaps this is one reason for its outmoded and blatant fawning upon aristocracy. The secrecy also forces the movement to argue that it can be judged by its individual members, although it takes no steps to ensure that Freemasons can be recognised as such by their fellow men. Mr Leonard Griffith, Minister at the City Temple in London, joined Freemasonry in Canada and was surprised to find how the movement differed in England in this important aspect.

Here in Britain Freemasonry is indeed a secret society. When you meet a man he gives you no intimation of whether or not he has any identification with Freemasonry. In North America the Freemason tends to advertise his association with his lodge; he wears insignia on his coat lapel, a ring on his finger, he seems anxious to identify with other Freemasons, and to advertise generally to the public that he is a member of this movement.

The widespread attitude in America that to be a Freemason is something to be proud of and to let the world know about is in quite remarkable contrast to the traditional attitude of British Masons and it is reflected at all levels. The United Grand Lodge of the State of New York employs a public relations officer, and one of his tasks is to publicise the award each year of the Grand Lodge Medal for Distinguished Achievement. A Past Grand Master of New York's Freemasons, M. W. H. Lloyd Jones told the Men's League of the Marble Collegiate Church in 1961:

I have long held the view that Freemasonry should adopt a more open policy so that non-Masons may know what it stands for and what its noble aims and purposes are. There are many misconceptions held by our non-Masonic friends which I feel should be cleared up. Again, a more widespread knowledge of our activities and of our mission in the world would help to correct misinformation that is spread abroad by those who are unfriendly to the Fraternity.

New York's World Fair in 1964 embraced a Masonic Centre where historical documents and other items were on exhibition to advertise the respectability of the movement and to emphasise the theme of brotherhood. American Masons were told that the Centre was a new concept, a break with the old tradition of secrecy, justified because it showed how Freemasonry 'illumined the lives of men and encouraged them to practise the art of brotherhood.' The slogan coined was: 'Brotherhood is our most important product.'

There was a predictable emphasis upon the names of Masons who have achieved world fame:[1] Bolivar, Robert Burns, Garibaldi, Goethe, Haydn, Kipling, Kitchener, Kossuth, Lessing, Mazzini, Mozart, Cecil Rhodes, Sir Walter Scott, Sibelius, Voltaire and many others. Special places were found, too, for Masonic relics of George Washington, Franklin and Paul Revere. Among other notable Masons publicised: Irving Berlin, Eddie Cantor, 'Buffalo Bill' Cody, LeRoy Gordon Cooper and his fellow astronaut Virgil Grissom, Henry Ford and Will Rogers.

Falling membership in America, partly accelerated by the loss through death of many of the men who joined in large numbers during the years between the world wars, has led to continuing campaigns to give Freemasonry there a positive image and to counter criticism. These publicity programmes involve television and radio spots and advertisement in all major daily newspapers to deal directly with questions asked about Freemasonry and religion, membership and secrecy. In 1988 the Masons of New York State were so eager to make their membership known that the Grand Lodge was asking for a change of law to permit vehicle licence plates with Masonic identification.

By comparison, British Freemasons remain tight-lipped, although a carefully controlled programme of publicity and media interviews was begun in 1984. This is conducted by the Grand Secretary of the United Grand Lodge of England, Commander (Royal Navy) Michael Higham, who takes part

---

[1] Sir Winston Churchill is said to have been initiated into a South African lodge, but was never prominent in Masonry. President Lyndon Johnson joined a lodge in Texas in 1937, but did not pursue the Masonic degrees because of political duties.

in selected radio and television programmes, usually those which use listeners and viewers to put questions. He also gives occasional press briefings and interviews. At the opening in 1986 of a permanent public Masonic exhibition in Freemasons' Hall, London, Commander Higham said that for many years Freemasons had been in a defensive posture and it had been decided to try to clear up some of the public misconceptions.

Another important distinction between British Freemasonry and the movement in America is that one is a society strictly for men, while the other reaches out to take in the whole family. Through a multiplicity of ancillary organisations there is a real place in the Freemasonry movement of America for wives, sons and daughters. The candidate for English Freemasonry is likely to be asked merely if he has discussed his intention to join with his wife and made it clear to her that should he do so he will be away from home several evenings in the year. After initiation, of course, he is bound by the oaths of secrecy to keep Masonry a private part of his life and a taboo subject for discussion with his wife.

The only contact the majority of Masonic wives in Britain have with the movement is on those occasions when they are invited to dine with lodge members. As a result, many women, apart from believing that Masonry helps men to get on, are convinced that it provides an excuse for husbands to have 'a night out with the boys', and that the secrecy and ritual add harmless excitement of the sort generated among the members of schoolboy gangs.

Other women, particularly those with deep religious convictions, find the allegiance of the husband to a movement cloaked in secrecy a barrier to a full partnership of lives and a threat to the marriage. A Mason's wife wrote to me:

I have talked with many wives of Freemasons about their husbands being involved in the movement and, apart from the three women, all were resentful in various degrees of their husbands having a life of which they had no part. Personally, I feel a barrier between my husband and myself on this subject and, although I should like him to resign, I see many years ahead of strained relations over Freemasonry.

My husband joined the Craft [another letter said] at the start of our married life and it was a severe shock to me when I discovered all it entailed.

It is obvious that from time to time the candidates for Masonry are appalled by its initiation ceremonies and do not talk about them, not merely because of the oath, but to avoid the charge that they have been made to look foolish. This secrecy, sustained afterwards by a sense of humiliation, is ridiculous when it is realised how successfully the movement has been penetrated and that some of the more sensational elements of lodge ceremonies are fairly common knowledge.

The British attitude towards Freemasonry expresses a love frequently deepening to worship of the old and the traditional. Most Freemasons in this country just cannot realise that their secrecy is outworn and in the modern world has become a barrier in the way of the expressed ambitions of the movement. It is nonsense today to speak of universal brotherhood within the context of a secrecy which forbids members of the movement to talk freely about it with their families or to invite worthy men beyond the family to join. Perhaps Freemasons in this country fear the admission of women would cause the order to degenerate into a social club; but this is no defence of its secrecy, and no ground for rejecting the American compromise of parallel organisations for women and youth.

Such a development would mean a gradual widening of the Freemasonry movement, a broader expression of its ideals in community service, and a steady diminution of the suspicions and fears fostered by secrecy. When Rotary, for example, protests that it is not a secret society and that its members devote themselves to projects outside politics, race and religion, the openness of the movement is a powerful argument for accepting the assurance. Rotary's luncheon meetings are reported by newspapers throughout the world and its literature is readily available. There is a reluctance to publicise charitable activities, for Rotary, like Freemasonry, has made good works a rule of membership and a duty to be performed without acclaim.

It is not uncommon, of course, in any group or club for motives of charity and social service to be diluted with those of self-interest: there is not a businessman who does not know that people are more prone to do a deal with those they know rather than with strangers. On these grounds Rotary has attracted similar criticism to that levelled against Freemasonry. The criticism does not carry the same weight, however, because Rotary meetings are not held in secret and the movement has set some limits upon its membership and so restricted the extent and power of its influence.

There is an important difference also between the constitution of Freemasons' lodges and local Rotary clubs. Only one representative from each of the various classifications of business and professional men is allowed to become a member of a Rotary Club. Certainly this rule is stretched to allow unexpected classifications; but Freemasonry, with no such restriction upon its lodges, has the opportunity to enlist a majority of men at the top of a particular profession or business or with considerable power in local affairs. There is, of course, no reason at all why such men should not form a club: but there is no reason either why worthy men professing worthy aims should feel it important to carry out ceremonial initiation rites in secret.

I know a surgeon who is adamant that Freemasonry is so widespread in the medical profession that many of his colleagues argue that it is difficult to make progress in London without becoming one. The idea finds oblique support in the fact that the 250th anniversary of the founding of the Grand Lodge of England in 1717 was celebrated by the establishment of a Trust Fund to add to research Fellowships provided by the Royal College of Surgeons.

Freemasonry is said to flourish among top doctors [Paul Ferris writes in *The Doctors*][1] and a non-Mason surgeon at a teaching

[1]Victor Gollancz, 1965.

hospital assured me that 'No one would become surgeon to the Queen unless he was a Mason. It's very difficult for a consultant to get to the top if he isn't one'.

Ferris adds, however, that these allegations were emphatically denied when he made inquiries at the Royal Masonic Hospital.

Dr Mervyn Stockwood, when Bishop of Southwark, expressed similar fears about the extent of Masonic influence in the Church of England.

A case known to me involved a particularly unfortunate appointment to an important living. The man, a Mason, had little to commend him. But he was approved by the diocesan, the suffragan and by the archdeacon—all of whom were Masons. I am prepared to believe that the hierarchy was innocent and never allowed the Masonic factor to determine their choice. But in the diocese it was widely believed that it was the golden handshake rather than the Holy Spirit that filled the vacant living.[1]

Only the removal of the veil of secrecy over the workings of Masonic lodges will convince many people that all that goes on there is neither cause for alarm nor for offence to conscience. If this is not yet possible, because of the secretive and ultra-conservative attitude of traditionalist Freemasons, they should at least recognise that much needs to be done to educate the public for the best purposes of the movement to be apparent. It is the scale of opportunity for misuse that Freemasonry offers, because of its great numerical strength, which affronts and, because of Masonic secrecy, appals.

[1]*Church of England Newspaper,* 6th July 1962.

CHAPTER X

The Spies and Cowans

A secret society has power, real or imaginary, all the while it hides within the shadows of its secrecy and fear attaches to those aspects of the organisation which are concealed. For this reason Freemasons deplore exposures: they destroy curiosity, invite hostility and may even reveal to many people that Freemasonry has no secret power or esoteric knowledge worth the degree of importance with which Masons cover themselves and the Craft. Any brother, therefore, who reveals the secrets is a traitor and a dishonoured individual whose evidence is worthless, as it comes from a man who has broken solemn obligations sworn on the sacred book of the lodge. Outsiders who seek to uncover the truth are known in the quaint language of Masonry as 'cowans', and their investigations frequently attributed to a desire to turn an easy penny.

Certainly disclosures have often been popular and therefore profitable, if sometimes only a little more so than the works which Freemasons publish for the edification of each other; but the earliest works revealing Masonry are by Masons themselves, the authors of the old manuscripts owe nothing to the profit motive. The documents most fruitful of details of early ritual are: The Edinburgh Register House Manuscript (*c.* 1696), the Chetwode Crawley Manuscript (*c.* 1700), the Sloane Manuscript (*c.*1700), the Haughfoot Fragment (1702), and the Trinity College, Dublin, Manuscript (*c.* 1711).

The Edinburgh Manuscript was found among archives about 1930 and contains a catechism, a description of the Five Points of Fellowship, the Mason Word, and a form of ceremonial within which to communicate that word. Much in the writing suggests, however, that he manuscript derives from an exposure lampooning Freemasonry. The Chetwode Crawley Manuscript, named after an Irish scholar, has so much in common with the Edinburgh Manuscript that it, too, may have derived from the same original but unknown source.

Both the Edinburgh and Sloane Manuscripts refer to only two degrees. The Sloane Manuscript gives a Masonic oath and mentions that it is sealed by kissing the book. This manuscript also affords support from the past for the rule that as few as five Masons constitute a lodge and form a quorum. 'If need require five will serve', says the Sloane Manuscript, and then stipulates that two Entered Apprentices, two Fellow Crafts, and one Master may become a lodge, 'on the highest hill or lowest valley of the world without a crow of a cock or the bark of a dog'.

The Scots Haughfoot Lodge is now extinct, but there remain its minutes from 1702 to 1763 and a fragment torn from the minute book by a zealously secretive brother which contains some ritual directions. This account of ceremonial is of particular significance, as it includes phrases to be found in the Edinburgh and the Chetwode Crawley Manuscripts. The Trinity College, Dublin, Manuscript, provides the earliest evidence of there being three separate classes of Freemasons each with different secrets. It is preserved in the library of Trinity College and is believed to be of purely Irish origin.

Just as these particular documents and the whole collection of manuscripts known as the 'Old Charges' are of great value to the Masonic historian, so, too, are the early printed exposés, for they provide the only evidence Freemasons have of workings in use before the Lodge of Reconciliation began its work of reconstructing the rituals under the United Grand Lodge in 1813. Two of these exposés published in the early eighteenth century contributed to the conflict between English Masons which began to develop around the 1720s and had repercussions which threw the whole movement in England into disrepute.

The first of these appeared in issues of the *Flying Post* in April 1723 under the title 'A Mason's Examination' and claimed to have been based upon the papers of a deceased Mason. The revelation included such interesting titbits of information as: 'To call a Mason out from among company, you must cough three times or knock against anything three times.'

Little more than a year later, 3rd September 1724, the *Daily Post* carried a notice from an anti-Masonic organisation calling itself the Gormogons. The style of the announcement indicated knowledge both of Masonic pretensions and ritual:

Whereas the truly Antient Noble Order of the Gormogons, instituted by Chin-Quaw Ky-Po, the first Emperor of China, many thousand years before Adam and of which the great Confucius was Oecumenical Volgee, has lately been brought into England by a Mandarin and he, having admitted several Gentlemen of Honour into the Mystery of that most illustrious order, they have determined to hold a Chapter at the Castle Tavern in Fleet Street, at the particular request of several persons of quality. This is to inform the public, that there will be no drawn Sword at the Door, nor Ladder in a dark Room, nor will any Mason be receiv'd as a Member till he has renounced his Novel Order and been properly degraded. . . . The Mandarin will shortly set out for Rome, having a particular Commission to make a Present of this Antient Order to his Holiness and it is believed the whole Sacred College of Cardinals will commence Gormogons.

The invitation to join the Gormogons brought at least one important recruit. According to the *British Journal* 12th December:

A peer of the first Rank, a noted Member of the Society of Free Masons, hath suffered himself to be degraded as a member of that Society and his Leather Apron and Gloves to be burnt and thereupon enter'd himself as a Member of the Society of Gormogons, at the Castle Tavern.

Masonic historians[1] believe that the Peer of the Realm was no less a person than the sixth Grand Master, Philip, Duke of Wharton—and that he may have founded the Gormogons. The gesture might not be so remarkable as it seems, for the Duke, while notorious for his high living and his part in founding Hell Fire Clubs, was also renowned for his cynical wit.

Vastly more successful than *A Mason's Examination* was Samuel Prichard's exposé, *Masonry Dissected*, published on 30th October 1730. The book became a world bestseller and was the first publication to give details of the rituals of three degrees. Its influence was so widespread among Masons themselves at a time when they relied solely upon an oral tradition for their knowledge of the Craft that Prichard inadvertently may have played an important part in the establishment of the present three-degree system and ceremonials.

The embarrassment and confusion caused by *Masonry Dissected* led the Grand Lodge of England to transpose the secret words of the first and second degrees in an attempt to keep Prichard Masons out of the lodges. The change not only put the English Masons out of step with those in other countries, it was one of the main causes of dissension between the 'Antients' and the 'Moderns'. The change was temporary in England, but became permanent in Dutch Grand Orient lodges.

The effect of the exposés on many members of the public was to make Freemasons the butt of ribald contempt. A few saw an opportunity to gain money or advantages from the knowledge and with it made themselves Prichard Masons and initiated others: a tavern notice of the time declared: 'Masons made here for 2*s*. 6*d*.' Processions of mock Masons became commonplace.

Even before *A Mason's Examination* and *Masonry Dissected* the public appetite for disclosures about the activities of the

[1]F. L. Pick and G. N. Knight, *Pocket History of Freemasonry*, Frederick Muller Ltd, London, 1953.

Freemasons had been titillated by satirists, often employing a vulgarity which would cause offence today. The title-page of a long poem published in 1723 bore the verse:

> All Secrets 'till they once are known,
> Are wonderful, all Men must own;
> But when found out we cease to wonder
> 'Tis equal then to FART and THUNDER.[1]

The poem's author says he was admitted into the Society of Masons and to ease his conscience about writing the poem received absolution from his oath of secrecy. His account of the Masonic initiation ceremony includes references to branding and whipping.

Mock Masonic ceremonials had sufficient public interest in 1731 for an opera[2] to be published at the price of a shilling a copy and to be performed in one of the booths of the Bartholomew Fair. Its title-page read:

The Generous Free Mason: or, The Constant Lady (With the Humours of Squire Noodle and his Man Doodle). A Tragi-Comi-Farcical Ballad Opera. In three acts.

Noodle, of course, is an oafish, simple fellow who during the opera is talked into mock Masonic ceremony.

During the eighteenth century most Freemasons met in a tavern or coffee-house and the lodge meeting was a remarkably convivial and informal affair, the ceremonial being accompanied by smoking and drinking. The 'lodge' was chalked on the floor, according to early custom by the Master and Wardens, but later by the Tyler, and after a candidate had been admitted he was given a mop and pail to wash out the drawing.

[1] *The Free Masons—An Hudibrastic Poem:* British Museum Ref. 164.1.25.
[2] *The Generous Free Mason:* British Museum Ref. 992 k. 8 (2).

William Hogarth, himself a Mason, depicts lodge members leaving a London tavern in his painting *Night* (1738). The print shows a lodge Master, or Past Master, the worse for drink, being escorted home by the Tyler, who still carries his sword. Two other lodge members, one with a mop in his hand, are facing the Salisbury Flying Coach which has run into a street bonfire and overturned. The street is believed to be Hartshorn Lane, Charing Cross, now part of Northumberland Avenue, with the statue of Charles I at the end. The tavern was presumably The Rummer, Charing Cross, and a coarse touch shows a chamber pot being emptied out of a first-floor window upon the lodge Master's hat.[1]

Smoking in the English Grand Lodge was prohibited in 1755 and in its current *Points of Procedure* the United Grand Lodge deprecates challenging and cross-toasting and drinking to an extent 'detrimental to congenial conversation'. These procedural notes also emphasise that Grand Lodge condemns any drinking upon lodge premises at the ceremony of installing the lodge Master. The reforms were too late, however, to prevent the aristocratic flavour of early Freemasonry creating suspicion among the lower classes and widespread distaste for the excesses Hogarth satirised.

On the Continent more official opposition was growing as the lodges there attracted men disposed to be against the old order and anti-clerical or anti-religion. The publication of exposés and of the *Constitutions of Grand Lodge* (a second edition of Dr James Anderson's Constitutions appeared in 1738) may have done much to harden Roman Catholic opposition to Freemasonry. At all events, in 1738 Pope Clement XII condemned the organisation and forbade Catholics to have anything to do with it under pain of excommunication. Denouncing the order, the Pope remarked: 'If they were not acting ill, they would not . . . have such hatred of the light.' In 1751 Pope Benedict XIV renewed the condemnation and

---

[1] The Master was identified as Sir Thomas de Veil, a member of Hogarth's own lodge, and the Tyler as a Grand Lodge Officer, Andrew Montgomerie.

pointed to the secularism, secrecy and revolutionary activities of the society. Successive Popes (Pius VI in 1775; Pius VII, 1821; Leo XII, 1825; Pius VIII 1829; Gregory XVI, 1832; and Pius IX, 1846) confirmed the attitude of the Roman Catholic Church, not always very effectively, perhaps, for Bernard E. Jones writes:

Although the Roman Catholic opposition to Freemasonry is common knowledge, it should be known also that there were originally a great many Roman Catholic Freemasons in all the countries where Freemasonry flourished, among them being priests and high dignitaries of the Church, a condition which held good for many years (indeed, all through the eighteenth century in some countries), even after Pope Clement XII in 1738 and Benedict XIV in 1751 had issued their Bulls denouncing Freemasonry. In Liège, Belgium (to cite an instance given by Count Goblet d'Alviella), the Roman Catholic Bishop Velbrück, who ruled his ecclesiastical Principality from 1772 to 1784, was a devoted Freemason, as were many of his canons and officials. One of these, the Rev. Canon de Geloes, was founder and first Master of *La Parfaite Intelligence*, at Liège, which was first a French and later a Belgian lodge, while another, the Rev. Canon Nicolas Devaux, was Master of another Liège lodge, *La Parfaite Egalité*; other instances could be given. It is to be assumed that it was the comparative inattention paid to the Bulls in some quarters that led to a whole series of Papal edicts, beginning in 1821, confirming and renewing them.[1]

The Papal condemnations were ignored by many Freemasons in England and in Ireland. Thomas Mathew, Grand Master of the rival English Grand Lodge, the Antients, from 1766 to 1770 was a Roman Catholic. In the other English Masonic encampment, the Moderns, the ninth Lord Petre, looked upon as a leader of the Catholic community, succeeded the Duke of Beaufort as Grand Master in 1772 and held office for five years. In Ireland, Daniel O'Connell was initiated a Freemason in 1799 and became Master of his lodge in Dublin; but in 1837 he declared publicly that he had renounced membership.

[1] *Freemasons' Guide and Compendium.*

Freemasons argued that the Popes had acted on wrong information and been excessively severe, yet in 1884 Pope Leo XIII issued another Encyclical, declaring Freemasonry utterly incompatible with the Christian religion, and forbidding Catholics to become Masons. A cartoon in the magazine *Puck* of 1884 depicted an argument between the Pope and Masons and commented that they were like 'two old women scolding each other', lots of noise but no one is ever hurt.

But at the time of the first Papal Bull lodges in Roman Catholic countries were closed, sometimes by mobs. Freemasonry had already been persecuted by the civil authorities in Holland in 1735 and in France and Italy in 1737. The Pope's condemnation forced it even deeper underground, where it prospered. Further persecution in Vienna in 1743 and in Switzerland in 1745 had the same beneficial results in numerical terms, but inevitable confusion followed as highly individualist, if imitative, organisations sprang up, led by political intriguers, revolutionaries, alchemists and charlatans. Even Jesuits joined the secret societies in order to denounce members to the Inquisition.[1]

The number of Masonic exposés continued to grow. From France came *L'Ordre des Francs-Maçons Trahi* (1745) and *Le Maçon Demasqué* (1751). In England two most important additions were extravagantly titled: *The Three Distinct Knocks on the Door of the Most Ancient Freemasonry opening to all men, neither naked nor clothed, barefooted nor shod* (1760); and *Jachin and Boaz, or an Authentic Key to the Door of Freemasonry* (1762).

There Distinct Knocks gives a formal opening for lodge proceedings and the three degree rituals are separated. There is also a ceremony for the installation of the lodge Master. *Jachin and Boaz,* upon its full title-page offers 'a safe and easy method proposed by which a man may obtain admittance into any lodge without passing through the form

---

[1] In Spain the Inquisition did not finally end until 1834.

required, and thereby save a guinea or two in his pockets'. The book provides very similar rituals to those printed in *Three Distinct Knocks*, but has caught up with the Grand Lodge switch of the secret words of the first and second degrees.

Answers to Prichard's *Masonry Dissected* had included a reply published with the unofficial sanction of Grand Lodge and reprinted at the end of Anderson's second edition of the *Constitutions*. Laurence Dermott, the Secretary of the Antients Grand Lodge, now reacted in much the same way to the anonymous *Jachin and Boaz* and went so far as to say that the author had cut his own throat 'in a fit of jealousy'. The next edition of *Jachin and Boaz* contained the reply:

The author presents his compliments to Mr Dermott, Secretary, and thanks him for the pity and compassion he has so kindly shown to his widow and numerous family, and begs him to alter that part of the preface which mentions the author of *Jachin and Boaz* being dead.

The semi-official denunciations of the exposés as worthless were in sharp contrast to the attention paid to them and the change in ritual which Grand Lodge felt compelled to make after the appearance of *Masonry Dissected*. The conclusion is inescapable: the exposés were substantially accurate, and this is borne out by the notice Masonic historians continue to take of them. More objective attitudes prevail now but the earlier response of Masonry to the eighteenth-century disclosures expressed resentment which found poetic expression in 1762 with the publication of *A Freemason's Answer*.[1]

> May he that proves false to the Brethren be curst
> With want of good liquor and unceasing thirst,
> May his days be all passed in dissention and strife;

[1]British Museum: Ref. 112.

At home may he ever be plagu'd by his wife;
Abroad may he ever meet troubles and crosses,
And still may his gains be outweigh'd by his
losses;
May he still in abhorence be everywhere held,
And with shame and disgrace from all company
expell'd.

The exposés and the public reactions they triggered threw Freemasonry into disrepute and this at a time when the movement in England was bitterly divided. Public processions by Freemasons were banned by Grand Lodge in 1747 and a further regulation in 1754 prevented a Mason joining a funeral, military recruiting parade, or any other public procession wearing his Masonic regalia. The decisions were most unpopular and added to the rancour growing between groups of English Masons.

Later, during the conflict between the two rival English Grand Lodges, this bitterness was to find expression in the widespread practice of 're-making'. Masons from lodges giving allegiance to one authority had to be 're-made' if they sought admission to a lodge under the jurisdiction of the other Grand Lodge. This could be a costly business although it was not unusual for lodges to waive part of the 're-making' fees.

A move which might have done a great deal to restore the dwindling prestige of Freemasonry with the public, or at any rate upper-class society, came from Henry, 5th Duke of Beaufort, Master of the Grand Lodge of England from 1767 to 1771. He believed that the Freemasons Society should have a Royal Charter of Incorporation and in 1769 Grand Lodge agreed, the lodges voting 168 to forty-three in favour.

Among Freemasons opposition to the idea grew. One of the opposed lodges under the Duke of Beaufort's authority, Caledonian Lodge, even had the temerity to enter a caveat with the Attorney-General, and only just escaped erasure for the move. The rival Grand Lodge of the Antients was firmly against the plan, which they considered directed against themselves. Finally, when the Bill was due to be moved in the House of Commons by the Duke's Deputy Grand Master, Charles Dillon, he moved instead that consideration should be adjourned *sine die*. To the accompaniment of jubilation from the rival Antient Masons, the Duke of Beaufort's scheme went into limbo.

Against this background of dissension the flow of exposés continued. A quite unusual offer was made in the *Newcastle Courant* of 4th January 1770, when an announcement informed the public that the landlady of the Crown Tavern had witnessed a lodge meeting of the 22nd Regiment. She had broken open a door to get into a room next to the one in which the lodge was being held and had seen all that went on through two spyholes in the wall. The announcement added that Mrs Bell was willing to pass on the secrets of Freemasonry to 'all her sex' and 'any lady desirous of learning' had only to apply.

A printed exposé found its way into the hands of John Wesley and on Friday, 18th June, 1773, he wrote in his journal:

I went to Ballymena, and read a strange tract, that professes to discover 'the inmost recesses of Freemasonry'; said to be 'translated from the French original, and lately published at Berlin'. I incline to think it is a genuine account. Only if it be, I wonder the author is suffered to live. If it be, what an amazing banter upon all mankind is Freemasonry! And what a secret is it which so many concur to keep! From what motive? Through fear—or shame to own it?

There is a note in the Oxford History of England[1] about the author of one of the most important exposés of Masonry in the nineteenth century, although the biographical details given there make no mention of his attack on the Craft.

Richard Carlile (1790–1843), s. of a shoemaker, b. Ashburton; a tinman until the depression of 1817, when he began to sell

[1]*Age of Reform 1815–1870*, E.L. Woodward.

periodicals; reprinted Paine's *Age of Reason* and other works of a radical kind. Between 1818 and 1843 Carlile spent over nine years in prison, mainly owing to his persistence in defying the law. His wife and sister were also imprisoned for assisting in his work.

Carlile was one of the writers and printers whose pamphleteering, despite libellous recklessness, did much to lay the foundation for a free Press.

While in gaol he was able to publish *The Republican* and by 1825 had included in numbers of this periodical all the material which was to appear as his *Manual of Freemasonry*. Carlile wrote, in his introduction to the manual:

The following forms of opening, working, and closing lodges, are literally and truly the formularies of the three common degrees in Masonic Lodges, or that secret system which is called Craft Masonry. It has been communicated to me by Masons; it has been confirmed by other Masons; it has been the Standard Manual of Masonry, since it was first published in *The Republican* in 1825; it has made many Masons, without the lodge initiations, and, by its direction, I have been assured, that men who were never in a lodge have successfully and *profitably* taught practical masonry. The higher degrees form the subject of other volumes. They are not common; are denominated orders of chivalry; and but very few Masons go beyond the Royal Arch Degree.

Another of Carlile's claims is of greater importance: it is that his disclosures in *The Republican* led to the publication of lodge secrets in America by William Morgan, for this in turn precipitated Freemasonry's big crisis in the United States. Morgan's revelations were first printed in 1826 and might have caused only a minor sensation had he not disappeared, supposedly abducted by revengeful Masons out to murder him. The rumour that he had been killed took such hold that an anti-Masonic movement arose.

The effects of this outcry on Freemasonry in America were dramatic as public disapproval mounted. In the six years following Morgan's disappearance 140 newspapers with anti-Masonic views were founded and lodges closed as businessmen found their association with the movement too costly to continue in the face of public antagonism. In 1832 an anti-Masonic candidate stood in the Presidential election, opposing Andrew Jackson, well known to be a Freemason. Jackson got elected; but the Morgan affair set back American Freemasonry for more that thirty years.

Morgan's fate remains a mystery. Masons were arrested and imprisoned for abducting him, but it could not be proved that they had done anything more. A body found in Lake Ontario and identified as Morgan's by his wife was demonstrated to be the corpse of another man who had committed suicide. Meanwhile, Morgan's book went through many editions on both sides of the Atlantic.

In contrast to the exposés which continued to appear during the remainder of the nineteenth century was a rather plaintive open letter published[1] in London in 1881, price one penny, with the self-explanatory title: *Letter from a Freemason to General H R H Albert Edward, Prince of Wales.* The author points out that the Prince having become a Freemason should realise Freemasonry stands for brotherhood, democracy and free thought. He then challenges the Prince:

Go to Ireland—not to Punchestown races, at a cost to the people of more than £2,000—but secretly amongst its poor, and learn their deep griefs. Walk in London, not in parade at its horse shows, where snobs bow and stumble, but in plain dress and unattended; in its Spitalfields, Bethnal Green, Isle of Dogs, and Seven Dials; go where the unemployed commence to cry in vain for bread. . . . As a Freemason you are bound to succour the oppressed of the world, but then it will be against your fellow-princes. As a Freemason you are bound to aid in educating the ignorant, but if you do this you teach them that the sole authority Kings can wield they derive from the people. . . . You were a prince by birth, it was your misfortune. You have enrolled yourself a Freemason by choice, it shall either

[1]Published by Annie Besant and Charles Bradlaugh. See Chapter VI, p. 104.

be your virtue or your crime—your virtue if you are true to its manly dutifulness; your crime if you dream that your blood royal is of richer quality than the poorest drop in the veins of a free and Accepted Mason.

Of the printed attacks on Freemasonry in this century, two are of particular note and are from clergymen who base their antipathy on theological grounds. The first, *The Menace of Freemasonry to the Christian Faith*, was written by the Rev C. Penney Hunt and published in 1926. The book so disturbed English Methodists that the following year they discussed Freemasonry at their Bradford Conference. A resolution passed by that Conference spoke of the 'purely Theistic nature' of Freemasonry and declared: 'The distinctive faith of Christianity can find no expression in its formulae.'

The Rev Penney Hunt's book, although it quoted the wording of Masonic oaths, was not strictly an exposé. The twin-barrelled blast of a clergyman's theological objections printed with the rituals of the first three degrees and other ceremonies came with *Darkness Visible*. This was published in 1952[1] and attracted a great deal of Press publicity. The author, the Rev Walton Hannah had been Priest in Charge of St Thomas's, Regent Street, and St Anne's, Soho, London. Then he had become Rector of Balcombe, Sussex, but resigned the living in 1947 to devote himself to study and writing.

Following the publication of *Darkness Visible*, he joined the Roman Catholic Church. He explained in an interview during 1965:

I had always been associated with High Church, the Anglo-Catholic school in the Church of England, and I came to the conclusion that the Church of England today did not have that spiritual authority to teach that Christ intended his Church to have.

[1]Augustine Press.

Undoubtedly, Father Hannah was disappointed with the results of attempts which he and Dr Hubert S. Box,[1] and others, made to raise the issue of Freemasonry in the Church of England. An article by Father Hannah entitled 'Should a Christian be a Freemason?' was published in the January 1951 edition of a specialist magazine, *Theology*,[2] and was taken up by the popular Press. The *Daily Express*, for example, in its issue of 15th January 1951, devoted four columns to a story with the headlines:

Are you a Mason? Row awaits. Foaming Archbishop—and he is!

Reynolds News of 4th February 1951 gave a five-column article under the headlines:

Church of England Sensation. King may act in Row over Freemasonry.

The stage was set, but for a damp squib. The theological controversy was not debated, as expected before the next Church of England Canterbury Convocation in May. According to Father Hannah, this was because of the intervention on the Masonic Bishop of Reading, Dr A. Groom Parham. There was a sequel in June, when the Freemasonry controversy came before the Church Assembly.

This body was not in any case competent to deal with the theological issues [Father Hannah says], but Masonic support could be relied on; critics of Masonry were frankly out-manoeuvred by the unexpectedness and speed with which Masons themselves with very little warning arranged the debate and placed it on a supplementary agenda, and the result was an appeal to sentimentality, to the social and ecclesiastical eminence of Masons, moral irrelevance, even including personal abuse, in which the theological issue was again completely sidestepped.[3]

The Rev R. Creed Meredith tabled a motion that a commission be appointed to report on Fr Hannah's article.

[1] Author of another book of theological objections to Masonry, *The Nature of Freemasonry*, Augustine Press, 1952.
[2] Published by the Society for Promoting Christian Knowledge.
[3] *Christian by Degrees.*

Freemasonry, he said, had been 'placed in the dock and pain and distress caused to hundreds of loyal Churchmen up and down the country. And he defended Freemasonry as:

A brotherhood of princes, prelates and peers, and a great body of ordinary men. . . . It is a brotherhood which seeks after truth, encourages members to uphold one another in the highest moral principles and strict honesty of purpose and integrity in all matters of business.

The Archbishop of York, who declared himself a non-Mason, told the Assembly:

Freemasonry in this country has always avoided the anti-clericalism which makes it offensive on the continent. It has never made any attack on Christianity and the Church.

Dr Garbett said that he found reassurance in the fact that the Archbishop of Canterbury (then Dr Fisher) was a Mason and that the Grand Master of the order was Lord Scarbrough. The motion for an inquiry was rejected with only a single vote in favour; and the result welcomed by its mover, the Rev R. Creed Meredith. The *Church Times*, 29th June 1951, commented:

There is sheer lack of logic in saying: 'We have absolutely nothing to fear from an enquiry. Therefore, there must on no account be an enquiry.'

Father Hannah recalled the debate in the interview quoted earlier:

I attended in person and most of the Masons who were speakers said that Mr Hannah could not possibly know what he was talking about; Mr Hannah was not a Mason—nobody who was not a Mason could ever know—therefore, Mr Hannah's criticisms are utterly valueless and worthless. So I was forced then into proving that Masonic secrecy is simply bluff, into publishing the book, with the entire Masonic ritual from beginning to end through the first three degrees.

The *Observer*, 15th June 1952, reported:

There are two new developments. Canon V.A.Demant, one of the Church of England's leading theologians, who is Regius Professor of Pastoral and Moral Theology at Oxford, has given it as his opinion that a Masonic oath is invalid for a Christian. The second development is that the Rev Walton Hannah, the man who originally started the controversy is shortly bringing out an astonishing book called *Darkness Visible*. Apparently several Christian Masons were so impressed by Canon Demant's ruling that they have come forward and given Mr Hannah what purports to be the facts about Masonic rituals.

Reynolds News of the same date carried an account of an attempt to suppress the book. Father Hannah told the newspaper that he had a telephone call asking him to be in the foyer of the Savoy Hotel, London. When out of curiosity he went there a man came up and offered him £1,000 in notes if he would sign an undertaking not to publish his book. Hannah refused and the man walked straight out of the hotel.

Four days later, on 19th June 1952, the *Daily Mirror* gave a page to Father Hannah's book. Around the headline *The Secret Signs of a Million Men* were pictures of Masonic grips and signs, amd the editorial was based on some nice filleting of Father Hannah's revelations of the secret words and the ceremonies containing them. In his second book, *Christian by Degrees* (devoted to the side degrees of Masonry open to men who have become Master Masons), Hannah commented:

Quite unconcerned with the religious issue, with my motives in writing the book, or indeed with anything beyond sensationalism and curiosity, Fleet Street unwittingly re-launched a theological controversy still unresolved and unanswered.

Certainly the press had made his earlier book, *Darkness Visible*, a best-seller: one can only speculate how many readers bought it for the theological arguments.

Father Hannah's disclosures of Masonic ceremonies were based on previous exposés, which he compared with modern rituals printed by Masonic publishers, and he confirmed his conclusions by checking Masonic commentaries and with two friends who had 'unquestionably been Masons'. He has been attacked for inviting his friends to forswear themselves, but many Masons who are men of integrity and aware of the long history of exposés simply cannot accept a vow of secrecy as still operative once the secret is known; or when in those circumstances conscience compels them to speak in order to achieve what they consider to be the good of other men.

Father Hannah's theological squib which seemed so damp at the Church of England's Convocation and Assembly of 1951 was set blazing briefly by the popular press. Despite this and sporadic public debate, the Church of England waited until 1985 before the General Synod passed a private member's motion calling for a report which considered the compatibility or otherwise of Freemasonry with Christianity. The report, endorsed by the General Synod two years later, presented various theological objections to Freemasonry and declared part of the Royal Arch rituals blasphemous, but it did not call upon Anglicans to give up membership of Masonic lodges.

Father Hannah's book and the publicity it received in the press was widely resented among Freemasons but dismissed as yet another unsuccessful attack on Freemasonry, simply the latest in a long line going back to the days before the first Grand Lodge. Freemasons were more disturbed by the first television programme about Freemasonry, a BBC documentary screened on 16 March 1965 and seen in 4,730,000 homes. The programme was produced by the author of this book without any help from the Grand Lodges of England, Scotland and New York. The Grand Lodges declined to take part, behaving as if the long line of exposures of Freemasonry did not exist. The BBC programme was the forerunner of other television and radio programmes exploiting the fact that, if Freemasonry's secrets were truly confined to its rituals and the secret recognition signs and codewords contained within them, these had been public property since the publication of Hannah's *Darkness Visible*.

It is inevitable that many Fremasons will object to books and television and radio programmes which expose their not so secret rituals and challenge cherished Masonic beliefs. The secrecy which still surrounds Freemasonry, and the opportunity for misuse this presents to such a large number of men, ensure that these investigations continue. The central difficulty with such journalism is the nature of the evidence uncovered by the researcher. Witnesses may rely on hearsay, as well as being prejudiced, and be so fearful of recriminations and reprisals from other Masons that they wish to remain anonymous. There are also proper legal constraints when its comes to naming names.

No legal problems exist, of course, when those accused of Masonic conspiracy are dead and not interested in libel actions. Stephen Knight in his book, *Jack the Ripper: The Final Solution*,[1] could freely advance his theory that a Freemason was responsible for the murders attributed to Jack the Ripper. He claimed that the prostitutes died by mutilation carried out according to the penalties set out in Masonic ritual and were murdered because they knew a state secret: that Prince Albert Victor Christian Edward, grandson of Queen Victoria and Heir Presumptive to the throne, had illegally married and fathered a child by a Roman Catholic commoner. The man behind the murders, said Knight, was Sir William Gull, Physician in Ordinary to the Queen, and the crimes were covered up by another eminent Freemason, Sir Charles Warren, the then commissioner of the Metropolitan Police.

'I am free to name only a small number of the many hundreds of people who have helped with advice and information,' wrote Knight introducing his next book about Freemasonry, *The Brotherhood*. This means, of course, that the serious allegations of Masonic conspiracy that the book contains cannot be properly tested. Nevertheless, it offers some

[1]Harrap, 1976.

documented cases of villainy among Masonic police officers and some not so well established evidence of Masonic influence among members of the Bar and the judiciary.

The Brotherhood caused a sensation on publication and within days there followed questions in the House of Commons. On 6th February 1984 Mr Austin Mitchell, Labour M P for Grimsby, asked Sir Michael Havers whether, in view of the evidence which had been sent to him that indicated that membership of Masonic lodges was detrimental to the fair and efficient exercise of their responsibilities by judges in the courts, the Lord Chancellor would make it a condition of their appointment that they were not Freemasons.

Sir Michael replied, No. The conditions for appointment to, and tenure of, judicial office, he added, were prescribed by statute, and no Minister had power to modify these or add to them. The independence of the judiciary from the Executive, thus guaranteed, was a principle of great constitutional importance.

Mr Austin Mitchell put a similar question to the Home Secretary, Mr Hurd, asking if he would take action to prohibit police officers from membership of Masonic lodges. Mr Hurd replied:

No. Such prohibition would be an unwarranted restriction on the private lives of police officers. Police regulations require police officers to abstain from any activity which is likely to interfere with the impartial discharge of their duties. Faiiure to comply with this requirement is a disciplinary offence and any specific evidence of such failure should be brought to the attention of the authorities in the usual way.

Knight's most sensational conclusion was more far-reaching and involved the security of the State. He claimed that the KGB is infiltrating Freemasonry and that the Russian intelligence organisation was behind the secret Italian Masonic lodge P2[1] and used it to destabilise

---

[1]For an authoritative investigation of P2 see *In God's Name*, David Yallop, Corgi Books, 1988.

174

Italy. The existence of the lodge came to the attention of the world's press in May 1981 when the Italian government published a list of names of men who were members. The 953 names on the list included two Cabinet ministers, 19 judges and many high-ranking army officers and prominent businessmen. They had been recruited by Lucio Gelli, a rich textile manufacturer from the Tuscan town of Arezzo and Master of P2.

Gelli was born in Pistoia, Central Italy, in 1919. In his mid-teens he was expelled from school and later joined the Italian Black Shirt Division to fight alongside the Fascists in Spain. During the Second World War he fought in Albania and then in Italy where he became involved in crimes against partisans. In 1954 he arrived in Argentina where he aligned himself with extreme right-wing groups and became a close friend of General Juan Peron. When the dictator was deposed after a military coup in 1956, Gelli quickly began befriending the incoming junta. He acquired dual nationality and drew around him a network of powerful people as he moved through a succession of business posts in South America and Italy. An important step on his road to power was his appointment in 1972 as Argentina's economic adviser to Italy and one of his principal tasks was to buy arms for the junta.

Gelli's Masonic career began in 1963 when he joined a conventional lodge under the Grand Orient of Italy. He was noticed by the Grand Master of Italy's Freemasons, Giordano Gamberini, and invited to form a group of influential men who would be useful to Freemasonry. The group was named Raggruppamento Gelli Propaganda Due,[1] P2 for short, and Gelli turned it into an illegal secret organisation comprising many of the most influential men in the country. Knight describes how Gelli did it:

[1] Propaganda was the name of an historic lodge constituted in Turin in the 19th century.

He had a genius for convincing people he had immense influence in public affairs, and many men joined P2 because they believed the Venerable Master's patronage was indispensable to the furtherance of their careers. By this self-perpetuating process, Gelli's purported power became real. Others joined the lodge because Gelli used ruthless blackmail. The 'Masonic dues' Gelli extracted from the brethren of lodge P2 were not primarily financial. What the Venerable Master demanded – and got – were secrets: official secrets which he could use to consolidate and extend his power, and personal secrets he could use to blackmail others into joining his lodge. This most sensitive information from all areas of government was passed to him by his members, who seem have obeyed him with unquestioning devotion.

Two of the names on the list of P2 members were those of Italian financiers, Michele Sindona and Roberto Calvi. Sindona, who had Mafia connections, had been sentenced to 25 years' imprisonment in June 1980 on charges arising from the collapse of the Franklin National Bank of New York. He was given another two and a half years for arranging his own false kidnapping so that he could go to Sicily on a desperate mission to tidy up his financial affairs. Before his arrest in New York, Sindona was wanted in Italy where he had been given another term in prison for misappropriating ten million pounds.

He successfully resisted extradition until 1985 when, while still serving time in America, he was sent for trial in Italy. On 18 March 1986, he was found guilty of ordering a murder and sentenced to life imprisonment, this to follow the remainder of his sentence in the United States. Faced with the prospect that he would die in prison, Sindona decided to betray the Mafia. Four days after being given the life sentence he was dead: he had drunk coffee that was poisoned.

Gelli was suspected of helping to arrange Sindona's 'kidnap' and in March 1981 Milan magistrates ordered a police raid on Gelli's home, Villa Wanda, outside Arezzo. Gelli and his wife, Wanda, had both fled to South America, but files of P2 lodge were there alongside secret government reports. The scandal that followed brought down the government and prompted further investigation into the affairs of Roberto Calvi. Within weeks he was found guilty of smuggling currency out of Italy and sentenced to four years' imprisonment and fined 16 billion lire. He appealed and was granted bail. Days later the board of Banco Ambrosiano, one of the country's largest banks, reconfirmed him as its chairman.

Like Sindona, Calvi was a close friend of Gelli. He was also associated with laundering Mafia money and was a financial adviser to the Vatican. Calvi, known as 'God's Banker', was one of the most powerful financiers in Italy and frequently conspired to fraud with Sindona. He was connected with the Vatican Bank, the IOR, and it is believed that the Vatican lost several million pounds when Calvi's Banco Ambrosiano crashed. Days before that, 18 June 1982, Calvi was found hanged under Blackfriars Bridge[1] in London. His body was weighted down with masonry. Half-bricks were in his pockets and down the front of his trousers and there was speculation that he had been the victim of a ritualistic Masonic killing. The first inquest into his death found that he had committed suicide, a second recorded an open verdict and, in January 1989, a court in Milan decided that Calvi was murdered.

Gelli is now believed to continue to control an international network of secret P2 lodges from a safe hiding in Brazil. Knight offered this verdict on KGB ambitions for the first lodge and his fears of similar success in Britain:

From the beginning, Lodge P2 was a KGB-sponsored programme aimed at destabilising Italy, weakening NATO's southern flank, sweeping the Communists into power in Italy and sending resultant shock waves throughout the western world. It achieved its first aim, partially succeeded in its second, came close to realising the

---

[1] The logo of the Grand Orient in Italy is the figure of a Blackfriar.

third, and all the but failed in the fourth ... The exploitation of Freemasonry by the KGB is not restricted to Italy. I can reveal that senior officers of British Intelligence are concerned that the KGB has been using Freemasonry in England for decades to help place its agents in positions of responsibility and influence ... According to the evidence now available the undoubted 'jobs for the brethren' aspect of British Freemasonry has been used extensively by the KGB to penetrate the most sensitive areas of authority, most spectacularly illustrated in the years since 1945 by its placing of spies at the highest levels of both MI5 and MI6.

Freemasonry, said Knight, got Sir Roger Hollis into MI5 and took him to the top: he was director-general from 1956 to 1965. Although it has been officially denied that Sir Roger, who died in 1981, was a Russian spy, according to Knight few people in MI5 doubted it. Sir Roger, he said, was poorly qualified as a recruit to MI5 on grounds of health and talent and only got into the service because he was a Freemason, as was the director-general at the time. Knight believed that Sir Roger became a Freemason when he worked for a tobacco company in Shanghai in the 1930s. Membership lists of the Shanghai lodges between the wars were among the most closely guarded secrets of the United Grand Lodge, and he added:

Several attempts by concerned members of the Brotherhood to get hold of these files through the ordinary channels have been blocked. It is evident that those lists of names contain something so explosive, so potentially damaging to the Brotherhood, that it will not permit them to be examined even by senior Masons. Whose name is being concealed, if not Hollis's?

In evidence to a working group of the Standing Committee of the General Synod of the Church of England, the United Grand Lodge of England said, 'Knight's claim that the registers of English lodges in the Far East were kept tightly secret for the period during which Sir Roger Hollis was in residence is nonsense. Sir Roger was in any case not a Mason'.

In the closing sections of his book Knight quoted extensively from a 'secret memorandum' which set out the dangers of KGB infiltration of Freemasonry. He said it was written in 1981 by a British diplomat who worked with MI6 for nearly 20 years. The memorandum suggests that Britain could be even more vulnerable to a Masonic scandal than Italy. KGB interest in British Freemasonry could lead to a plot to provoke public outrage following a P2-type scandal. The author of the memorandum is so unconcerned at the reality of the dangers to the State that he envisages, or so fearful of some sort of reprisal should his name be known, that his warnings lack the authority of a signature. Knight calls him 'Chinaman'.

In a sequel to Knight's book[1] Martin Short dismisses the Chinaman's theory that the KGB uses Freemasonry to infiltrate British society. He points out that there is no proof of the existence of KGB Freemasons and that spies might more usefully join other British institutions, such as exclusive clubs or the House of Commons.

Short also rebuts Knight's suggestion that Lodge P2 was the centre of a KGB plot to weaken NATO and to destabilise Italy. Knight's source in British intelligence, he writes, 'filled him with disinformation'. Knight was misled, claims Short, possibly to protect the image of a reformed Grand Orient tradition by placing the P2 scandal at the door of the KGB and, at the same time, to reduce embarrassment arising from the continuing recognition of Italy's Grand Orient by the United Grand Lodge of England.

[1]*Inside the Brotherhood*, Grafton Books, 1989.

CHAPTER XI

The Ordeal of a Master Mason

CEREMONY OF INITIATION

The lodge has opened in the First Degree. Outside the Temple are Tyler and candidate. The candidate is blindfold and wears a noose around his neck. His left breast is bared and the right sleeve of his shirt rolled above the elbow. His left trouser leg is rolled up above the knee and on his right foot he wears a slipper. His money, watch, cuff links and any articles of metal have been left in the anteroom. The Tyler knocks upon the door of the Temple.[1] Within the Inner Guard parodies a military salute by taking the Masonic step and giving the First Degree sign before addressing the Junior Warden. The step is made by taking a short pace forward with the left foot and bringing the right heel into the instep to form a 'T'. The First Degree sign is given by bringing the outstretched thumb of the right hand to the left of the windpipe and keeping the elbow horizontal to the body.

INNER GUARD. (*To Junior Warden.*) Brother Brown, there is a report.
JUNIOR WARDEN. (*Knocks with his gavel. Rises and takes step and makes sign of the First Degree as he turns to the Worshipful Master.*) Brother Grey, there is a report.
WORSHIPFUL MASTER. Brother Brown, inquire who wants admission.

---

[1] Three evenly spaced knocks for First Degree ceremonies. For Second Degree one knock followed by two quick ones. For Third Degree two quick knocks followed by one.

JUNIOR WARDEN. (*Cuts sign by drawing right hand across throat and dropping arm to side. Sits down.*) Brother Green [Inner Guard], see who wants admission.

INNER GUARD. (*Cuts sign. Opens door and talks with Tyler.*) Whom have you there?

TYLER. Mr John Smith, a poor candidate in a state of darkness who has been well and worthily recommended, regularly proposed and approved in open Lodge, and now comes of his own free will and accord, properly prepared, humbly soliciting to be admitted to the mysteries and privileges of Freemasonry.

INNER GUARD. How does he hope to obtain those privileges?

CANDIDATE. (*Repeating the words after Tyler.*) By the help of God, being free and of good report.

INNER GUARD. Halt while I report to the Worshipful Master. (*Shuts door. Takes step and makes sign.*) Worshipful Master, Mr John Smith, a poor candidate in a state of darkness ... (*repeating Tyler's speech above*) ... humbly soliciting to be admitted to the mysteries and privileges of Freemasonry.

WORSHIPFUL MASTER. How does he hope to obtain those privileges?

INNER GUARD. By the help of God, being free and of good report.

WORSHIPFUL MASTER. The tongue of good report has already been heard in his favour; do you, Brother Inner Guard,[1] vouch that he is properly prepared?

INNER GUARD. I do, Worshipful Master.

WORSHIPFUL MASTER. Then let him be admitted in due form. (*Inner Guard drops sign.*) Brother Deacons. (*Senior Deacon puts a kneeling stool in north-east corner. At door Candidate is met by Inner Guard who pricks his bared left breast with the point of a poniard.*)

INNER GUARD. Do you feel anything?

CANDIDATE. Yes. (*The Inner Guard holds up poniard to show the Worshipful Master that the ceremony has been*

---

[1]Surnames are normally used; for simplicity, titles have been substituted.

observed and allows Candidate to be escorted to kneeling stool by Junior Deacon.)

WORSHIPFUL MASTER. Mr John Smith, as no person can be made a Mason unless he is free and of mature age, I demand of you, are you a free man and of the full age of twenty-one years?

CANDIDATE. I am.

WORSHIPFUL MASTER. Thus assured, I will thank you to kneel (*Candidate kneels*) while the blessing of Heaven is invoked on our proceedings. (*Worshipful Master gives a single knock, which is answered by the Wardens. The Brethren stand and give sign of Reverence, made by placing the right hand on the left breast. Deacons cross wands over Candidate's head. The Worshipful Master or Chaplain says following prayer.*) Vouchsafe Thine aid, Almighty Father and Supreme Governor of the Universe, to our present convention, and grant that this Candidate for Freemasonry may so dedicate and devote his life to Thy service as to become a pure and faithful Brother among us. Endue him with a competency of Thy Divine Wisdom, that, assisted by the secrets of our Masonic art, he may the better be enabled to unfold the beauties of true Godliness, to the honour and glory of Thy Holy Name.

IMMEDIATE PAST MASTER. So mote it be. (*All cut sign of Reverence and Deacons lower wands.*)

WORSHIPFUL MASTER. In all cases of difficulty and danger, in whom do you put your trust?

CANDIDATE. In God.

WORSHIPFUL MASTER. Right glad am I to find your faith so well founded: relying on such sure support you may safely rise and follow your leader with a firm but humble confidence, for where the name of God is invoked we trust no danger can ensue.

(*Junior Deacon helps Candidate rise, and Senior Deacon pulls away kneeling-stool. The Worshipful Master and Brethren sit down.*)

WORSHIPFUL MASTER. (*Gives single knock, answered in turn by the Wardens.*) The Brethren from the north, east, south and

182

west will take notice that Mr John Smith is about to pass in view before them, to show that he is the Candidate properly prepared, and a fit and proper person to be made a Mason.

(*Senior Deacon puts the kneeling-stool in front of Worshipful Master's pedestal, and gives him the poniard. Junior Deacon takes Candidate's right hand and leads him up the north, across the east and down the south. He 'squares' the Lodge at the corners by coming to a halt, turning, and leading off again with the left foot. Stopping by Junior Warden, he taps Junior Warden's right shoulder three times with Candidate's right hand.*)

JUNIOR WARDEN. Whom have you there?

JUNIOR DEACON. Mr John Smith, a poor candidate in a state of darkness . . . (*And on as before.*)

JUNIOR WARDEN. How does he hope to obtain those privileges?

JUNIOR DEACON. By the help of God, being free and of good report.

JUNIOR WARDEN. (*Takes Candidate's right hand.*) Enter, free and of good report.

(*The Junior Deacon leads Candidate to Senior Warden, squaring the Lodge at the south-west corner. The same examination is repeated by the Senior Warden and they then pass to the left of the Senior Warden and face east.*)

SENIOR WARDEN. (*Takes step and gives sign.*) Worshipful Master, I present to you Mr John Smith, a Candidate properly prepared to be made a Mason.

WORSHIPFUL MASTER. Brother Senior Warden, your presentation shall be attended to, for which purpose I shall address a few questions to the Candidate, which I trust he will answer with candour.

Do you seriously declare on your honour that, unbiased by the improper solicitation of friends against your own inclination, and uninfluenced by mercenary or other unworthy motive, you freely and voluntarily offer yourself a Candidate for the mysteries and privileges of Freemasonry?

CANDIDATE. I do.

WORSHIPFUL MASTER. Do you likewise pledge yourself that you are prompted to solicit those privileges by a favourable opinion preconceived of the Institution, a general desire of knowledge, and a sincere wish to render yourself more extensively serviceable to your fellow-creatures?

CANDIDATE. I do.

WORSHIPFUL MASTER. Do you further seriously declare on your honour, that avoiding fear on the one hand, and rashness on the other, you will steadily persevere through the ceremony of your initiation, and if once admitted, you will afterwards act and abide by the ancient usages and established customs of the order?

CANDIDATE. I do.

WORSHIPFUL MASTER. Brother Senior Warden, you will direct the Junior Deacon to instruct the Candidate to advance to the pedestal in due form.

SENIOR WARDEN. Brother Junior Deacon, it is the Worshipful Master's command that you instruct the Candidate to advance to the pedestal in due form.

(*Junior Deacon takes Candidate near to pedestal and directs him to stand with his heels together and his feet at right angles, left foot facing east and right foot facing south.*)

JUNIOR WARDEN. Take a short pace with your left foot, bringing the heels together in the form of a square. Take another, a little longer, heel to heel as before. Another still longer, heels together as before.

(*Candidate should now be able to kneel before the pedestal. The Senior Deacon comes and stands on Candidate's left. The Junior Deacon is on his right and all three face Worshipful Master.*)

WORSHIPFUL MASTER. It is my duty to inform you that Masonry is free, and requires a perfect freedom of inclination in every Candidate for its mysteries. It is founded on the purest principles of piety and virtue; it possesses great and invaluable privileges; and in order to secure those privileges to worthy men, and we trust to worthy men alone, vows of fidelity are required; but let me assure you that in those vows there is nothing incompatible with your civil, moral, or religious duties; are you therefore willing to take a Solemn Obligation, founded on the principles I have stated, to kep inviolate the secrets and mysteries of the Order?

CANDIDATE. I am.

WORSHIPFUL MASTER. Then you will kneel on your left knee, your right foot formed in a square, give me your right hand which I place on the Volume of the Sacred Law, while your left will be employed in supporting these compasses, one point presented to your naked left breast.

(The Master gives a single knock. The Wardens do so. Brethren stand with the sign of the Degree as right thumb to the left of the windpipe, elbow horizontal. Deacons cross their wands over the Candidate's head, and give the sign with their right hands.)

WORSHIPFUL MASTER. Repeat your name at length, and say after me:

OBLIGATION

CANDIDATE. I, John Smith, in the presence of the Great Architect of the Universe, and of this worthy, worshipful, and warranted Lodge of Free and Accepted Masons, regularly assembled and properly dedicated, of my own free will and accord, do hereby *(Worshipful Master touches Candidate's right hand with his left hand)* and hereon *(Worshipful Master touches the Bible with his left hand)* sincerely and solemnly promise and swear, that I will always hele[1], conceal, and never reveal any part or parts, point or points of the secrets or mysteries of or belonging to Free and Accepted Masons in Masonry, which may heretofore have been known by me, or shall now or at any future period be communicated to me, unless it be to a true and lawful Brother or Brothers, and not even to him or them, until after due trial, strict examination, or sure information from a well-known Brother, that he or they are worthy of that confidence, or in the body of a just, perfect, and regular Lodge of Ancient Freemasons. I further solemnly promise that I will not write those secrets, indite, carve, mark, engrave or otherwise them

[1]Hele: from the Anglo-Saxon meaning to cover.

delineate, or cause or suffer it to be so done by others, if in my power to prevent it, on anything movable or immovable, under the canopy of Heaven, whereby or whereon any letter, character or figure, or the least trace of a letter character or figure, may become legible, or intelligible to myself or anyone in the world, so that our secret arts and hidden mysteries may improperly become known through my unworthiness. These several points I solemnly swear to observe, without evasion, equivocation, or mental reservation of any kind, under no less a penalty, on the violation of any of them, I shall be branded as a wilfully perjured individual, void of all moral worth, and totally unfit to be received into this worshipful Lodge, or any other warranted Lodge or society of men, who prize honour and virtue above the external advantages of rank and fortune. So help me, God, and keep me steadfast in this my Great and Solemn Obligation of an Entered Apprentice Freemason.

(*All drop sign, Deacons lower wands, and Worshipful Master takes compasses from Candidate.*)

WORSHIPFUL MASTER. What you have repeated may be considered but a serious promise; as a pledge of your fidelity, and to render it a Solemn Obligation, you will seal it with your lips on the Volume of the Sacred Law. (*Candidate obeys.*) Having been kept for a considerable time in a state of darkness, what in your present situation is the predominant wish of your heart?

CANDIDATE. Light.

WORSHIPFUL MASTER. Brother Junior Deacon, let that blessing be restored to the Candidate.

(*Worshipful Master waves his gavel left, right, then down on to the pedestal and the Brethren give a single clap. Junior Deacon removes blindfold and shields Candidate's eyes so that they look to the Bible. He then removes noose and Candidate rises.*)

Having been restored to the blessing of material light, let me point out to your attention what we consider the three great, though emblematical lights in Freemasonry; they are, the Volume of the Sacred Law, the Square, and Compasses;

the Sacred Writings are to govern our faith, the Square to regulate our actions, and the Compasses to keep us in due bounds with all mankind, particularly our Brethren in Freemasonry. (*He takes the Candidate's right hand in his.*) Rise, newly obligated Brother among Masons. You are now enabled to discover the three lesser lights; they are situated east, south, and west, and are meant to represent the Sun, Moon, and Master of the Lodge; the Sun to rule the day, the Moon to govern the night, and the Master to rule and direct his Lodge. Brother John Smith, by your meek and candid behaviour this evening, symbolically you have escaped two great dangers, but there is a third which traditionally, would have awaited you until the latest period of your existence.

The dangers you have escaped are those of stabbing and strangling, for on your entrance into the Lodge this poniard (*Shows it*) was presented to your naked left breast, to imply that, had you rashly attempted to rush forward you would have been accessory to your own death by stabbing, whilst the Brother who held it would have remained firm and done his duty; there was likewise this cable-tow (*Shows it*) with a running noose about your neck which would have rendered any attempt at retreat equally fatal. But the danger which, traditionally, would have awaited you until your latest hour was the physical penalty at one time associated with the Obligation of a Mason had you improperly disclosed the secrets of Masonry, that of having the throat cut across, the tongue torn out by the root and buried in the sand of the sea at low-water mark or a cable's length from the shore, where the tide regularly ebbs and flows twice in twenty-four hours. The inclusion of such a penalty is unnecessary, for the Obligation you have taken this evening is binding upon you for so long as you shall live.

Having taken the Great and Solemn Obligation of a Mason, I am now permitted to inform you that there are several degrees in Freemasonry, and peculiar secrets restricted to each; these, however, are not communicated indiscriminately, but are conferred on Candidates according to merit and abilities. I shall, therefore, proceed to entrust you

187

with the secrets of this degree, or those marks by which we are known to each other, and distinguished from the rest of the world; but must premise for your general information that all squares, levels, and perpendiculars are true and proper signs, to know a Mason by. You are therefore expected to stand perfectly erect, your feet formed in a square, your body being thus considered an emblem of your mind, and your feet of the rectitude of your actions.

You will now take a short pace towards me with your left foot, bringing the right heel into its hollow. That is the first regular step in Freemasonry, and it is in this position that the secrets of the degree are communicated. They consist of a sign, token, and word.

Place your hand in this position with the thumb extended in the form of a square to the left of the windpipe. The sign is given by drawing the hand smartly across the throat and dropping it to the side. (*He demonstrates and Candidate copies.*) This is in allusion to the symbolic penalty of the degree, which implied that, as a man of honour, a Mason would rather have had his throat cut across (*Makes sign*) than improperly disclose the secrets entrusted to you. The grip or token is given by a distinct pressure of the thumb on the first joint of the hand (*Demonstrates*); this, when regularly given and received, serves to distinguish a Brother by night as well as by day. This grip or token demands a word, a word highly prized amongst Masons as a guard to their privileges. Too much caution, therefore, cannot be observed in communicating it; it should never be given at length, but always by letters or syllables; to enable you to do which, I must first tell you what that word is: it is BOAZ.

CANDIDATE. Boaz.

WORSHIPFUL MASTER. B—O—A—Z.

CANDIDATE. (*Also spelling it.*) B—O—A—Z.

WORSHIPFUL MASTER. As in the course of the ceremony you will be called on for this word, the Junior Deacon will now dictate the answers you are to give.

WORSHIPFUL MASTER. (*Gives grip.*) What is this?

CANDIDATE. (*Prompted by Junior Deacon.*) The grip or token of an Entered Apprentice Freemason.

WORSHIPFUL MASTER. What does it demand?

CANDIDATE. A word.

WORSHIPFUL MASTER. Give me that word.

CANDIDATE. At my initiation I was taught to be cautious; I will letter or halve it with you.

WORSHIPFUL MASTER. Which you please, and begin.

CANDIDATE. BO.

WORSHIPFUL MASTER. AZ.

CANDIDATE. BOAZ.

WORSHIPFUL MASTER. This word is derived from the left-hand pillar at the porchway or entrance of King Solomon's Temple, so named after Boaz, the great-grandfather of David, a Prince and Ruler in Israel. The import of the word is 'in strength'. Pass, Boaz.

(*Junior Deacon leads Candidate to Junior Warden's pedestal, 'squaring' south-east corner.*)

JUNIOR DEACON (*Step and sign.*). Brother Junior Warden, I present to you Brother John Smith on his Initiation.

JUNIOR WARDEN. I will thank Brother John Smith to advance to me as a Mason. (*Candidate takes step and makes sign.*) Have you anything to communicate?

CANDIDATE. I have. (*Gives grip helped by Junior Deacon.*)

JUNIOR WARDEN. What is this?

CANDIDATE. The grip or token of an Entered Apprentice Freemason.

JUNIOR WARDEN. What does it demand?

CANDIDATE. A word.

JUNIOR WARDEN. Give me that word.

CANDIDATE. At my initiation I was taught to be cautious; I will letter or halve it with you.

JUNIOR WARDEN. Which you please, and begin.

CANDIDATE. B.

JUNIOR WARDEN. O.

CANDIDATE. A.

JUNIOR WARDEN. Z.

CANDIDATE. BO.

189

JUNIOR WARDEN. AZ.

CANDIDATE. BOAZ.

JUNIOR WARDEN. Pass, Boaz.

(Junior Deacon leads Candidate to Senior Warden's pedestal, where he takes step and gives sign.)

JUNIOR DEACON. Brother Senior Warden, I present to you Brother John Smith on his Initiation. *(Cuts sign.)*

SENIOR WARDEN. I will thank Brother John Smith to advance to me as a Mason. *(Candidate takes step.)* What is that?

CANDIDATE. The first regular step in Freemasonry.

SENIOR WARDEN. Do you bring anything else?

CANDIDATE. I do. *(Gives sign.)*

SENIOR WARDEN. What is that?

CANDIDATE. The sign of an Entered Apprentice Freemason.

SENIOR WARDEN. To what does it allude?

CANDIDATE. The symbolic penalty of the degree, which implied that, as a man of honour, a Mason would rather have had his throat cut across *(Draws thumb across throat)* than improperly disclose the secrets entrusted to me.

SENIOR WARDEN. Have you anything to communicate?

CANDIDATE. I have. *(Gives grip.)*

SENIOR WARDEN. What is this?

CANDIDATE. The grip or token of an Entered Apprentice Freemason.

SENIOR WARDEN. What does it demand?

CANDIDATE. A word.

SENIOR WARDEN. Give me that word.

CANDIDATE. At my initiation I was taught to be cautious; I will letter or halve it with you.

SENIOR WARDEN. Which you please, and begin. *(They halve the word.)* Whence is this word derived?

CANDIDATE. From the left-hand pillar at the porchway or entrance to King Solomon's temple, so named after Boaz, the great-grandfather of David, a Prince and Ruler in Israel.

SENIOR WARDEN. The import of the word?

CANDIDATE. In strength.

SENIOR WARDEN. Pass, Boaz.

(*Junior Deacon leads Candidate to Worshipful Master.*)

(*Step and sign.*) Worshipful Master, I present to you Brother John Smith on his Initiation, for some mark of your favour.

WORSHIPFUL MASTER. Brother Senior Warden, I delegate you to invest him with the distinguishing badge of a Mason. (*Senior Warden and Junior Deacon invest Candidate with Entered Apprentice's apron. While he speaks Senior Warden holds lower right-hand corner of apron in his right hand.*)

SENIOR WARDEN. Brother John Smith, by the Worshipful Master's command, I invest you with the distinguishing badge of a Mason. It is more ancient than the Golden Fleece or Roman Eagle, more honourable than the Garter or any other Order in existence, being the badge of innocence and the bond of friendship. I strongly exhort you ever to wear and consider it as such; and further inform you that if you never disgrace that badge (*Senior Warden strikes Candidate's apron with right hand and the Brethren simultaneously strike theirs*) it will never disgrace you.

WORSHIPFUL MASTER. Let me add to the observations of the Senior Warden that you are never to put on that badge should you be about to visit a Lodge in which there is a Brother with whom you are at variance, or against whom you entertain animosity. In such cases it is expected that you will invite him to withdraw, in order amicably to settle your differences, which being happily effected, you may then clothe yourselves, enter the Lodge, and work with that love and harmony which should at all times characterise Freemasons. But if, unfortunately, your differences be of such a nature as not to be so easily adjusted, it were better that one or both of you retire than that the harmony of the Lodge should be disturbed by your presence. Brother Junior Deacon, you will place our new-made Brother at the north-east part of the Lodge. (*On arrival both face south.*)

JUNIOR DEACON. Left foot across the Lodge, right foot down the Lodge, pay attention to the Worshipful Master.

191

WORSHIPFUL MASTER. It is customary, at the erection of all
stately and superb edifices, to lay the first or foundation-
stone at the north-east corner of the building. You, being
newly admitted into Masonry, are placed at the north-east
part of the Lodge, figuratively to represent that stone, and
from the foundation, laid this evening, may you raise a
superstructure perfect in its parts and honourable to the
builder. You now stand, to all external appearance, a just
and upright Mason, and I give it you in strong terms of
recommendation ever to continue and act as such. Indeed,
I shall immediately proceed to put your principles, in some
measure, to the test, by calling upon you to exercise that
virtue which may justly be denominated the distinguishing
characteristic of a Freemason's heart—I mean Charity. I
need not here dilate on its excellences; no doubt it has
often been felt and practised by you. Suffice it to say, it
has the approbation of Heaven and earth, and, like its
sister, Mercy, blesses him who gives as well as him who
receives.

In a society so widely extended as Freemasonry, the
branches of which are spread over the four quarters of
the globe, it cannot be denied that we have many members
of rank and opulence; neither can it be concealed that,
among the thousands who range under its banners, there
are some who, perhaps from circumstances of unavoid-
able calamity and misfortune, are reduced to the lowest
ebb of poverty and distress. On their behalf it is our usual
custom to awaken the feelings of every new-made Brother
by such a claim on his charity as his circumstances in life
may fairly warrant. Whatever therefore you feel disposed
to give you will deposit with the Junior Deacon; it will be
thankfully received and faithfully applied.

JUNIOR DEACON. (*Offering alms dish.*) Have you anything
to give in the cause of charity?
(*Candidate, embarrassed, explains that he has no money with
him.*)
Were you deprived of everything valuable previously to
entering the Lodge? (*Candidate to answer 'yes'.*) If you had

'Whom have you there?'

The Inner Guard holds a dagger to the candidate's breast

The Junior Deacon leads the candidate around the lodge

The Senior Warden presents a candidate 'properly prepared to be made a Mason'

The candidate's right hand is placed on the Bible

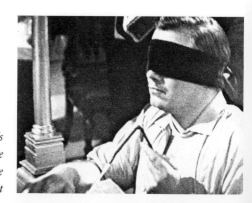

The candidate holds the compasses, one point to his bare breast

He swears to keep the Masonic secrets

The candidate's head is directed towards the Bible

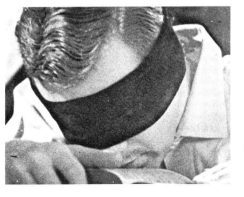

He seals his Solemn Obligation with a kiss

'Rise, newly obligated Brother among Masons'

The Masonic step, right heel in the hollow of the left foot

The First Degree sign

The First Degree grip, thumb pressing the first joint of the forefinger

The Inner Guard holds a square to the candidate's breast

The candidate wears the apron of the First Degree with its triangular flap turned up

The candidate takes the oath of the Second Degree

The Worshipful Master demonstrates the sign of Fidelity and the Hailing sign

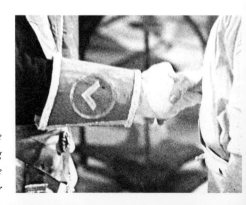

The Second Degree grip, thumb pressing the first joint of the second finger

The Brethren stand holding the Penal sign

The Master Mason awaits his 'last and greatest trial'

A 'death' blow from the Worshipful Master's maul

The Master Mason is lowered to the floor

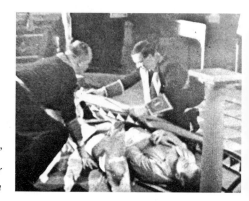

The Wardens 'bury' the new Master Mason

The Master Mason lies in his mock grave

not been so deprived would you give freely? (*Candidate to answer 'yes', but should not be prompted.*)

(*Step and sign.*) Worshipful Master, our new-made Brother affirms that he was deprived of everything valuable previously to entering the Lodge, or he would give freely. (*Cuts sign.*)

WORSHIPFUL MASTER. I congratulate you on the honourable sentiments by which you are actuated, likewise on the inability which in the present instance precludes you from gratifying them; believe me, this trial was not made with a view to sport with your feelings; far be from us any such intention; it was done for three especial reasons—first, as I have already premised, to put your principles to the test; secondly, to evince to the Brethren that you had neither money nor metallic substance about you, for if you had, the ceremony of your initiation, thus far, must have been repeated; and thirdly, as a warning to your own heart, that should you at any future period meet a Brother in distressed circumstances, who might solicit your assistance, you will remember the peculiar moment you were received into Masonry, poor and penniless, and cheerfully embrace the opportunity of practising that virtue you have professed to admire. (*Junior Deacon places Candidate before Worshipful Master.*)

I now present to you the working tools of an Entered Apprentice Freemason; they are the twenty-four-inch Gauge, the common Gavel and Chisel. The twenty-four-inch Gauge is to measure our work; the common Gavel to knock off all superfluous knobs and excrescences, and the Chisel to further smooth and prepare the stone and render it fit for the hands of the more expert workman. But, as we are not all operative Masons, but rather free and accepted or speculative, we apply these tools to our morals. In this sense, the twenty-four-inch Gauge represents the twenty-four hours of the day, part to be spent in prayer to Almighty God, part in labour and refreshment; and part in serving a friend or Brother in time of need, without detriment to

193

ourselves or connections. The common Gavel represents the force of conscience, which should keep down all vain and unbecoming thoughts which might obtrude during any of the aforementioned periods, so that our words and actions may ascend unpolluted to the Throne of Grace. The Chisel points out to us the advantages of education, by which means alone we are rendered fit members of regularly organised society.

As in the course of the evening you will be called on for certain fees for your initiation, it is proper you should know by what authority we act. This is our Charter or Warrant from the Grand Lodge of England (*Shows it*), which is for your inspection on this or any future evening. This is the Book of Constitutions (*Gives copy to Candidate*) and these are our by-laws (*Presents copy*), both of which I recommend to your serious perusal, as by one you will be instructed in the duties you owe to the Craft in general, and by the other in those you owe to this Lodge in particular.

You are now at liberty to retire, in order to restore yourself to your personal comforts, and on your return to the Lodge I shall call your attention to a Charge, founded on the excellences of the Institution and the qualifications of its members.

(*Junior Deacon leads Candidate to left of Senior Warden, and tells Candidate to salute Worshipful Master as a Mason, with step and sign. Candidate withdraws to put on his ordinary clothing, including his apron. On his return, Junior Deacon goes to door and takes the Candidate's hand. He again orders him to salute the Worshipful Master as a Mason. The Charge after Initiation is then given by the Worshipful Master, by a Past Master, or by a Warden.*)

CEREMONY OF PASSING TO THE SECOND DEGREE

(*The Lodge is opened in the First Degree, and the Candidate examined according to the following catechism, which he should have learnt.*)

194

WORSHIPFUL MASTER. Brethren, Brother John Smith is this evening a Candidate to be passed to the Second Degree, but it is first requisite that he give proofs of proficiency in the former; I shall therefore proceed to put the necessary questions:

Where were you first prepared to be made a Mason?

CANDIDATE. In my heart.

WORSHIPFUL MASTER. Where next?

CANDIDATE. In a convenient room adjoining the Lodge.

WORSHIPFUL MASTER. Describe the mode of your preparation.

CANDIDATE. I was divested of metal and hoodwinked, my right arm, left breast, and knee were made bare, my right heel was slipshod, and a cable-tow placed about my neck.

WORSHIPFUL MASTER. Where were you made a Mason?

CANDIDATE. In the body of a Lodge, just, perfect, and regular.

WORSHIPFUL MASTER. And when?

CANDIDATE. When the sun was at its meridian.

WORSHIPFUL MASTER. In this country Freemasons' Lodges are usually held in the evening; how do you account for that which at first view appears a paradox?

CANDIDATE. The Earth constantly revolving on its axis in its orbit round the Sun, and Freemasonry being universally spread over its surface, it necessarily follows that the Sun must always be at its meridian with respect to Freemasonry.

WORSHIPFUL MASTER. What is Freemasonry?

CANDIDATE. A peculiar system of morality, veiled in Allegory, and illustrated by Symbols.

WORSHIPFUL MASTER. Name the grand principles on which the Order is founded.

CANDIDATE. Brotherly Love, Relief, and Truth.

WORSHIPFUL MASTER. Who are fit and proper persons to be made Masons?

CANDIDATE. Just, upright, and free men, of mature age, sound judgement, and strict morals.

WORSHIPFUL MASTER. How do you know yourself to be a Mason?

CANDIDATE. By the regularity of my initiation, repeated trials and approbations, and a willingness at all times to undergo an examination when properly called on.

WORSHIPFUL MASTER. How do you demonstrate the proof of your being a Mason to others?

CANDIDATE. By signs, tokens, and the perfect points of my entrance.

WORSHIPFUL MASTER. These are the usual questions. I will put others if any Brother wishes me to do so. (*A right seldom exercised.*) Do you pledge your honour as a man, and your fidelity as a Mason that you will steadily persevere through the ceremony of being passed to the Degree of a Fellow Craft?

CANDIDATE. I do.

WORSHIPFUL MASTER. Do you likewise pledge yourself that you will conceal what I shall now impart to you with the same strict caution as the other secrets in Masonry?

CANDIDATE. I do.

WORSHIPFUL MASTER. Then I will entrust you with a test of merit, which is a pass grip and a pass word leading to the Degree to which you seek to be admitted. The pass grip is given by a distinct pressure of the thumb between the first and second joints of the hand. This pass grip demands a pass word which is SHIBBOLETH.

CANDIDATE. (*Prompted by Junior Deacon.*) Shibboleth.

WORSHIPFUL MASTER. Shibboleth denotes plenty, and is usually depicted in our Lodges by an ear of corn near to a fall of water. You must be particularly careful to remember this word, as without it you cannot gain admission into a Lodge in a superior degree. Pass, Shibboleth. (*Junior Deacon takes Candidate to door, instructing him to salute the Worshipful Master as a Mason. He retires to be prepared and meanwhile the Lodge is opened or resumed in the Second Degree. The Candidate is no longer divested of metals, blindfolded, or haltered. Again, his left breast is bared, but the other members are reversed; left arm, right knee are bared, and left foot slipshod. He wears his Apprentice apron with the triangular flap turned up. The Tyler gives the First Degree knocks on the door.)*

INNER GUARD. *(With step and Second Degree Sign—right hand on left breast, thumb vertical.)* Brother Junior Warden, there is a report.

JUNIOR WARDEN. *(Step and sign.)* Worshipful Master, there is a report.

WORSHIPFUL MASTER. Brother Junior Warden, inquire who wants admission.

JUNIOR WARDEN. *(Cuts sign.)* Brother Inner Guard, see who wants admission.

INNER GUARD. *(Cuts sign. Opens door.)* Whom have you there?

TYLER. Brother John Smith, who has been regularly initiated into Freemasonry, and has made such progress as he hopes will recommend him to be passed to the Degree of a Fellow Craft, for which ceremony he is properly prepared.

INNER GUARD. How does he hope to obtain the privileges of the Second Degree?

TYLER. By the help of God, the assistance of the Square, and the benefit of a pass word.

INNER GUARD. Is he in possession of the pass word?

TYLER. Will you prove him?

(Inner Guard extends right hand, and Candidate gives pass grip and pass word.)

INNER GUARD. Halt, while I report to the Worshipful Master. *(Closes door. Step and sign.)* Worshipful Master, Brother John Smith, who has been regularly initiated into Freemasonry, and has made such progress as he hopes will recommend him to be passed to the Degree of a Fellow Craft, for which ceremony he is properly prepared.

WORSHIPFUL MASTER. We acknowledge the propriety of the aid by which he seeks admission; do you, Brother Inner Guard, vouch that he is in possession of the pass word?

INNER GUARD. I do, Worshipful Master.

WORSHIPFUL MASTER. Then let him be admitted in due form. (*Inner Guard cuts sign.*) Brother Deacons.

Candidate is received at door by Deacons and Inner Guard. The Inner Guard places the square upon Candidate's breast, and holds it aloft to show that he has done so. Senior Deacon leads Candidate to kneeling stool left of Senior Warden, and directs him to advance as a Mason, Candidate takes step and gives First Degree sign—right thumb to the left of the windpipe, elbow horizontal.)

Let the Candidate kneel, while the blessing of Heaven is invoked on what we are about to do.

(*One knock, followed by Wardens. The Brethren stand, giving sign of Reverence—right hand on left breast. Deacons cross wands over Candidate's head.*)

WORSHIPFUL MASTER or CHAPLAIN. We supplicate the continuance of thine aid, O Merciful Lord, on behalf of ourselves, and him who kneels before thee; may the work, begun in Thy Name, be continued to Thy Glory, and evermore established in us by obedience to Thy precepts.

IMMEDIATE PAST MASTER. So mote it be.[1] (*Deacons lower wands. All drop sign.*)

WORSHIPFUL MASTER. Let the Candidate rise.

(*Junior Deacon takes kneeling stool and places it before the Master's pedestal. Senior Deacon leads Candidate round the Lodge 'squaring' the corners, ordering him to salute the Worshipful Master as a Mason as he passes him. They arrive at Junior Warden's pedestal.*)

SENIOR DEACON. Advance to the Junior Warden as such, showing the sign and communicating the token and word. (*Candidate takes step and gives sign.*)

JUNIOR WARDEN. Have you anything to communicate?

CANDIDATE. I have. (*Gives First Degree grip.*)

JUNIOR WARDEN. What is this?

---

[1]Mote: from the Anglo-Saxon meaning to be allowed.

CANDIDATE. The grip or token of an Entered Apprentice Freemason.

JUNIOR WARDEN. What does it demand?

CANDIDATE. A word.

JUNIOR WARDEN. Give me that word, freely and at length.

CANDIDATE. BOAZ.

JUNIOR WARDEN. Pass, Boaz.

(*Senior Deacon and Candidate halt before Senior Warden. Candidate takes step and gives sign.*)

WORSHIPFUL MASTER. (*Gives single knock, repeated by Wardens.*) The Brethren will take notice that Brother John Smith, who has been regularly initiated into Freemasonry, is about to pass in view before them to show that he is the Candidate properly prepared to be passed to the degree of a Fellow Craft.

(*Senior Deacon again leads Candidate round Lodge, directing him to salute the Worshipful Master and Junior Warden as he passes them. He then conducts him to right of the Senior Warden.*)

SENIOR DEACON. Advance to the Senior Warden as such, showing the sign and communicating the pass grip and pass word you received from the Worshipful Master previously to leaving the Lodge. (*Candidate takes step and gives First Degree sign.*)

SENIOR WARDEN. Have you anything to communicate?

CANDIDATE. I have (*Gives the pass grip—a thumb press between first and second fingers.*)

SENIOR WARDEN. What is this?

CANDIDATE. The pass grip leading from the First to the Second Degree.

SENIOR WARDEN. What does this pass grip demand?

CANDIDATE. A pass word.

SENIOR WARDEN. Give me that pass word.

CANDIDATE. SHIBBOLETH.

SENIOR WARDEN. What does Shibboleth denote?

CANDIDATE. Plenty.

SENIOR WARDEN. How is it usually depicted in our Lodges?

CANDIDATE. By an ear of corn near to a fall of water.

SENIOR WARDEN. Pass, Shibboleth.

(*Senior Deacon leads Candidate to Senior Warden's left, where they face East.*)

SENIOR WARDEN. (*With sign of Fidelity—right hand on left breast, thumb vertical.*) Worshipful Master, I present to you Brother John Smith, a Candidate properly prepared to be passed to the Second Degree.

WORSHIPFUL MASTER. Brother Senior Warden, you will direct the Senior Deacon to instruct the Candidate to advance to the east in due form.

SENIOR WARDEN. (*Cuts sign.*) Brother Senior Deacon, it is the Worshipful Master's command that you instruct the Candidate to advance to the east in due from.

SENIOR DEACON. (*Places Candidate in the north.*) The method of advancing from west to east in this degree is by five steps, as if ascending a winding staircase. For your information I will go through them, and you will afterwards copy me.

(*Senior Deacon stands with right foot pointing to Senior Warden, and left left foot pointing to Junior Warden. He steps off with the left foot, lifting the feet at each step as if going up a stair. A quarter circle wheel of five steps brings him in front of the Worshipful Master's pedestal. He returns to Candidate and they take the five steps together.*)

WORSHIPFUL MASTER. As in every case the Degrees in Freemasonry are to be kept separate and distinct, another Obligation will now be required of you, in many respects similar to the former; are you willing to take it?

CANDIDATE. I am.

WORSHIPFUL MASTER. Then you will kneel on your right knee, your left foot formed in a square, place your right hand on the Volume of the Sacred Law, while your left arm will be supported in the angle of the Square. (*Gives single knock, answered by the Deacons. Brethren stand, giving sign of Fidelity—right hand on left breast, thumb vertical. Deacons cross wands over Candidate's head.*)

Repeat your name at length, and say after me:

200

OBLIGATION

CANDIDATE. I, John Smith, in the presence of the Grand Geometrician of the Universe, and of this worthy and worshipful Lodge of Fellow Craft Freemasons, regularly held, assembled, and properly dedicated, of my own free will and accord do hereby solemnly promise and swear that I will always hele, conceal and never improperly reveal, any or either of the secrets or mysteries of or belonging to the Second Degree in Freemasonry, denominated the Fellow Crafts, to him who is but an Entered Apprentice, any more than I would either of them to the uninstructed and popular world who are not Masons. I further solemnly pledge myself to act as a true and faithful Craftsman, answer signs, obey summonses, and maintain the principles inculcated in the former Degree. These several points I solemnly swear to observe, without evasion, equivocation, or mental reservation of any kind. So help me Almighty God, and keep me steadfast in this my Solemn Obligation of a Fellow Craft Freemason.

WORSHIPFUL MASTER. As a pledge of your fidelity, and to render this a Solemn Obligation which might otherwise be considered but a serious promise, you will seal it with your lips twice on the Volume of the Sacred Law. (*Candidate does so.*) Your progress in Masonry is marked by the position of the Square and Compasses. When you were made an Entered Apprentice, both points were hid; in this degree one is disclosed, implying that you are now in the midway of Freemasonry, superior to an Entered Apprentice, but inferior to that to which I trust you will hereafter attain. Rise, newly obligated Fellow Craft Freemason. Having taken the Solemn Obligation of a Fellow Craft, I shall proceed to entrust you with the secrets of the Degree. You will therefore advance to me as at your initiation. (*Candidate takes step and sign of the First Degree—right thumb to the left of the windpipe, elbow horizontal.*) You will now take another short pace towards me with your left foot, bringing the right heel into its hollow as before. That is the second regular step in Freemasonry, and it is in this position that the secrets of the Degree are communicated. They consist, as in the former instance, of a sign, token, and word, with this difference, that in this Degree the sign is of a threefold nature. The first part of the threefold sign is called the sign of Fidelity, and is given by placing the right hand on the left breast with the thumb extended in the form of a square (*Demonstrates and Candidate copies*), emblematically to shield the repository of your secrets from the attacks of the insidious. The second part is called the Hailing sign, or sign of Perseverance, and is given by throwing up the left hand (horizontal from the shoulder to the elbow, and perpendicular from the elbow to the fingertips) with the thumb level extended in the form of a square. This took its rise at the time that Joshua fought the battles of the Lord, when it was in this position he prayed fervently to the Almighty to continue the light of day, that he might complete the overthrow of his enemies. The third part is the Penal sign, and is given by dropping the left hand, drawing the right smartly across the breast and dropping it to the side. This is in allusion to the symbolic penalty at one time included in the Obligation in this degree had he improperly disclosed the secrets entrusted to him, which implied that, as a man of honour, a Fellow Craft Freemason would rather have had the left breast laid open, the heart torn therefrom, and given to the ravenous birds of the air, or devouring beasts of the field as a prey. The grip or token is given by a distinct pressure of the thumb on the second joint of the hand. (*Demonstrates*). This grip or token demands a word, a word to be given with the same strict caution as that in the former Degree; that is to say, never at length, but always by letters or syllables, to enable you to do which, I must tell you that the word is JACHIN. (*Senior Deacon and Candidate repeat the word. The Worshipful Master then spells it, and so do Junior Deacon and Candidate.*) As in the course of this ceremony you will be called on for this word, the Senior Deacon will now dictate the answers you are to give. What is this?

CANDIDATE. (*Prompted by Senior Deacon.*) The grip or token of a Fellow Craft Freemason.

WORSHIPFUL MASTER. What does it demand?

CANDIDATE. A word.

WORSHIPFUL MASTER. Give me that word.

CANDIDATE. I was taught to be cautious in this Degree as well as in the former. I will letter or halve it with you.

WORSHIPFUL MASTER. Which you please, and begin.

(*The word is halved.*)

This word is derived from the right-hand pillar at the porchway or entrance of King Solomon's temple, so named after Jachin, the Assistant High Priest who officiated at its dedication. The import of the word is to establish, and when conjoined with that in the former degree, stability, for God said: 'In strength I will establish this Mine house to stand firm for ever.'

Pass, Jachin.

(*Senior Deacon leads Candidate to right of Junior Warden, squaring Lodge corner.*)

SENIOR DEACON. (*Step and sign.*) Brother Junior Warden, I present to you Brother John Smith, on his being passed to the Second Degree. (*Cuts sign.*)

JUNIOR WARDEN. I will thank Brother John Smith to advance to me as a Fellow Craft. (*Candidates takes step and gives Second Degree sign.*) Have you anything to communicate?

CANDIDATE. I have. (*Gives grip.*)

JUNIOR WARDEN. What is this?

CANDIDATE. The grip or token of a Fellow Craft Freemason.

JUNIOR WARDEN. What does it demand?

CANDIDATE. A word.

JUNIOR WARDEN. Give me that word.

CANDIDATE. I was taught to be cautious in this Degree as well as in the former. I will letter or halve it with you.

JUNIOR WARDEN. Which you please, and begin.

(*The word is lettered and halved.*)

Pass, Jachin.

203

(*Senior Deacon, squaring Lodge, takes Candidate to Senior Warden.*)

SENIOR DEACON. (*Step and sign.*) Brother Senior Warden, I present to you Brother John Smith on his being passed to the Second Degree.
(*Cuts sign.*)

SENIOR WARDEN. I will thank Brother John Smith to advance to me as a Fellow Craft, first as an Entered Apprentice. (*Candidate takes step and gives First Degree sign, then takes second step.*) What is that?

CANDIDATE. The second regular step in Freemasonry.

SENIOR WARDEN. Do you bring anything else?

CANDIDATE. I do. (*Gives sign of Fidelity.*)

SENIOR WARDEN. What is that?

CANDIDATE. The sign of Fidelity, emblematically to shield the repository of my secrets from the attacks of the insidious.

SENIOR WARDEN. Do you bring anything else?

CANDIDATE. I do. (*Gives Hailing sign.*)

SENIOR WARDEN. What is that?

CANDIDATE. The Hailing sign, or sign of perseverance.

SENIOR WARDEN. When did it take its rise?

CANDIDATE. At the time that Joshua fought the battles of the Lord, when it was in this position he prayed fervently to the Almighty to continue the light of day, so that he might complete the overthrow of his enemies.

SENIOR WARDEN. Do you bring anything else?

CANDIDATE. I do. (*Gives Penal sign.*)

SENIOR WARDEN. What is that?

CANDIDATE. The Penal sign.

SENIOR WARDEN. To what does it allude?

CANDIDATE. The symbolic penalty of this degree, which implied that, as a man of honour, a Fellow Craft Freemason would rather have had his heart torn from his breast than improperly disclose the secrets entrusted to me.

SENIOR WARDEN. Have you anything to communicate?

CANDIDATE. I have. (*Gives grip.*)

SENIOR WARDEN. What is this?

CANDIDATE. The grip or token of a Fellow Craft Freemason.

SENIOR WARDEN. What does is demand?

CANDIDATE. A word.

SENIOR WARDEN. Give me that word.

CANDIDATE. I was taught to be cautious in this Degree as well as in the former. I will letter or halve it with you.

SENIOR WARDEN. Which you please, and begin. (*They halve it.*) Whence is this word derived?

CANDIDATE. From the right-hand pillar at the porchway or entrance of King Solomon's temple so named after Jachin, the Assistant High Priest who officiated at its dedication.

SENIOR WARDEN. The import of the word?

CANDIDATE. To establish.

SENIOR WARDEN. And when conjoined with that in the former degree?

CANDIDATE. Stability, for God said: 'In strength I will establish this Mine house to stand firm for ever.'

SENIOR WARDEN. Pass, Jachin. (*Gives sign of Fidelity.*) Worshipful Master, I present to you Brother John Smith on his being passed to the Second Degree, for some further mark of your favour.

WORSHIPFUL MASTER. Brother Senior Warden, I delegate you to invest him with the distinguishing badge of a Fellow Craft Freemason.

SENIOR WARDEN. (*Cuts sign, and invests Candidates with Fellow Craft apron.*) Brother John Smith, by the Worshipful Master's command, I invest you with the distinguishing badge of a Fellow Craft Freemason, to mark the progress you have made in the science.

WORSHIPFUL MASTER. Let me add to what has been stated by the Senior Warden that the badge with which you have now been invested points out that, as a Craftsman, you are expected to make the liberal arts and sciences your future study, that you may the better be enabled to discharge your duties as a Mason, and estimate the wonderful works of the Almighty. Brother Senior Deacon, you will place our Brother at the south-east part of the Lodge. (*Senior Deacon does so.*)

SENIOR DEACON. Right foot across the Lodge, left foot down the Lodge; pay attention to the Worshipful Master.

WORSHIPFUL MASTER. Masonry being a progressive science, when you were made an Entered Apprentice you were placed at the north-east part of the Lodge, to show that you were newly admitted; you are now placed at the south-east part to mark the progress you have made in the science. You now stand to all external appearance a just and upright Fellow Craft Freemason, and I give it you in strong terms of recommendation ever to continue and act as such; and, as I trust, the import of the former charge neither is, nor ever will be, effaced from your memory, I shall content myself with observing that, as in the previous degree you made yourself acquainted with the principles of moral truth and virtue, you are now permitted to extend your researches into the hidden mysteries of nature and science.

(*Senior Deacon leads Candidate to Worshipful Master's Pedestal.*)

I now present to you the working tools of a Fellow Craft Freemason; they are the Square, Level, and Plumb Rule. The Square is to try and adjust rectangular corners of buildings, and assist in bringing rude matters into due form; the Level to lay levels and prove horizontals; the Plumb Rule to try and adjust uprights, while fixing them on their proper bases. But as we are not all operative Masons, but rather free and accepted or speculative, we apply these tools to our morals. In this sense, the Square teaches morality, the Level equality, and the Plumb Rule justness and uprightness of life and actions. Thus by square conduct, level steps and upright intentions we hope to ascend to those immortal mansions whence all goodness emanates.

You are now at liberty to retire in order to restore yourself to your personal comforts, and on your return to the

Lodge I shall call your attention to an explanation of the Tracing Board.

SENIOR DEACON. Salute the Worshipful Master as a Fellow Craftsman, first as an Entered Apprentice.

(*Candidates does so, and then Senior Deacon leads him to the door. Candidate retires and on his return the Tracing-Board lecture of the Second Degree may be delivered.*)

CEREMONY OF RAISING TO THE THIRD DEGREE
(*The Lodge is opened in the Second Degree, and the Candidate examined according to the following catechism.*)

WORSHIPFUL MASTER. Brethren, Brother John Smith is this evening a Candidate to be raised to the Third Degree, but it is first requisite that he give proofs of proficiency in the Second. I shall therefore proceed to put the necessary questions. How were you prepared to be passed to the Second Degree?

CANDIDATE. In a manner somewhat similar to the former, save that in this Degree I was not hoodwinked. My left arm, breast, and right knee were made bare, and my left heel was slipshod.

WORSHIPFUL MASTER. On what were you admitted?

CANDIDATE. The Square.

WORSHIPFUL MASTER. What is a Square?

CANDIDATE. An angle of ninety degrees, or the fourth part of a circle.

WORSHIPFUL MASTER. What are the peculiar objects of research in this Degree?

CANDIDATE. The hidden mysteries of Nature and Science.

WORSHIPFUL MASTER. As it is the hope of reward that sweetens labour, where did our ancient Brethren go to receive their wages?

CANDIDATE. In the middle chamber of King Solomon's temple.

WORSHIPFUL MASTER. How did they receive them?

CANDIDATE. Without scruple or diffidence.

WORSHIPFUL MASTER. Why in this peculiar manner?

207

CANDIDATE. Without scruple, well knowing they were justly entitled to them; and without diffidence, from the great reliance they placed on the integrity of their employers in those days.

WORSHIPFUL MASTER. What were the names of the two great pillars which were placed at the porchway or entrance of King Solomon's temple?

CANDIDATE. That on the left was called Boaz, and that on the right, Jachin.

WORSHIPFUL MASTER. What are their separate and conjoint significations?

CANDIDATE. The former denotes in strength, the latter, to establish; and when conjoined, stability, for God said, 'In strength will I establish this Mine house to stand firm for ever.'

WORSHIPFUL MASTER. There are the usual questions. I will put others if any Brother wishes me to do so. (*They seldom do.*)

Do you pledge your honour as a man and your fidelity as a Craftsman that you will steadily persevere through the ceremony of being raised to the sublime Degree of a Master Mason?

CANDIDATE. I do.

WORSHIPFUL MASTER. Do you likewise pledge yourself that you will conceal what I shall now impart to you with the same strict caution as the other secrets in Masonry?

CANDIDATE. I do.

WORSHIPFUL MASTER. Then I will entrust you with a test of merit, which is a pass grip and a pass word, leading to the Degree to which you seek to be admitted. The pass grip is given by a distinct pressure of the thumb between the second and third joints of the hand. This pass grip demands a pass word, which is TUBAL CAIN.

Tubal Cain was the first artificer in metals. The import of the word is worldly possessions. You must be particularly careful to remember this word, as without it you cannot gain admission into a Lodge in a superior Degree. Pass, Tubal Cain.

(*Senior Deacon leads Candidate to door, where he salutes the*

208

Worshipful Master with signs of first two Degrees. He retires to be prepared for the ceremony. Both arms, breasts, and knees are bared and both feet slippered. He wears the Fellow Crafts apron. Meanwhile, the Lodge is opened in the Third Degree. The Deacons lay a sheet upon the floor near to the Worshipful Master's pedestal. On the sheet is drawn an 'open grave', surrounded by skulls and cross-bones. The Tyler gives the Second Degree knocks.)

INNER GUARD. (*Step and Penal sign of Third Degree—right thumb to the left of the navel, thumb at right angle to hand held palm down.*) Brother Junior Warden, there is a report.

JUNIOR WARDEN. (*Step and sign.*) Worshipful Master, there is a report.

WORSHIPFUL MASTER. Brother Junior Warden, inquire who wants admission.

JUNIOR WARDEN. (*Cuts sign.*) Brother Inner Guard, see who wants admission.

INNER GUARD. (*Cuts sign, opens the door.*) Whom have you there?

TYLER. Brother John Smith, who has been regularly initiated into Freemasonry, passed to the Degree of a Fellow Craft, and has made such further progress as he hopes will entitle him to be raised to the sublime Degree of a Master Mason, for which ceremony he is properly prepared.

INNER GUARD. How does he hope to obtain the privileges of the Third Degree?

TYLER. By the help of God, the united aid of the Square and Compasses, and the benefit of a pass word.

INNER GUARD. Is he in possession of the pass word?

TYLER. Will you prove him? (*Inner Guard offers right hand, and receives pass grip and pass word from Candidate.*)

INNER GUARD. Halt, while I report to the Worshipful Master. (*Closes door, takes step and sign.*) Worshipful Master, Brother John Smith, who has been regularly initiated into Freemasonry, passed to the Degree of Fellow Craft, and has made such further progress as he hopes will entitle him to be raised to the sublime Degree of a Master Mason, for which ceremony he is properly prepared.

WORSHIPFUL MASTER. How does he hope to obtain the privileges of the Third Degree?

INNER GUARD. By the help of God, the united aid of the Square and Compasses, and the benefit of a pass word.

WORSHIPFUL MASTER. We acknowledge the powerful aid by which he seeks admission; do you, Brother Green, vouch that he is in possession of the pass word?

INNER GUARD. I do, Worshipful Master.

WORSHIPFUL MASTER. Then let him be admitted in due form. Brother Deacons. (*All lights are put out except the candle by the Worshipful Master's pedestal. Junior Deacon puts kneeling stool in position, and both Deacons go to door. Inner Guard opens it and places the points of an open pair of compasses to the Candidate's breasts. He holds the compasses aloft to show that he has done so. Senior Deacon leads Candidate to kneeling stool.*)

SENIOR DEACON. Advance as a Fellow Craft, first as an Entered Apprentice. (*Candidate takes step and gives First Degree sigh, then another step and makes Second Degree sign.*)

WORSHIPFUL MASTER. Let the Candidate kneel while the blessing of Heaven is invoked on what we are about to do.

(*Worshipful Master gives a knock, repeated by Wardens. All stand with sign of Reverence, right hand on left breast. Deacons cross wands over Candidate's head.*)

WORSHIPFUL MASTER. or CHAPLAIN. Almighty and Eternal God, Architect and Ruler of the Universe, at whose creative fiat all things first were made, we the frail creatures of Thy Providence, humbly implore thee to pour down on this convocation assembled in Thy Holy name the continual dew of Thy blessing. Especially, we beseech thee, to impart Thy grace to this Thy servant, who offers himself a Candidate to partake with us the mysterious secrets of a Master Mason. Endue him with such fortitude that in the hour of trial he fail not, but that, passing safely under Thy protection through the valley of the shadow of death, he may finally rise from the tomb of transgression, to shine as the stars for ever and ever.

IMMEDIATE PAST MASTER. So mote it be. (*Deacons lower wands, and Brethren cut sign.*)

WORSHIPFUL MASTER. Let the Candidate rise. (*He does so. The kneeling stool is taken to Worshipful Master's pedestal. Senior Deacon takes Candidate's right hand, and begins the perambulations of the Lodge, 'squaring' the corners. They stop for Candidate to salute the Worshipful Master as a Mason, then advance to Junior Warden's pedestal.*)

SENIOR DEACON. Advance to the Junior Warden as such, showing the sign and communicating the token and word.

(*Candidate takes step and gives First Degree sign.*)

JUNIOR WARDEN. Have you anything to communicate?

CANDIDATE. I have. (*Gives First Degree grip.*)

JUNIOR WARDEN. What is this?

CANDIDATE. The grip or token of an Entered Apprentice Freemason.

JUNIOR WARDEN. What does it demand?

CANDIDATE. A word.

JUNIOR WARDEN. Give me that word, freely and at length.

CANDIDATE. BOAZ.

JUNIOR WARDEN. Pass, Boaz.

(*Senior Deacon continues round Lodge with Candidate. They halt before Senior Warden, and Candidate salutes as a Mason with step and First Degree sign. The perambulation continues, squaring the Lodge, to the Worshipful Master. Candidate salutes as a Fellow Craft, with step and Second Degree sign, right hand on left breast, thumb vertical. Continuing round Lodge, he salutes Junior Warden as a Fellow Craft, and on to Senior Warden again.*)

SENIOR DEACON. Advance to the Senior Warden as such, showing the sign, and communicating the token and word of that Degree.

(*Candidate takes step and gives sign.*)

SENIOR WARDEN. Have you anything to communicate?

CANDIDATE. I have (*Gives grip.*)

SENIOR WARDEN. What is this?

CANDIDATE. The grip or token of a Fellow Craft Free-mason.

SENIOR WARDEN. What does it demand?

CANDIDATE. A word.

SENIOR WARDEN. Give me that word freely and at length.

CANDIDATE. JACHIN.

SENIOR WARDEN. Pass, Jachin.

WORSHIPFUL MASTER. (*Gives single knock, repeated by Wardens.*) The Brethren will take notice that Brother John Smith, who has been regularly initiated into Free-masonry, and passed to the Degree of a Fellow Craft, is about to pass in view before them, to show that he is the Candidate properly prepared to be raised to the Sublime Degree of a Master Mason. (*Senior Deacon leads Candidate round Lodge for the third time, followed by Junior Deacon. They halt before Worshipful Master's pedestal, where Candidate salutes as a Fellow Craft, then on to Junior Warden, who is saluted. They then go to the right of the Senior Warden.*)

SENIOR DEACON. Advance to the Senior Warden as such, showing the sign and communicating the pass grip and pass word you received from the Worshipful Master previously to leaving the Lodge. (*Candidate takes step and gives Fellow Craft sign.*)

SENIOR WARDEN. Have you anything to communicate?

CANDIDATE. I have. (*Gives pass grip to the Third Degree, a thumb press between the second and third fingers.*)

SENIOR WARDEN. What is this?

CANDIDATE. The pass grip leading from the Second to the Third Degree.

SENIOR WARDEN. What does this pass grip demand?

CANDIDATE. A pass word.

SENIOR WARDEN. Give me that pass word.

CANDIDATE. TUBAL CAIN.

SENIOR WARDEN. What was Tubal Cain?

CANDIDATE. The first artificer in metals.

SENIOR WARDEN. The import of the word?

212

CANDIDATE. Worldly possessions.

SENIOR WARDEN. Pass, Tubal Cain. (*Senior Warden takes step and gives Penal Sign of Third Degree—right thumb to the left of the navel, thumb at right angle to hand held palm down.*) Worshipful Master I present Brother John Smith, a Candidate properly prepared to be raised to the Third Degree.

WORSHIPFUL MASTER. Brother Senior Warden, you will direct the Deacons to instruct the Candidate to advance to the east by the proper steps.

SENIOR WARDEN. Brother Deacons, it is the Worshipful Master's command that you instruct the Candidate to advance to the east by the proper steps.

SENIOR DEACON. The method of advancing from west to east in this Degree is by seven steps, the first three as if stepping over a grave. For your information I will go through them, and you will afterwards copy me. (*The steps are taken diagonally to and fro. They start at the west or head of the grave as drawn on the sheet. The first step is taken to the north-east, the second south-east, and the third brings Candidate to foot of 'grave', facing due east. After each step the heels are brought together with the feet squared. Four ordinary steps, taken east, bring Candidate before Worshipful Master's pedestal.*)

WORSHIPFUL MASTER. It is but fair to inform you that a most serious trial of your fortitude and fidelity and a more solemn Obligation await you. Are you prepared to meet them as you ought?

CANDIDATE. I am.

WORSHIPFUL MASTER. Then you will kneel on both knees, place both hands on the Volume of the Sacred Law. (*Candidate does so. The Worshipful Master gives one knock, answered by Wardens. Brethren stand with Penal sign of Third Degree. Deacons cross wands over Candidate's head.*)

Repeat your name at length, and say after me:

OBLIGATION

CANDIDATE. I, John Smith, in the presence of the Most High, and of this worthy and worshipful Lodge of Master Masons, duly constituted, regularly assembled, and properly dedicated, of my own free will and accord, do hereby and hereon most solemnly promise and swear that I will always hele, conceal, and never reveal any or either of the secrets or mysteries of or belonging to the Degree of a Mason to anyone in the world, unless it be to him or them to whom the same may justly and lawfully belong, and not even to him or them until after due trial, strict examination, or full conviction that he or they are worthy of that confidence, or in the body of a Master Masons' Lodge duly opened on the Centre. I further solemnly pledge myself to adhere to the principles of the Square and Compasses, answer and obey all lawful signs, and summonses sent to me from a Master Mason's Lodge, if within the length of my cable-tow, and plead no excuse except sickness or the pressing emergencies of my own public or private avocations.

I further solemnly engage myself to maintain and uphold the Five Points of Fellowship in act as well as in word; that my hand given to a Master Mason, shall be a sure pledge of brotherhood; that my feet shall travel through dangers and difficulties to unite with his in forming a column of mutual defence and support; that the posture of my daily supplications shall remind me of his wants and dispose my heart to succour his weakness and relieve his necessities, so far as may fairly be done without detriment to myself or connections; that my breast shall be the sacred repository of his secrets when entrusted to my care—murder, treason, felony, and all other offences contrary to the laws of God and the ordinances of the realm being at all times most especially excepted.

And finally, that I will maintain a Master Mason's honour and carefully preserve it as my own; I will not injure him myself, or knowingly suffer it to be done by others if in my power to prevent it; but on the contrary, will boldly repel the slanderer of his good name, and most strictly respect the chastity of those nearest and dearest to him, in the person of his wife, his sister, and his child.

All these points I solemnly swear to observe, without evasion, equivocation, or mental reservation of any kind. So help me the Most High, and keep me steadfast in this my solemn Obligation of a Master Mason.

WORSHIPFUL MASTER. As a pledge of your fidelity and to render this binding as a Solemn Obligation for so long as you shall live, you will seal it with your lips thrice on the Volume of the Sacred Law. (*Candidate does so.*) Let me once more call your attention to the position of the Square and Compasses. When you were made an Entered Apprentice, both points were hid; in the Second Degree one was disclosed, in this the whole is exhibited, implying that you are now at liberty to work with both those points in order to render the circle of your Masonic duties complete. Rise, newly obligated Master Mason. (*Deacons and Candidate back to foot of 'grave'.*)

Having entered upon the Solemn Obligation of a Master Mason, you are now entitled to demand that last and greatest trial, by which alone you can be admitted to a participation of the secrets of this Degree. But it is first my duty to call your attention to a retrospect of those Degrees in Freemasonry through which you have already passed, that you may the better be enabled to distinguish and appreciate the connection of our whole system, and the relative dependency of its several parts. Your admission among Masons in a state of helpless indigence was an emblematical representation of the entrance of all men on this, their mortal existence. It inculcated the useful lessons of natural equality and mutual dependence. It instructed you in the active principles of universal beneficence and charity, to seek the solace of your own distress by extending relief and consolation to your fellow creatures in the hour of their affliction. Above all, it taught you to bend with humility and resignation to the will of the Great Architect of the Universe; to dedicate your heart, thus purified from every baneful and malignant passion, fitted only for the reception of truth and wisdom, to His glory and the welfare of your fellow mortals.

Proceeding onwards, still guiding your progress by the principles of moral truth, you were led in the Second Degree to contemplate the intellectual faculty, and to trace it from its development, through the paths of heavenly science, even to the Throne of God Himself. The secrets of Nature and the principles of intellectual truth were then unveiled to your view. To your mind, thus modelled by virtue and science, Nature, however, presents one great and useful lesson more. She prepares you, by contemplation, for the closing hour of existence; and when by means of that contemplation she has conducted you through the intricate windings of this mortal life, she finally instructs you how to die.

Such, my Brother, are the peculiar objects of the Third Degree in Freemasonry; they invite you to reflect on this awful subject and teach you to feel, that, to the just and virtuous man, death has no terrors equal to the stain of falsehood and dishonour. Of this great truth the annals of Masonry afford a glorious example in the unshaken fidelity and noble death of our Master, Hiram Abiff, who was slain just before the completion of King Solomon's temple, at the construction of which he was, as no doubt you are well aware, the principal architect. The manner of his death was as follows. Brother Wardens.

(Wardens come up and stand either side of Candidate, who is told to cross his feet right over left.)

Fifteen Fellow Crafts of that superior class appointed to preside over the rest, finding that the work was nearly completed, and that they were not in possession of the secrets of the Third Degree, conspired to obtain them by any means, even to have recourse to violence. At the moment, however, of carrying their conspiracy into execution, twelve of the fifteen recanted, but three, of a more determined and atrocious character than the rest, persisted in their impious design, in the prosecution of which they planted themselves respectively at the east, north and south entrances of the temple, whither our Master had retired to pay his adoration to the Most High, as was his wonted custom at the hour of high twelve. Having finished his devotions, he attempted to return by the south entrance, where he was opposed by the first of those ruffians, who, for want of other weapon, had armed himself with a heavy Plumb Rule, and in a threatening manner demanded the secrets of a Master Mason, warning him that death would be the consequence of a refusal. Our Master, true to his Obligation, answered that those secrets were known to but three in the world, and that without the consent and cooperation of the other two he neither could nor would divulge them, but intimated that he had no doubt patience and industry would, in due time, entitle the worthy Mason to a participation of them, but that, for his own part, he would rather suffer death than betray the sacred trust reposed in him.

This answer not proving satisfactory, the ruffian aimed a violent blow at the head of our Master, but, being startled at the firmness of his demeanour, it missed his forehead and only glanced on his right temple (*Junior Warden touches Candidate's right temple with the Plumb Rule*), but with such force as to cause him to reel and sink on his left knee. (*Candidate drops on to his left knee.*) Recovering from the shock (*Candidate rises*), he made for the north entrance, where he was accosted by the second of those ruffians, to whom he gave a similar answer with undiminished firmness, when the ruffian, who was armed with a Level, struck him a violent blow on the left temple (*Senior Warden touches Candidate's left temple with the Level*), which brought him to the ground on his right knee. (*Candidate drops on to his right knee, and recovers.*) Finding his retreat cut off at both these points, he staggered faint and bleeding to the east entrance, where the third ruffian was posted, who received a similar answer to his insolent demand—for even at this trying moment our Master remained firm and unshaken—when the villain, who was armed with a heavy Maul, struck him a violent

217

blow on the forehead. (*The Worshipful Master makes a gesture as if slaying Candidate with the Maul*), which laid him lifeless at this feet. (*Wardens lower Candidate backwards into the 'grave'. A clock or gong may sound twelve, or the Lodge Organist play the Dead March from* Saul *while Ecclesiastes 12, 'Remember now thy Creator', is recited.*)

The Brethren will take notice that in the recent ceremony, as well as in his present situation, our Brother has been made to represent one of the brightest characters recorded in the annals of Masonry, namely, Hiram Abiff, who lost his life in consequence of his unshaken fidelity to the sacred trust reposed in him, and I hope this will make a lasting impression on his and your minds, should you ever be placed in a similar state of trial.

Brother Junior Warden, you will endeavour to raise the representative of our Master by the Entered Apprentice's grip.

(*Junior Warden lifts Candidate's right arm with his left, gives First Degree grip with his right hand and lets it slip, lowering Candidate's arm again.*)

JUNIOR WARDEN. (*Step and sign.*) Worshipful Master, it proves a slip. (*Cuts sign.*)

WORSHIPFUL MASTER. Brother Senior Warden, you will try the Fellow Craft's.

(*Senior Warden tries Second Degree grip and lets it slip.*)

SENIOR WARDEN. (*Step and sign.*) Worshipful Master, it proves a slip likewise. (*Cuts sign.*)

WORSHIPFUL MASTER. Brother Wardens, having both failed in your attempts, there remains a third method, by taking a more firm hold of the sinews of the hand and raising him on the Five Points of Fellowship, which, with your assistance, I will make trial of.

(*Worshipful Master goes to Candidate's feet and uncrosses them. He then takes Candidate's right hand in Third Degree grip, places his right foot to Candidate's right foot, and then, as Wardens raise Candidate, places right knee to right knee, right breast to right breast, and left hand over Candidate's back.*)

(*Holding the Five Points of Fellowship*.) It is thus all Master Masons are raised from a figurative death to a reunion with the former companions of their toils. Brother Wardens, resume your seats.

Let me now beg you to observe that the light of a Master Mason is darkness visible, serving only to express that gloom which rests on the prospect of futurity. It is that mysterious veil which the eye of human reason cannot penetrate unless assisted by that light which is from above. Yet, even by this glimmering ray, you may perceive that you stand on the very brink of the grave into which you have just figuratively descended, and which, when this transitory life shall have passed away, will again receive you into its cold bosom. Let the emblems of mortality which lie before you lead you to contemplate on your inevitable destiny, and guide your reflections to that most interesting of all human studies, the knowledge of yourself. Be careful to perform your allotted task while it is yet day; continue to listen to the voice of Nature, which bears witness, that even in this perishable frame resides a vital and immortal principle, which inspires a holy confidence that the Lord of Life will enable us to trample the King of Terror beneath our feet, and lift our eyes to that bright Morning Star, whose rising brings peace and salvation to the faithful and obedient of the human race.

(*Worshipful Master moves to the north and faces south. Candidate stands in the south facing north.*)

I cannot better reward the attention you have paid to this exhortation and charge than by entrusting you with the secrets of the Degree. You will therefore advance to me as a Fellow Craft, first as an Entered Apprentice. (*Candidate does so.*) You will now take another short pace towards me with your left foot, bringing the right heel into its hollow as before. That is the third regular step in Freemasonry, and it is in this position that the secrets of the degree are communicated. They consist of signs, a token and word.

219

Of the signs, the first and second are Casual, the third Penal. The first Casual sign is called the sign of Horror, and is given from the Fellow Crafts. Stand to order as a Fellow Craft, by dropping the left hand into this position (*Down, palm outwards as if shielding eyes from something on the ground*), elevating the right (*Back of hand to face, shielding eyes*), with the head turned over the right shoulder, as if struck with horror as some dreadful and afflicting sight.

The second Casual sign is called the sign of Sympathy, and is given by bending the head forward, and smiting the forehead gently with the right hand.

Place your hand in this position (*Forearm parallel with ground and in line with navel, palm downwards*), with the thumb extended in the form of a square. (*Tip of thumb touching body.*) The Penal sign is given by drawing the hand smartly across the body, dropping it to the side, and recovering with the thumb to the navel. This is in allusion to the symbolic penalty at one time included in the Obligation in this degree had he improperly disclosed the secrets entrusted to him, which implied that, as a man of honour, a Master Mason would rather have been severed in two, the bowels burned to ashes, and those ashes scattered over the face of the earth and wafted by the four cardinal winds of heaven, that no trace or remembrance of so vile a wretch may longer be found among men, particularly Master Masons. (*As Worshipful Master demonstrates each sign Candidate copies.*)

The grip or token is the first of the Five Points of Fellowship. They are hand to hand, foot to foot, knee to knee, breast to breast, and hand over back (*Worshipful Master demonstrates with Candidate*), and may be thus briefly explained. (*He goes through each point with Candidate as he explains it.*)

Hand to hand, I greet you as a brother; foot to foot I will support you in all your laudable undertakings; knee to knee the posture of my daily supplications shall remind me of your wants; breast to breast, your lawful secrets when entrusted to me as such I will keep as my own; and hand over back, I will support your character in your absence as in your presence. It is in this position, and this only, and then only in a whisper, except in open Lodge, that the word is given; it is MACHABEN or MACHBINNA.

You are now at liberty to retire in order to restore yourself to your personal comforts, and on your return to the Lodge, the sign, tokens and word will be further explained.

(*Senior Deacon takes Candidate to door, instructing him to salute Worshipful Master in the three degrees, but only with penal sigh in Third Degree. The lodge lights are put on again. The Candidate's return is announced by Third Degree knocks from Tyler. Senior Deacon leads Candidate to north of Senior Warden.*)

SENIOR WARDEN. (*Step and sign.*) Worshipful Master, I present to you Brother John Smith on his being raised to the Third Degree, for some further mark of your favour.

WORSHIPFUL MASTER. Brother Senior Warden, I delegate you to invest him with the distinguishing badge of a Master Mason. (*Senior Warden cuts sign, and invests Candidate with apron. He holds right-hand corner of apron in his left hand during his next speech.*)

SENIOR WARDEN. Brother John Smith, by the Worshipful Master's command I invest you with the distinguishing badge of a Master Mason to mark the further progress you have made in the science.

WORSHIPFUL MASTER. I must state that the badge with which you have now been invested not only points out your rank as a Master Mason, but is meant to remind you of those great duties you have just solemnly engaged yourself to observe, and whilst it marks your own superiority, it calls on you to afford assistance and instruction to the Brethren in the inferior degrees. We left off at that part of our traditional history which mentions the death of our Master Hiram Abiff. A loss so important as that of the principal architect could not fail of being generally and severely felt. The want of those plans and designs which had

221

hitherto been regularly supplied to the different classes of workmen was the first indication that some heavy calamity had befallen our Master. The Menatschin or Prefects, or more familiarly speaking, the Overseers, deputed some of the most eminent of their number to acquaint King Solomon with the utter confusion into which the absence of Hiram had plunged them, and to express their apprehension that to some fatal catastrophe must be attributed his sudden and mysterious disappearance. King Solomon immediately ordered a general muster of the workmen throughout the different departments, when three of the same class of overseers were not to be found. On the same day the twelve Craftsmen who had originally joined in the conspiracy came before the King and made a voluntary confession of all they knew, down to the time of withdrawing themselves from the number of conspirators. This naturally increased the fears of King Solomon for the safety of his chief artist. He therefore selected fifteen trusty Fellow Crafts, and ordered them to make diligent search after the person of our Master, to ascertain if he were yet alive, or had suffered death in the attempt to extort from him the secrets of his exalted Degree.

Accordingly, a stated day having been appointed for their return to Jerusalem, they formed themselves into three Fellow Craft Lodges, and departed from the three entrances of the temple. Many days were spent in fruitless search; indeed, one class returned without having made any discovery of importance. A second, however, were more fortunate, for on the evening of a certain day, after having suffered the greatest privations and personal fatigues, one of the Brethren, who had rested himself in a reclining posture, to assist his rising caught hold of a shrub that grew near, which to his surprise came easily out of the ground. On a closer examination he found that the earth had been recently disturbed. He therefore hailed his companions and with their united endeavours reopened the ground, and there found the body of our Master very indecently interred. They covered it again with all respect

222

and reverence, and to distinguish the spot, stuck a sprig of acacia at the head of the grave.

They then hastened to Jerusalem to impart the afflicting intelligence to King Solomon. He, when the first emotions of his grief had subsided, ordered them to return and raise our Master to such a sepulture, as became his rank and exalted talents, at the same time informing them that by his untimely death the secrets of a Master Mason were lost. He therefore charged them to be particularly careful in observing whatever casual sign, token, or word might occur whilst paying this last sad tribute of respect to departed merit. They performed their task with the utmost fidelity, and on reopening the ground one of the Brethren looking round observed some of his companions in this position (*Demonstrates sign of Horror*), struck with horror at the dreadful and afflicting sight, while others viewing the ghastly wound still visible on his forehead, smote their own in sympathy with his sufferings. (*Demonstrates sign of Sympathy.*) Two of the Brethren then descended the grave and endeavoured to raise him by the Entered Apprentice's grip, which proved a slip. They then tried the Fellow Craft's which proved a slip likewise. Having both failed in their attempts, a zealous and expert brother took a more firm hold on the sinews of the hand, and with their assistance raised him on the Five Points of Fellowship; while others, more animated, exclaimed MACHABEN or MACHBINNA, both words having a nearly similar import, one signifying the death of the builder, the other the builder is smitten. King Solomon therefore ordered that those casual signs, and that token and word, should designate all Master Masons throughout the universe, until time or circumstances should restore the genuine.

It only remains to account for the third class, who had pursued their researches in the direction of Joppa, and were meditating their return to Jerusalem, when, accidentally passing the mouth of a cavern, they heard sounds of deep lamentation and regret. On entering the cave to ascertain the cause, they found three men answering the description of those missing, who, on being charged with the murder, and finding all chance of escape cut off, made a full confession of their guilt. They were then bound and led to Jerusalem, when King Solomon sentenced them to that death the heinousness of their crime so amply merited. (*Rest of Traditional History given from tracing board.*)

Our Master was ordered to be re-interred as near to the Sanctum Sanctorum as the Israelitish law would permit; there in a grave, from the centre three feet east and three feet west, three feet between north and south, and five feet or more perpendicular. He was not buried in the Sanctum Sanctorum, because nothing common or unclean was allowed to enter there; not even the High Priest, but once a year; nor then until after many washings and purifications against the great day of expiation for sins; for by the Israelitish law, all flesh was deemed unclean. The same fifteen trusty Fellow Crafts were ordered to attend the funeral, clothed in white aprons and gloves as emblems of their innocence. You have already been informed that the working tools with which our Master was slain were the Plumb Rule, Level, and heavy Maul. The ornaments of a Master Masons' Lodge are the Porch, Dormer, and Square Pavement. The Porch was the entrance to the Sanctum Sanctorum, the Dormer the window that gave light to the same, and the Square Pavement for the High Priest to walk on.

The High Priest's office was to burn incense to the honour and glory of the Most High, and to pray fervently that the Almighty, of His unbounded wisdom and goodness, would be pleased to bestow peace and tranquillity on the Israelitish nation during the ensuing year. The coffin, skull and crossbones, being emblems of mortality, allude to the untimely death of our Master Hiram Abiff. He was slain three thousand years after the creation of the world. (*End of tracing-board explanation.*) In the course of the ceremony you have been informed of three signs in this Degree. The whole of them are five, corresponding in number with the Five Points of Fellowship. They are the sign of Horror, the sign of Sympathy, the Penal sign, the sign of Grief and Distress, and the sign of Joy and Exultation, likewise called the Grand or Royal sign. For the sake of regularity I will go through them and you will copy me.

This is the sign of Horror; this, of Sympathy; this, the Penal sign. The sign of Grief and Distress is given by passing the right hand across the face, and dropping it over the left eyebrow in the form of a square. This took its rise at the time our Master was making his way from the north to the east entrance of the temple, when his agony was so great that the perspiration stood in large drops on his forehead, and he made use of this sign (*Demonstrates and Candidate copies*) as a temporary relief to his sufferings. This tis the sign of Joy and Exultation. (*Hands raised above head, with palms facing.*) It took its rise at the time the temple was completed, and King Solomon with the princes of his household went to view it, when they were so struck with its magnificence that with one simultaneous motion they exclaimed, 'O wonderful Masons!'

On the Continent of Europe the sign of Grief and Distress is given in a different manner, by clasping the hands and elevating them with their backs to the forehead, exclaiming, 'Come to my assistance, ye children of the widow', on the supposition that all Master Masons are Brothers to Hiram Abiff, who was a widow's son. In Scotland, Ireland and the States of America the sign of Grief and Distress is given in a still different manner by throwing up the hands with the palms extended towards the Heavens, and dropping them, with three distinct movements to the sides, exclaiming, 'O Lord my God, O Lord my God, O Lord my God, is there no help for the widow's son?' (*Candidate copies each sign as it is demonstrated.*)

I now present to you the working tools of a Master Mason. They are the Skirret, Pencil, and Compasses. The Skirret is an implement which acts on a centre pin, whence a line is drawn to mark out ground for the foundation of the intended structure. With the Pencil the skilful artist delineates the building in a draft or plan for the instruction and guidance of the workman. The Compasses enable him, with accuracy and precision, to ascertain and determine the limits and proportions of its several parts. But as we are not all operative Masons, but rather free and accepted, or speculative, we apply these tools to our morals.

In this sense, the Skirret points out that straight and undeviating line of conduct laid down for our pursuit in the Volume of the Sacred Law. The Pencil teaches us that our words and actions are observed and recorded by the Almighty Architect, to whom we must give an account of our conduct through life. The compasses remind us of His unerring and impartial justice, who, having defined for our instruction the limits of good and evil, will reward or punish, as we have obeyed or disregarded His Divine commands. Thus the working tools of a Master Mason teach us to bear in mind, and act according to, the laws of our Divine Creator, that when we shall be summoned from this sublunary abode, we may ascend to the Grand Lodge above, where the world's Great Architect lives and reigns for ever.

CHAPTER XII

Law and Order

Freemasonry among policemen has a long history but it was not until May 1972 following an article in *Police Review*, a weekly news magazine for the police service, that speculation about its influence began to assume the proportions of a public debate. The author, Sergeant Peter J. Welling, of Nottinghamshire police, proposed that the Police Federation and the Home Office should both press for legislation to prohibit a police officer from taking an oath in a secret society, and to compel new recruits to renounce any such affiliation. Sergeant Welling did not believe that a police officer who is a Freemason can be impartial and held that his proposed ban on membership would avoid the danger of policemen having divided loyalties. He wrote:

It is a fact that when a police officer is appointed he takes an oath of allegiance to the Queen and the community to carry out his duties 'without fear or favour, malice or ill will'. It is not commonly known that on enrolment to a Freemasonry lodge a Freemason also takes an oath. I do not profess to know what form this oath takes or how it is administered, but it is most certainly an oath of allegiance not only to members of his own Lodge but to all members of the Freemasonry movement. To assist him to recognise other Freemasons he is taught secret handshakes and other secret signs. This type of association taken throughout the country forms a formidable chain of contact and associates from all walks of life.

Sergeant Welling also noted that the police service was changing and there was 'an increasing awareness among junior members that, after passing the appropriate examinations, a sure way to promotion is through the Freemasonry

227

movement'. Many officers would protest at his proposed ban on their being Masons on the grounds that it was a further restriction on a policeman's private life. Such officers had to answer two questions. What benefit does a secret society gain from having a police officer as a member? What does a police officer gain from being a member of a secret society?

Freemasons were briefed with the official reply to Sergeant Welling's article, which received widespread newspaper coverage and some attention from television, in the editorial of the June issue of *Masonic Record*:

He (Welling) contrasts the Freemason's oath with the oath a policeman takes on his appointment ... No Freemason could have any difficulty in reconciling these two oaths, and it reveals no secret to say that for a policeman the Freemason's oath does no more than underwrite the honourable intentions required of him when he enters the force. So far as a Freemason is required to give an additional allegiance, it is in charity and brotherhood, but always within the larger context of his duty to his family and the community as a whole.

For the policeman there is only a problem of divided loyalties when there is someone in his own family who is in conflict with the law. Freemasonry has never asked for divided loyalties on its own account, has always been careful to put the higher first ... It must always be hard for a policeman to exercise the requirements of the law against someone he knows and respects, whether a neighbour, a member of the Watch Committee, a local personality, a member of the church, a doctor, a lawyer, even a fellow member of the police force. It would be dehumanising indeed if service in the police should seek to deny a man all off-duty relationships with his fellows that might seem to create loyalties. Fellowship in Freemasonry creates no new problems for the policeman. It should strengthen him in his duties, not confuse him.

The following month the *Masonic Record* returned to the subject and a contributor specifically answered the two questions posed by Sergeant Welling to those Masonic policemen who would object to his proposed ban on their membership. The Freemasons, said the writer, gained with every man entering of his own free will and accord, a just, upright and free man. The police officer gained from his Freemasonry an opportunity to relax and to mix freely with men of like ideals. On the question of promotion preferment for Masonic police officers, the writer added:

The wise man, whatever his senior position, will not allow his social life to affect his judgement, but it may give him the opportunity of assessing another's capabilities, or otherwise, which might not be apparent in their business life.

In fact, it was not until sixteen years later that a Bill came before Parliament which, if it became law, would require any police officer who was a Freemason to resign either from his lodge or from the police. When it arrived the Bill owed nothing to the Police Federation or the Home Office. The debate which Sergeant Welling initiated finally reached the House of Commons because of a sequence of events: the exposure of widespread corruption among Metropolitan policemen linked with Freemasonry; the publication of a book making sensational claims about the degree of Masonic influence within the police, the Bar, the judiciary and local government; and publicly aired concerns that Masonic conspiracy had affected the careers of two senior police officers.

Among investigations into corruption involving the police in Britain which made headlines in the 1970s was an operation to uncover corrupt CID officers responsible for policing vice and pornography in London's Soho. For more than three years detectives sought the truth behind allegations that policemen among the Obscene Publications Squad were taking bribes.

More than twenty detectives were sacked from the force during the inquiries and after trial in 1977 two senior police officers were imprisoned for twelve years. They were Commander Wallace Virgo, who had been in charge of specialist detective squads including those investigating drugs and pornography, and Detective Chief Superintendent William Moody, a subordinate and former head of the OPS. A serious Masonic connection was established: some officers of the OPS, including Moody, belonged to a lodge in South London where a number of distributors of pornography were also members.

Another much publicised investigation into police corruption in London started in August 1978 and was dubbed 'Operation Countryman' because it was originally led by senior officers from Dorset. It concerned allegations that police officers were involved in three big armed robberies. These took place at the offices of the *Daily Express* in 1976, a branch of Williams and Glyn's bank in the City in 1977 and at the *Daily Mirror* in 1978.

In his book *The Brotherhood* Stephen Knight wrote:

Operation Countryman, the biggest investigation ever conducted into police corruption in Britain, would never have come about if the Commissioner of the City of London Police between 1971 and 1977 had not been corrupted and unduly influenced by Freemasonry. Indeed, there seems little doubt that if James Page had refused to join the Brotherhood, he would not have been appointed Commissioner in the first place . . . These crimes would never have occured if Page had not committed himself to Freemasonry to assure himself of the Commissioner's job. If he hadn't done so, he would not have become Commissioner in 1971.

Knight built his case against Page on information he was given by people who did so only on the understanding that they must remain anonymous. As a result his book is seriously flawed and its sources suspect. His statement that if Page had not been a Freemason, he would not have been appointed Commissioner has been refuted by United Grand Lodge.[1] Page, says the statement, did not join the Craft until after he became Commissioner.

Knight gives the pseudonym 'Commander Dryden' to one informant, described as among the highest-ranking officers in the force. This man, says Knight, advised Page on no account to promote two City police officers whom he knew to be corrupt. The pseudonyms given by Knight to these two corrupt

[1]Evidence to working group of General Synod of Church of England

officers are 'Tearle' and 'Oates' and this is the conclusion of his chapter on Operation Countryman:

If Page had not been a Freemason, he would have heeded Dryden's warning in 1969 never to promote Tearle and Oates, when both of them were in the less influential rank of detective chief inspector. As it was, he promoted them because he and they were part of the same Brotherhood. They achieved high rank under Page. Commander Dryden told me: 'If Tearle and Oates had not been promoted others would not have been promoted because they - Tearle and Oates - came to have influence over other promotions. Once they were in a position of control, they then promoted their Masonic brethren, many of whom were in on the corruption with them. This brought about an ease of communication and a whole corrupt Masonic network was set up within the force. Tearle and Oates colluded with some of these newly promoted Masons and played a part in setting up the Williams and Glyn's and the *Mirror* jobs, and they helped out after the event at the *Express*. Mason police shared out around £60,000 from one job.'
Oates and some of the worst of their accomplices have now gone from the force, but Tearle remains, terrified that his name will be connected publicly with the crimes in which he has taken part if one of his former colleagues decides there is no longer anything to be gained by protecting him. One of the men who is thinking very seriously of 'shopping' Tearle, Oates and the rest of the crew told me, 'One word from me and they go down for a long, long while.' So far that word has not been forthcoming.

Not surprisingly, the official verdict on Operation Countryman makes no mention of Freemasonry or James Page. *The Times* of 19 June 1981 carried this report:

Operation Countryman, the inquiry into allegations of police corruption in London, is being wound up leaving eight officers awaiting trial and three acquitted after almost three years' work at a cost of nearly £2m.
In the wake there are 83 cases of alleged corruption, not central to the Countryman brief, which are being dealt with by Scotland Yard officers. They involve up to 200 alleged offences and investigations will continue for a further 18 months. The most serious cases involve the miscarriage of justice connected with armed robberies.

231

Announcing the end of Countryman yesterday, Deputy Commissioner Patrick Kavanagh accused the press of blowing the inquiry up out of all proportion. It had revealed neither widespread corruption nor had it implicated senior officers.

Many of the 83 cases would have come to Scotland Yard's attention anyway, Mr Kavanagh said. He added: 'The Metropolitan Police is more honest than it has ever been.'

Knight, calling for an independent inquiry into Freemasonry in the Police, claimed:

Many people want to see Masonry banned in the police. This would inflict damage to the personal happiness of many thousands of upright Masonic policemen and to the principle of individual freedom that might overweigh any good effect. But a compulsory register on which police officers have to list their affiliation to secret societies, and their status within such societies, is the minimum requirement if a grave situation is to be improved.

Knight's book also raised serious questions about Masonic influence among members of the Bar and the judiciary. While there is no question that a number of judges are Freemasons, nothing has come to light to call into question their integrity; and Knight's investigations into Masonic influence within the judiciary and legal profession suffered from the quality of the evidence produced. For example, an unnamed senior official in the Lord Chancellor's Department told Knight that joining the right lodge was an important step towards appointment as a judge because those who selected and recommended candidates considered that Freemasons made the best judges. Knight added that, without knowing it, the Lord Chancellor was fed recommendations of Freemasons by Freemasons.

Lord Hailsham told the *Law Society Gazette* in July 1984, 'Not merely am I not myself a Mason, but not one of those on my staff who advises me on judicial appointments is one either . . . To suggest that, in making judicial appointments, I am fed recommendations of Freemasons by Freemasons is therefore the purest nonsense.' More publicly in letters to *The Times*, the *Telegraph* and the *Guardian* Lord Hailsham denied

232

that the Lord Chancellor's patronage office was staffed by Freemasons.

Parliament was told in December 1985 that judges and justices of the peace would not be required to declare membership of Freemasonry. The Solicitor General said that to ask for such a declaration of interest would be 'a very dangerous infraction of personal privacy and personal freedom'. He continued:

There is no evidence to justify the discrimination between Free-masonry and other forms of voluntary association. In the case of justices of the peace, they are also free to join political associations and campaigning bodies so long as they remain within the law, behave in a manner not calculated to bring the magistracy into disrepute, and disqualify themselves from sitting in cases in which it might reasonably be supposed that they were emotionally or personally involved.

A few weeks after the publication of Knight's book The *Observer*[1] said it had evidence that Freemasons who were senior policemen and officials on the staff of the Director of Public Prosecutions had been directly involved in unsuccessful corruption inquiries concerning fellow Masons. Much of the article concerned the claim of Detective Chief Inspector Brian Woollard that his police career had been ruined by Freemasons after he had formally interviewed an official of the DPP during investigations into alleged corruption in the allocation of council contracts in Islington, north London, in 1982. The *Observer* reported:

In a statement given to the Home Office, Detective Chief Inspector Brian Woollard says he was removed from the Islington inquiry after seeking explanations from a senior DPP official of why the official had intervened in the case.
After 26 years' service, Mr Woollard was transferred in 1981 to an offshoot of the Fraud Squad, the Public Sector Corruption Squad. He was later assigned to lead an inquiry into a department of Islington Council.

[1]Report by David Leigh and Paul Lashmar, 25 March 1984.

Newspaper allegations had been made of council officers' collusion with contractors to deprive the council of many thousands of pounds. It was claimed that council officers had been entertained at expensive nightclubs. Mr Woollard says information was being passed secretly between Masons, documents needed in the inquiry were not available and certain council officers who were not the subject of allegations appear to have been helping fellow Masons who were implicated.

When he was approached by a senior member of the DPP's office Mr Woollard took the unprecedented step of interviewing the DPP official, who he concluded was a Mason. He then went to Scotland Yard to explain his actions. Later the same day he was removed from the case and shortly afterwards transferred to administrative duties in Wembley. Scotland Yard's Deputy Assistant Commissioner, Richard Wells, said yesterday that he felt Mr Woollard was having difficulty in coming to terms with the investigation of fraud, and that was one of the reasons for his removal from the case.

The Islington inquiry was handed over to a fellow Public Sector Corruption Squad officer, DCI Robert Andrews. He was himself a Mason. He eventually sent a report to the DPP's office. The DPP decided that there was insufficient evidence for a prosecution.

In June 1981 Mr Andrews had been in charge of a similar inquiry in Newham after detailed allegations of corruption in the council. The LWT 'London Programme' had revealed that a substantial number of councillors and council officers were in the same Masonic lodge and some were involved with the allegations over housing allocations, payments and preferential treatment for Masons.

A report of the police inquiry in that case was passed to the DPP's office too and it also recommended no prosecution.

Mr Andrews told us that he was no longer a Mason but declined to say when he had resigned.

'It has no bearing on my job and has not influenced me at all. Both those investigations were done quite properly,' he said.

The *Observer* does not suggest that Mr Andrews acted in any way improperly. Fraud Squad investigations are long and difficult and result in a low rate of prosecutions. But clearly there are problems if both the investigator and investigated are Masons.

Brian Woollard started to campaign for an inquiry into the circumstances of his removal from the Public Sector

Corruption Squad and early in August such an inquiry, to be led by Mr Tom Meffen, an Assistant Chief Constable of West Midlands Police, was announced. The *Daily Telegraph*, 6 August 1984, reported:

Towards the end of last year Mr Woollard, who served for 14 years in the Special Branch, complained to the Parliamentary Commissioner and Parliament that the then Home Secretary, Viscount Whitelaw, had 'obstructed' an independent inquiry into his complaints against the then Deputy Commissioner of the Metropolitan Police, Mr Patrick Kavanagh, and Deputy Assistant Commissioner, Mr Ronald Stevenson. He claimed that they had obstructed him 'in the execution of my duties into an investigation into public sector corruption'. Both officers have since retired.

A month later the Deputy Commissioner of the Metropolitan Police, Mr Albert Laugharne, issued guidance to his officers concerning membership of Freemasonry. It was supported by the Metropolitan Police Commissioner, Sir Kenneth Newman. All Freemasons in the Force were asked to consider whether Freemasonry was compatible with their duties to the service and to the public.

'The discerning officer,' they were told, 'will probably consider it wise to forego the prospect of pleasure and social advantage in Freemasonry so as to enjoy the unreserved regard of all those around him.' All chief officers of police were sent copies of the Metropolitan Police guidance, which was said by the *Observer*, 9 September 1984, to have caused 'intense embarrassment' within the Directorate of Public Prosecutions where many officials were Masons. The report continued:

The former Director of Public Prosecutions for 13 years, Sir Norman Skelhorn, who was a prominent Freemason, was appointed Senior Grand Deacon in 1976 while still in office.
The present deputy DPP, Mr Kenneth Dowling, and one of the key assistant directors, Mr Richard Thomas, are both said to be Masons. Asked by the *Observer* whether that was so, both refused to say.

Many prominent members of the 'law and order' establishment and an unknown number of their juniors are Masons. Sir Ian Percival, MP, until recently junior law officer in the Thatcher administration, and Lord Whitelaw, until recently Home Secretary, are Masons.

Dozens of magistrates, judges and prosecuting barristers are rank and file Masons, and we have identified at least 36 judges who have held senior Masonic office.

They range from the House of Lords (Lord Justice Templeman) to the Old Bailey (Judge Abdela) and the High Court (the former Lord Chief Justice, the late Lord Widgery).

Early in April 1985 the Director of Public Prosecutions, Sir Thomas Hetherington, received the report of the police investigation into Chief Inspector Brian Woollard's complaints. Mr Thomas Meffen and his team of hand-picked detectives who were not Freemasons, had found that there was no Masonic influence on either the Islington corruption inquiry or Woollard's career. The *Daily Telegraph*, 15 April 1985, which leaked the report, said:

Now Sir Thomas will have to decide whether there should be any prosecutions arising from it. Mr Woollard, however, has already said through his solicitor that he will not accept any finding from Sir Thomas's department, and has made complaints of Masonic influence there. He wants a wholly independent inquiry to make recommendations about his future career prospects and his loss of seniority in the CID. He also wants the Parliamentary Commissioner, the Ombudsman, to have the power to investigate complaints about alleged maladministration made by members of the public services. The Ombudsman has already told him he has no remit to investigate such complaints.

Woollard continued his campaign but his appeals to the Commissioner of Police, Home Secretary, the Parliamentary Commissioner for Administration and Prime Minister were referred back to the officers against whom his complaints were made in the first place. At the end of a year, Woollard's petition for an independent inquiry into his case and for the introduction of an independent complaints procedure for internal complaints within the Police was presented to the House of Commons. It got nowhere, it was left to lie upon the table.

The pursuit of his complaints placed Woollard under such stress that he became ill. After his recovery, he wrote to the Police Commissioner that he would refuse to return to work alongside Freemasons and he was suspended. Sympathetic colleagues were helping him to compile a file of evidence to prove that some Freemasons at all levels in the Police use their Masonic connections improperly. The most important piece of evidence to come his way was a list of members of the Manor of St James's Lodge No. 9179,[1] a lodge founded in January 1986 by police officers who had served in 'C' or St James's district of the Metropolitan Police.

On the lodge list Woollard found the names of at least nine of the men who had important influence over his career from 1982, the year of his corruption inquiry into a department of Islington council, until he finally refused to report for work in 1987. One was the name of a senior officer instrumental in his removal from the Public Sector Corruption Squad. Three of his immediate superiors at the London division to which he was posted were listed, as was a man with whom he worked every day. Another member of the lodge was the officer responsible for Woollard's career development in the Force. The most shocking discovery for Woollard was the inclusion of the Police Federation official with whom he had discused his complaints.

The *Observer*, 30 November 1986, based a story about the Manor of St James's Lodge on secret lodge documents in its possession and said:

There are at least 100 Masons in the lodge, most of them present or former Scotland Yard officers. Members include Commander Malcolm Campbell, head of the Metropolitan Police fraud branch, who is lodge treasurer; anti-terrorist squad leader, Commander

---

[1]The term Manor is the colloquial expression used by police officers when referring to their own district or place of duty.

Kenneth Churchill-Coleman; and Commander William Gibson, a lodge officer, of the Met's North West area. Former Met officers who belong includee retired Commander John Cass, who led the police inquiry into the death of Blair Peach, allegedly killed by police at an anti-National Front demonstration seven years ago.

The Sunday Times, 10 April 1988, said that the newspaper had a list of 100 senior Scotland Yard officers who were active Masons and that the Commissioner had up to 5,000 Masons in his force. The list of 100 was the membership list of the Manor of St James's Lodge sent to Mr Woollard and the basis of a story in the *Observer*, 30 November 1986. Some more names of lodge members were revealed by *The Sunday Times* which said that Anthony Speed, in charge of detective training at the Hendon police college, was among them and went on:

At least four detective chief superintendents are on the list. One, David Stephenson, heads the squad that investigates computer and charity frauds. Another, Ron Hay, is a member of the complaints investigation bureau, at present inquiring into alleged links between Commander Ray Adams and Kenneth Noye, now serving 14 years for conspiring to dispose of bullion from the £26m Brink's-Mat robbery.

The Sunday Times also named two important men who, the paper claimed, were involved in establishing the St James's Lodge:

Some of Britain's highest-ranking Masons helped to launch the lodge, including Lord Farnham, the Masonic order's Assistant Grand Master, and Sir Peter Lane, chairman of the executive committee of the National Union of Conservative Associations. Farnham refused to comment. Lane, a key figure at Tory conferences, said:
'I assisted Lord Farnham when this lodge was formed, but, for a variety of reasons, I haven't attended any of its meetings since. There are those who see evil and corruption everywhere, but I would be very surprised if this lodge had any influence at all.'

238

Another Masonic lodge made headlines in August 1986 when it held an unprecedented press conference. Journalists and television cameramen were invited into the Manchester Temple of the East Lancashire Province of Freemasons to hear denials of newspaper reports that Freemasons were involved in the suspension of John Stalker, Deputy Chief Constable of the Greater Manchester Police. Two years earlier Stalker had been asked to set up an inquiry into the killings of six men by the Royal Ulster Constabulary in three separate incidents in 1982. The killings had prompted speculation that the RUC has a 'shoot to kill' policy against the IRA.

Stalker in a bestseller[1] about his experiences during and after his investigations says that his removal from the inquiry was a hasty decision made against the background of the political situation in Ulster. He was nearing the completion of his task at the end of May 1986 when he was told that allegations had been made against him that might indicate a disciplinary offence on his part. During an interview, Colin Sampson, Chief Constable of West Yorkshire and the officer appointed to investigate, invited him to take extra leave and said that he was to consider himself off the Northern Ireland inquiry forever; that would be taken over by Sampson, using Stalker's team.

At the end of June Stalker was formally suspended from duty. The day before, a Sunday newspaper carried a story that Stalker's troubles were due to co-ordinated Masonic influence in the RUC, the Orange Order (a Masonic organisation in Northern Ireland), and Greater Manchester Police. It was these allegations which led to the Freemasons' press conference at which the East Lancashire Provincial Grand Secretary, Mr Colin Gregory, denied any Masonic involvement in Stalker's case. He told reporters there were 17,000 Masons in the Province, but would not say how many were policemen in the Greater Manchester Force, nor how many

[1]*Stalker*, Harrap, 1988. My edition, is that published by Penguin Books with revisions to the chapter entitled 'Conclusions', 1988.

239

were senior officers. It had been alleged that the chairman of the Greater Manchester Police Committee, councillor Norman Briggs, was part of a Masonic conspiracy to discredit Stalker. Mr Briggs collapsed and died a week after the allegations were first published, and at the Masons' press conference they were strongly denied by his family and the Freemasons. In his book Stalker says:

Norman Briggs was not a Freemason. I felt his death deeply. Salford had lost a good councillor, and the community had lost an honest servant. Despite everything, I would have trusted him to be fair and of independent mind when the report about me was placed before him ... The Northern headquarters of the Freemasons' Society threw open their doors for a press conference to say that 'to the best of their knowledge' there had been no Masonic conspiracy in the Stalker affair. Their spokesman invited the public to test the openness of Masons about their membership. 'Ask them,' he said, 'they will tell you. We are not ashamed of being Masons.' Two days later, on 8 August, Sir Philip Myers[1] was bluntly asked by a Police Committee member whether he was a Mason. He replied, 'Some time ago I was sent a questionnaire (by Stephen Knight, author of the book *The Brotherhood*) asking the same question. I threw it in the wastepaper basket, and I propose to do the same with your question.' He is reported not to have responded to an appeal for him to investigate links between police Masons in Manchester and Belfast. I mention these matters not to suggest that Sir Philip is a Freemason – if he is, he is entitled to be so – or that there were any Masonic links. I just do not know. I am not a Freemason but I know many good and efficient policemen who are.

The main and very serious charge against Stalker was that he had been associating with people involved with crime and it first surfaced at the beginning of his investigations in Northern Ireland. A remark made in Manchester by a businessman to a senior policeman during a game of golf led to a report being sent to James Anderton, Chief Constable of Greater Manchester Police, who told Sir Philip Myers,

[1]Inspector of Constabulary (North West).

the Regional Inspector of Constabulary[1]. The report was prepared by Chief Superintendent Peter Topping, number two in the CID, and Stalker believes that no value was attached to it until reasons were being sought to take him out of Northern Ireland. The allegations against Stalker were found to be totally without foundation and on 23 August 1986 he returned to work as Deputy Chief Constable. In his book Stalker recounts a confrontation he had with Topping on 26 September 1986:

I told him he had presented an over-inflated story to the Chief Constable, who had acted on it to the extreme detriment of the Force, himself, and me and my family. Topping said, 'I did not. I was only doing my job. I referred everything to Assistant Chief Constable Lees. He did the rest. It was not my fault.' I asked him whether the press reports were true, that since his appointment to the CID, the Drugs Squad and the Fraud Squad had all come to be members of Masonic Lodges. I made it clear that I was not being critical – I merely wished to know. He said, 'They are there on ability. I emphatically deny any wrongful influences.' I said to him that I was not suggesting there were any, but that some people might see it as unhealthy. He said, 'I would welcome any scrutiny of their activities. I choose people on their ability – nothing else – and I resent any inference that I do not.' I asked him whether he would always exercise a preference for a fellow Mason, all other things being equal. Topping replied, 'Yes, I would, and I do: and I see nothing wrong with that. In sensitive departments I need to know I can trust my officers. The ones I have chosen are all there on personal merit. I *know* without doubt I can trust them; others I only think I can trust.'

Stalker was dismayed at the way he was treated throughout the investigation into the allegations made against him and highly critical of the Sampson report at the end of the inquiry, a copy of which he received from David Leigh of the *Observer*. He was further disillusioned by the treatment he received when he returned to his post.

[1] Sir Philip received Stalker's acceptance of leadership of the Northern Ireland investigation, gave him an early briefing and was in touch with progress.

Stalker shows an admirable objectivity; although he re-counts Chief Superintendent Peter Topping's clear prefer-ence for working with Masonic officers, he refrains from comment. Stalker, unlike Brian Woollard, believes himself a victim of political rather than Masonic forces. Woollard, even after his suspension, rigorously pursues his claims that Freemasonry is rife at senior levels in the Metropolitan Police and that Masons are favoured for promotion, and Masonic influence was responsible for his removal from an investiga-tion into alleged corruption at Islington council.

The *Daily Telegraph*, 7 April 1988, reported the Metropol-itan Police Commissioner, Mr Peter Imbert, as saying there were no Freemasons among the six top-ranking officers of the force. There were Freemasons among his officers, but they were not in policy-making positions. The story, which followed a radio interview given by Mr Imbert, quoted him as saying:

If the allegations that you can only have promotion if you are a Freemason were correct, somehow my deputy, myself and my three predecessors have slipped through the net. So I think we ought to nail that ghost.

The questions raised by Sergeant Peter Welling in 1972 about the compatibility of Masonic oaths with the oath of allegiance by policemen on appointment were put before Parliament at the end of June 1988. So too was the case of Detective Chief Inspector Brian Woollard.

Mr Dale Campbell-Savours, the Labour member for Workington, brought in a bill to amend the service declara-tion made by all newly appointment policemen to undertake that they would 'abstain from any activity which is likely to interfere with the impartial discharge of my duties or which is likely to give rise to the impression amongst members of the public that it may so interfere.' The amendment to the law was designed specifically to stop practising Freemasons from serving as police officers.

Over many years, he said, there had been widespread

anxiety over allegations that Freemasons in the police force had received preferential treatment over appointments, promotion, disciplinary procedures and, most important, that they might not be impartially investigating criminal cases in which other Freemasons were involved.

His attack was not on the altruistic principles of Freemasonry and he applauded the charitable activities of Freemasons. The present secretive form of Freemasonry, however, made it inappropriate, not only for police officers, but also for the judiciary and those responsible for public administration to be Masons. If Freemasonry were to transform itself and shed its secrecy, exclusivity and its oath of allegiance, he would have no objection to police officers being members. As things stood, police officers should not be Freemasons, and those who were already Masons should resign either from the lodge or from the police force.

Mr Campbell-Savours said that Sir Kenneth Newman, former Commissioner of the Metropolitan Police, had drawn attention to the possible conflict between the Freemason's oath, and the police officer's declaration of impartiality and sworn obligation to avoid any activity likely to interfere with impartiality or to give the impression that it might do so. He went on:

In response, Freemasonry closed ranks. The new and powerful lodge of St James was forged, made up almost exclusively of Metropolitan police officers, some say as an act of defiance and a calculated insult to the commissioner. Its tentacles ran deep, with strong Conservative connections.

Sir Kenneth's concerns were prompted by a long history of problems involving freemasonry in the police force. One example that he must have had in mind was Operation Countryman, in the mid–1970s, when over 250 police officers were forced to resign and many faced criminal charges after investigations revealed that police membership of particular lodges formed the nucleus of a criminal conspiracy. If revelations of wrongdoing and insidious corruption are not enough, what about the worries of the sergeant on the beat passed over for promotion for a less experienced or less able but better-connected colleague, the disciplinary complaint against an official inexplicably overlooked, or the drunken driver who is not breathalysed?

Mr Campbell-Savours spoke too about Detective Chief Inspector Brian Woollard's campaign against 'the unacceptable influence of Freemasonry within the Metropolitan police'. Woollard's career had brought him seven commendations. He had served at Downing Street, at Buckingham Palace, with the anti-terrorist squad, with the public sector corruption squad, and as personal protection officer to a former Home Secretary. His diligent investigation of criminal conspiracy involving Freemasonry had ruined his career. 'The mistake that he made was to question a senior DPP official who showed an unprecedented interest in his case. Of course, that official turned out to be a Freemason.'

Mr Campbell-Savours's bill was supported by 117 votes in favour to 16 against, but had no chance of becoming law. It was introduced under the ten-minute rule procedure, a device for getting a debate. This consisted almost entirely of Mr Campbell-Savours's speech which closed with a condemnation of Freemasonry and the secrecy surrounding the organisation.'

Freemasonry is plagued with contradictions. It claims to be open to all, yet it bars women. It makes high moral claims, yet it offends the Church. It contains some of the most powerful and respected people in the land, yet subjects them to bizarre ritual that invites ridicule. I argue that Freemasons should not serve as police officers and that police officers should sever their links with their lodges. Their inter-tribal oath of loyalty is utterly incompatible with the duty to serve the whole community impartially. The secrecy of the organisation makes it impossible to check whether impartiality might be at risk in a particular case.
I submit that the police force is considerably damaged by its links with Freemasonry. Good policemen are embarrassed. We all recognise that the police depend on the full co-operation of the public in solving crime. That co-operation depends in turn on trust and a belief in their impartiality. Undermine that trust, and one undermines the fight against crime. The police force is an important

institution pledged to uphold the principles of an open, free and democratic society. We all support it. It is unhealthy that large numbers of its officers should be involved in an organisation whose practices are so entirely out of keeping with those principles.

MPs continued to press the Home Secretary to hold an inquiry into the case of Detective Chief Inspector Brian Woollard but this was refused. Mr Douglas Hogg, the Home Office Under-Secretary, in a Commons written reply at the end of July, said such an inquiry would be inappropriate. Mr Woollard had appeared before a disciplinary board on 25 May charged with being absent from duty. He was dismissed from the force and had appealed to the Commissioner, Sir Peter Imbert. Mr Woollard is now preparing a civil action for damages for wrongful dismissal and, with the support of a number of MPs, continues his campaign for the appointment of an Ombudsman for the police and public services.

CHAPTER XIII

The Christian Dilemma

Freemasonry continues to attract partly because in an increasingly secular environment men (and women) are the more prone to yearn for comfort from the esoteric to replace that which formal religion once provided. Freemasonry is well adapted to fill such a need. It offers all the advantages of a movement which is religious without being a religion. Its symbolism can be freely interpreted and Masons may choose their own metaphysics unhampered by theology. They are required only to believe in God, a system of morality, and a general brotherhood of men—with special reference to other Freemasons. So Freemasonry is able to claim that it upholds theistic religion: not any one particular religion, but all religions acknowledging a God ordering the Universe and having a personal relation to His creatures. As result Freemasonry attracts men who find within the Masonic system a substitute religion, and even inspiration for mysticism, as well as those who hold orthodox religious convictions and see nothing in Masonry to conflict with them.

During a television interview I asked Dr David Steel, a Church of Scotland minister, how Freemasonry integrated with his Christian beliefs and he replied:

I find no difficulty whatsoever in this. My impression is that Freemasonry is much more concerned with conduct than with faith. Where the Christian Church defines faith as faith in God through Jesus Christ and, of course, we see Him in Jesus Christ, I would say that the Masonic movement makes no attempt to give any particular content to the term God. That being so any Christian can insert into this term God as used in Freemasonry whatever content he cares to give it. In my case it is, of course, a Christian content, and so it is for other Christians.

The official attitude on the relationship of Masonry and religion is expressed in a report[1] approved by Grand Lodge on 12 September 1962. This is the crux of the statement:

It cannot be too strongly asserted that Masonry is neither a religion nor a substitute for religion. Masonry seeks to inculcate in its members a standard of conduct and behaviour which it believes to be acceptable to all creeds, but studiously refrains from intervening in the field of dogma or theology. Masonry, therefore, is not a competitor with religion though in the sphere of human conduct it may be hoped that its teaching will be complementary to that of religion. On the other hand its basic requirement that every member of the Order shall believe in a Supreme Being and the stress laid upon his duty towards Him should be sufficient evidence to all but the wilfully prejudiced that Masonry is an upholder of religion since it both requires a man to have some form of religious belief before he can be admitted as a Mason, and expects him when admitted to go on practising his religion.

At the same time Grand Lodge also approved some new regulations. These confined Masonic rites, prayers and ceremonies to the lodge room, and said that dispensation to wear regalia in public would be granted 'only in exceptional cases'. Masons are not to take any active part, as Masons, at the burial service or cremation of a brother and there are to be no Masonic prayers, readings or exhortations either then or at the graveside subsequent to the interment, 'since the final obsequies of any human being, Mason or not, are complete in themselves and do not call in the case of a Freemason for any additional ministrations'. References to the Masonic life and actions of a deceased brother are to be made in the lodge, or at a specifically arranged memorial service. The order of service for any act of corporate worship is to be arranged by the officiating minister, or his superior.

[1]For full Statement see Appendix 2.

From the statements of Grand Lodge itself emerge both the main grounds upon which a number of Christian churches have seen fit to declare their opposition to Freemasonry and the official defence. The temples of Masonry are imitative of churches and chapels and the ceremonies performed in the lodges borrow freely from religious practices while excluding any mention of Christ and the Trinity. Like churches, lodges are placed east to west, and the Master's pedestal, set in the east, is 'in a sense a combination of altar and desk'.[1] In some lodges there is a separate altar immediately in front of the Master's pedestal. All lodges are consecrated according to a form of ceremony which has never been laid down, but which has evolved.

The ceremony is conducted by the Consecrating Officer, acting on behalf of the Grand Master, who opens the lodge in the three degrees. The lodge warrant is then read and those Masons who petitioned for its foundation asked to approve the appointment of the officers named in it. There follow prayers, Scripture readings and addresses. Then the lodge board is uncovered by the Consecrating Officer, who scatters it with corn, the symbol of plenty; pours wine, the symbol of joy and cheerfulness; pours oil, the symbol of peace and unanimity; and sprinkles salt, the symbol of fidelity and friendship. Finally, after the Consecrating Officer has dedicated the lodge, the Chaplain takes the censer three times round and offers the prayer of dedication.

A Freemason is encouraged to refer to the lodge in which he was initiated as his 'mother lodge' and to regard his proposer as his Masonic 'god father'. At one time in the United States a ritual for Masonic Baptism was prepared.[2] On behalf of the parents it is said that they 'place these children under the protection of the great Masonic Brotherhood . . . in the hope of ensuring for them that purity of soul and stainlessness of life which are symbolised by Masonic

[1] *Freemasons' Guide and Compendium.*
[2] For the Supreme Council 33 for the Southern Jurisdiction of the US 1871. British Museum Ref. 4782. h. 13.

Baptism'. The climax of the ceremony, open to boys until the age of twelve and girls till eighteen, is the point at which the lodge Master dips the child's hand or finger in perfumed water and oil, and anoints the child with a delta on the forehead. The gist of the formulae spoken is: 'I devote thee to the service of Virtue and Truth ... I set upon thy forehead the old symbol of the Wisdom, Power, and Love of God.'

Freemasons, although today they may not attend funerals in their regalia or in procession, sometimes drop into the open grave of a Masonic brother a sprig of acacia; a reminder of the ritual of the third degree, for when the Fellow Crafts discovered the grave of their Master, Hiram Abiff, they stuck a sprig of acacia at his head to distinguish it. Up until the present century it was quite common in England for lodges of Sorrow to be held and such a lodge was opened in 1901 by Canadian Freemasons in memory of Queen Victoria, Patroness of the Masonic Order.

The Greek Orthodox Church, condemning Freemasonry,[1] mentioned Masonic ceremonies of adoption, or baptism; of 'conjugal acknowledgement', or marriage; the masonic memorial service; and the lodge consecration service. These have largely fallen into disuse and only the consecration service and the placing on a Mason's grave of the sprig of acacia are now practised in this country.

Of course, the Greek Orthodox Church had strong theological arguments to reinforce its objection that not only does Freemasonry affect the outward appearances of a religious movement but seeks to usurp the role of religion. The Greek bishops considered Masonry a mystery religion both alien to the Christian faith and seeking to become a super-religion above all others. They found that the ceremonials suggested that only in the lodge were men shaped towards perfection, and that by Masonic initiation a Christian might become a brother of men of other religions, but only at the cost of having to regard fellow Christians

[1] *Eklesia*, No. 48, 4th December 1933.

who were not Masons as outsiders. Christianity, maintained the bishops, is a religion of Revelation, demanding of faith and proclaiming Divine Grace. Freemasonry, on the other hand, is a secret organisation which deifies rationalism and encourages men to look for redemption and moral perfection outside Christ.

The Roman Catholic and Greek Orthodox Churches are not alone in their condemnations of Freemasonry.[1] General Bramwell Booth of the Salvation Army wrote to his officers in 1925:

No language of mine could be too strong in condemning any Officer's affiliation with any Society which shuts Him outside its temples; and which in its religious ceremonies gives neither Him nor His Name any place ... the place where Jesus Christ is not allowed is no place for any Salvation Army Officer. As for the future, the Army's views upon this matter will be made known to all who wish to become Officers, and acceptances of these views will be necessary before candidates can be received for training; and, further, from this time it will be contrary to our regulations for any Officer to join such a Society.

Despite this firm line many Salvationists throughout the world have become Freemasons. The Army's rules have been interpreted not as a ban on full-time officers becoming Masons but simply as official discouragement. In any event no restriction applies to retired or part-time officers and in 1949 an unofficial Salvation Army Lodge[2] was constituted in London. Five years later it sponsored another[3] and a third lodge consisting of Salvationists[4] was consecrated in 1974, this time in the Province of East Lancashire.

The Reformed Presbyterian Church of Ireland will not allow members to be Masons and, in 1927, the same ruling

[1]For a closer look at the Catholic attitude, see pp. 338–342.
[2]Standard Lodge No. 6820.
[3]Constant Trust No. 7347.
[4]Jubilate No. 8561.

was made by the Free Presbyterian Church of Scotland. The English Methodist Church in 1927 passed a motion censuring the purely theistic nature of Freemasonry. A committee of the Orthodox Presbyterian Church of America condemned Masonry in 1942 and some Lutheran churches in America followed suit. The Dutch Reformed Church of South Africa (Cape Synod) also held a commission into Freemasonry in 1942 and came out strongly against the movement.

It should be emphasised, however, that many lay and ordained members of Christian churches are also Freemasons, and some clergy and laity maintain their loyalty to the lodge although their church has ruled against the Craft. This is because the theological issues cannot be reduced to a single completely convincing argument. One tempting over-simplification runs: the fundamental belief of Christianity is in an historical Christ, the Son of God, and as He has no place in Masonic rites, Freemasonry is anti-Christian or, at least, detrimental to the Christian faith.

The central theological conflicts around Freemasonry are those of deepest importance to Christians who are both orthodox and conservative. Christians who accept Christ as a personal Saviour, believe that Christianity is the only true religion and that through its Sacraments they are sanctified and saved to eternal life. They cannot but react with revulsion to the claims of Freemasonry, its pretensions of special brotherhood and, more importantly, its references to a Great Architect of the Universe and complete omission of the name of Jesus Christ.

Such Christians are unlikely to be convinced by Dr William Baxter, another Church of Scotland minister with whom I spoke, when he says: 'In the course of our ordinary ceremonies we are instructed to think about God ... the reason why Freemasons don't insist that they use the name of Jesus Christ in connection with God is that this society is meant to give us a fellowship with people of other faiths and many people have testified that that's been a great thing for them.' For many Christians, Freemasonry,

251

denying Christ, is so substandard a fellowship and so in error at the heart of its moral teaching as to be something which especially degrades a clergyman.

Others find the orthodox and conservative view an over-simplification and for them the first issue to surface is whether or not Freemasonry is a religion. Critical non-Masons point to these facts: lodges meet in places called 'temples'; Masons use hymns, prayers and Scripture readings, but exclude the name of Christ; there are lodge Chaplains willing to officiate and to exclude the name of Christ; the Bible or another Holy Book is open in the lodge and oaths are taken upon it; and Masonry has a theology expressed in its ritual, lectures, and the 'Old Charges' or directives of the movement. A formidable case, but not unanswerable.

Although unlike Masonry they are open to public appraisal, there are many movements correctly described as religious in that they try to make use of religious emotions and call upon God to provide an elevated sense of purpose. British Guides and Scouts, and the younger children in the Brownies and Cubs, promise at their enrolment 'to do their best to do their duty to God'. In 'open', as opposed to 'church', troops there is no mention of Christ in their promise and they are merely encouraged to be loyal members of their own religious community whatever that may be. Baden-Powell might have been speaking for Grand Lodge when he said:

There is no religious side to the movement, the whole of it is based on religion, that is, on the realisation and service of God.

Freemasonry, however, may be included among organisations like the Scouting Movement, Moral Rearmament and Alcoholics Anonymous, as invoking a God which is not the Triune God of the Christian religion but one left deliberately ill-defined enough to be embraced by men of differing creeds. The idea of a God other than a Triune God is also not theologically defenceless. Christians, while finding a Unitarian God a barren expression of their ideas and beliefs, will concede that the God of the Old Testament was not worshipped as a triune God, although the idea of the 'Spirit of God' is found in the Old Testament.

At one level Masonry has no theology at all: it is simply a series of morality plays in which the initiate is asked to take part. On the other hand, it is not just a movement using a religious atmosphere: it seeks to turn the willing candidate into a new man. The morality plays are acted out in the solemn atmosphere of a temple and to the accompaniment of prayers and Scripture readings and prefaced by vows. The religious overtones run like threads through the ceremonies.

The prayer said by the lodge Master after the entrance of the candidate for initiation ends with the words: 'Endue him [the candidate] with a competency of Thy Divine Wisdom, that, assisted by the secrets of our Masonic art, he may the better be enabled to unfold the beauties of true Godliness, to the honour and glory of Thy Holy Name.' The phrase 'by the secrets of our Masonic art' clearly implies esoteric knowledge. Within the context of the prayer, it also clearly means knowledge conferring illumination likely to assist religious understanding, something not promised by the formulae of open Scout troops, or those organisations calling upon God to sanction broad humanitarian purposes.

The first degree ceremony also puts forward a firm belief in an after life. The tracing-board lecture declares: 'The way by which we, as Masons, hope to arrive there is by the assistance of a ladder, in Scripture called Jacob's ladder. It is composed of many staves or rounds, which point out as many moral virtues, but three principal ones, which are Faith, Hope and Charity: Faith in the Great Architect of the Universe, Hope in salvation, and to be in Charity with all men. It reaches to the Heavens, and rests on the Volume of the Sacred Law, because by the doctrines contained in that Holy Book we are taught to believe in the dispensations of Divine Providence, which belief strengthens our faith and enables us to ascend the first step; this Faith naturally creates in us a Hope of becoming partakers of the blessed promises therein recorded, which Hope enables us to ascend the second step; but the third and last, being Charity, comprehends the whole and the Mason who is possessed of this virtue in its most ample sense may justly be deemed to have attained the summit of his profession; figuratively speaking an Ethereal Mansion, veiled from mortal eyes, by the starry firmament. . . .'

If these injunctions are seen as articles of faith in the religious sense and not as merely an elaboration of a theistic backcloth to a society devoted to the support of certain moral attitudes, the Christian objections are obvious. The central doctrine of salvation won by the death of Christ is cast aside; and the inspiration of the Bible is placed no higher than that of the Koran or the Vedic Books, or those portions of the Bible acceptable to an orthodox Jew. From the same standpoint Freemasonry is also vulnerable to the criticism that it rests upon the false teaching that man can perfect himself by his own efforts.

The lodge Master in his charge to the initiated candidate tells him: 'No institution can boast a more solid foundation than that on which Freemasonry rests, the practice of every moral and social virtue.' If Freemasonry is considered a religion, then Christians have a particularly appropriate Scriptural authority for its rejection:

The stone which was set at nought of you builders is become the head of the corner. Neither is there salvation in any other: for there is none other name under Heaven given among men, whereby we must be saved (Acts 4: 11–12).

Article XI of the Church of England declares:

We are accounted righteous before God, only for the merit of our Lord and Saviour Jesus Christ by Faith, and not for our own works or deservings. Wherefore, that we are justified by faith only is a most wholesome doctrine, and very full of comfort.

The article is based on the life of St Paul, who despite his elaborate attention to the law of the Jewish faith, could find no peace with God (Rom. 7: 7–8); that peace was to come only when he abandoned striving to earn or deserve his own salvation by 'works of the law' (Rom. 5: 1–11; 8: 1–17; Gal. 2: 16; Gal. 4: 28–51). The late Professor E. J. Bicknell has written:

This doctrine is, as the Article says, *a most wholesome doctrine and very full of comfort*. If our acceptance with God depended upon our having attained to a certain standard of holiness, we could never be quite sure that we had reached it: God would always seem to be standing over us as a critic and a judge. But the knowledge that God justifies us saves us both from hard thoughts of God and from morbid brooding over our own weakness and failures. It bids us look not at our very unsatisfactory selves, but at God and God's love and mercy as manifested in Christ. This attitude is the only sure foundation of a joyous and happy faith. Much of the gloominess of religious people is due to a neglect of 'justification by faith'.[1]

On the other hand, there is in Christian teaching no promise of salvation which does not lead on to good works. As Bicknell points out:

We have indeed an apparent contradiction between the teaching of St Paul and St James on this point. St James can write 'What doth it profit . . . if a man say he hath faith, but have not works? can that faith save him?' (2:14). 'Faith if it have not works is dead in itself' (5:17). 'By works a man is justified and not only by faith' (5:24). . . . They were dealing with different types of error from a practical point of view . . . both use 'to justify' in a forensic sense, but St James has in view the final judgment (2:14), St Paul the initial act by which the soul is placed in right relation to God. . . . St James wishes to rebuke a barren orthodoxy, divorced from life; St Paul is opposing a Jewish legalism, the spirit of the Pharisee who supposed that by the excellency of his works he could earn God's favour. . . . There is no real contradiction between them.

[1] *A Theological Introduction to the Thirty-Nine Articles*, Longmans, Green and Co (3rd edition, 1955).

The argument is enlarged, however, by Article XIII, which raises complications at the pivot of much of today's lack of certainty in the Church of England. The Article states:

Works done before the grace of Christ and the Inspiration of His Spirit, are not pleasant to God, forasmuch as they spring not of faith in Jesus Christ, neither do they make men meet to receive grace, or deserve grace of congruity: yea rather, for that they are not done as God hath willed and commanded them to be done, we doubt not but they have the nature of sin.

The problem here is particularly relevant to those raised by Freemasonry. The phase 'forasmuch as they spring not of faith in Jesus Christ', however, indicts the efforts of all good and conscientious non-Christians. It permits of no compromise and so has prompted many Christian doubts and reservations. The late Dr William Temple described the Article as 'unfortunately, even calamitously expressed'.[1]

Returning to the Masonic ceremonies and those aspects of them which Christians regard as implicit evidence that the Craft is a religion, the death and resurrection ceremony of the third degree must be considered. Christian critics have argued that this is presented as a religious rite, for the lodge Master says to the newly raised Master Mason, 'It is thus all Master Masons are raised from a figurative death to a reunion with the former companions of their toils ... let me now beg you to observe that the light of a Master Mason is darkness visible, serving only to express that gloom which rests on the prospect of futurity. It is that mysterious veil which the eye of human reason cannot penetrate unless assisted by that light which is from above. Yet, even by this glimmering ray, you may perceive that you stand on the very brink of the grave into which you have just figuratively descended, and which, when this transitory life shall have passed away, will again receive you into its cold bosom. Let the emblems of mortality which lie before

[1] *Nature, Men and God.*

256

you lead you to contemplate on your inevitable destiny, and guide your reflections to that most interesting of all human studies, the knowledge of yourself. Be careful to perform your allotted task while it is yet day; continue to listen to the voice of Nature, which bears witness, that even in this perishable frame resides a vital and immortal principle, which inspires a holy confidence that the Lord of Life will enable us to trample the King of Terror beneath our feet, and lift our eyes to that bright Morning Star, whose rising brings peace and salvation to the faithful and obedient of the human race.'

The theme of higher initiations is frequently that of symbolic death followed by resurrection in a new state and in this ceremony—although the candidate is told that he has been made to represent Hiram Abiff, the martyr of Masonry—there is nothing to suggest that in turn Hiram Abiff is a Christ figure. Father Hannah comments:

If, however, Hiram represents Christ, we are faced at once with the fact that this degree teaches a Gnostic heresy rather than Christian orthodoxy. The death of Hiram in itself, even though symbolising the death of Christ, avails nothing; it is not an objective propitiatory sacrifice wrought *for* the Candidate, but rather a type of experience which the Candidate himself, representing Hiram, must undergo by his own efforts in his quest for light. This is precisely how the Gnostics roundly condemned by the Church, regarded the crucifixion.[1]

It would seem that the criticism, at all events officially, has been taken care of, for Father Hannah himself admits later:

The present century, with its greater emphasis on the universality of Freemasonry, has seen the abandonment of this historically untenable claim that the Hiramic legend was originally intended as a Christian allegory. Few would maintain that this is *the* interpretation and key of the mystery, but merely that it is a valid and permissive one.

[1]*Christian by Degrees.*

The official moral allegory contained in the ceremony may simply be that death is to be preferred to dishonour; but the contention that it is all play-acting to bring home that message to the candidate is weakened by the words of the prayer said over the candidate by the lodge Master or Chaplain. This ends: 'Endue him with such fortitude that in the hour of trial he fail not, but that, passing safely under Thy protection through the valley of the shadow of death, he may finally rise from the tomb of transgression, to shine as the stars for ever and ever.' These phrases would certainly seem to support the charge of Gnosticism and, as Father Hannah says elsewhere,[1] the ritual 'clearly indicates that through Masonry one may ascend to the "Grand Lodge above"—by a short-cut which completely by-passes Calvary'.

The fact remains, however, that Freemasonry makes no official claim to be a religion and, indeed, Grand Lodges strenuously deny that it is anything more than a system of morality. It must be admitted also that Freemasonry does not behave like a religion: it is not evangelistic; it makes no attempt in Britain to include within its ranks women and children; discussion of religious matters at its meetings is expressly forbidden; and it demands of members initiation fees.

In these and other aspects Freemasonry is limited from the point of view of Christian revelation; but how many Christians today really believe the doctrine that outside the Church there is no salvation? To do so is to deny the hope of salvation to Buddhists, Jews, Muslims, Unitarians, and others sincerely devout who do not accept Atonement through a self-sacrificing Christ.

Father Hannah in *Darkness Visible* comments:

No one would be so narrow or so dogmatic as to assert that those who live and die without Christ are bereft of all hope of salvation, if they live according to the light that is in them in good faith, for that would be limiting the infinite mercies of God, who is not bound

[1] *Why shouldn't I be a Freemason?* Pamphlet, Augustine Press, 1955.

by His own laws though man is so bound. But if it is blasphemous to limit God's uncovenanted mercies, it is equally presumptuous of man to take them for granted.

For the Christian, the limitations of Freemasonry are obvious not only from its officially defined objectives, but from the pastiche nature of the ceremonies with their occasional evocations of the ancient heathen mystery religions and cults and the cumbersome and dowdy prose which betrays lack of inspiration. These aspects should in themselves be sufficient to convince a Christian that Freemasonry offers him no substitute for his faith.

It is too hasty a judgement, however, to maintain that because Freemasonry is sub-Christian, it is anti-Christian. Although historically on the Continent this has often been the case, in Britain and other countries Freemasonry might be regarded as supporting Christianity and other religions. Morality is a part of all religions, and Masonic lodges use as the 'Volume of Sacred Law' any book accepted as sacred by lodge members and call upon members to regulate their actions according to the precepts of their chosen sacred book. Similarly, in justice to Freemasonry, it should be emphasised that during the ritual of admission of a candidate the lodge Master assures him that 'in these vows there is nothing incompatible with your civil, moral, or religious duties'.

Many churchmen see in Freemasonry the dangerous concept of a non-Christian super-religion, sharing with the old mystery religions a vagueness of religious emotions and a shifting popular theology permitting an unquestioning tolerance of widely divergent beliefs. Dr Hubert Box says:

The basic error of Freemasonry is its naturalism ... it puts itself above the Mystical Body of Christ and aims at drawing all states and nations into a naturalistic supranational unity.[1]

[1]*The Nature of Freemasonry.*

259

Others do not find Masonry incompatible with their Christian faith and appear confident that Freemasonry reinforces and supplements the work of the Church by assisting the building of character and good citizenship. It may well be that in many cases Freemasonry is a successful competitor with the Church; but then so are other organisations which, like Freemasonry, make mention of high moral purposes but say nothing of forgiveness and redemption. The Mason who seeks from his organisation a religion is asking for something which it makes no claim to provide. If he insists that it is there he has not realised the real spiritual needs of his soul. The Christian who becomes a Freemason must, if he is to be true to his faith, recognise that Masonry is sub-Christian and offers no substitute for Christian belief, worship and service. He may also wonder to what extent participation in Masonry represents a rejection of some part of fundamental Christian dogma and a failure to make a complete response to the implicit demand of his Church for the total loyalty of its members.

Many of these issues, important as they are, have been overshadowed by the controversy which has gathered around the oaths which Freemasons are called upon to take during the initiation ceremonies, and the secrecy they are meant to protect. The commonly accepted Christian position on the taking of oaths is that they are contrary to the spirit of Christ and would rightly be abolished in a truly Christian society.

Nevertheless, although Quakers, for example, have refused to use oaths and affirm instead, Christians generally act as members of the State in this matter and conform to the State's rules, as indeed Christ was prepared to do, for He was willing to be put on oath by Caiaphas and recognised the authority of the State (Matthew 26: 63).

The oaths of a Freemason have as part of their purpose the protection of Masonic secrecy, though the third-degree obligation involves much more than this: 'I further solemnly engage myself to maintain and uphold the Five Points of Fellowship in act as well as in word; that my hand, given to a Master Mason, shall be a sure pledge of brotherhood; that

260

my feet shall travel through dangers and difficulties to unite with his in forming a column of mutual defence and support; that the posture of my daily supplications shall remind me of his wants and dispose my heart to succour his weakness and relieve his necessities, so far as may fairly be done without detriment to myself or connections; that my breast shall be the sacred repository of his secrets when entrusted to my care—murder, treason, felony, and all other offences contrary to the laws of God and the ordinances of the realm being at all times most especially excepted.

'And finally, that I will maintain a Master Mason's honour and carefully preserve it as my own; I will not injure him myself, or knowingly suffer it to be done by others if it in my power to prevent it; but on the contrary, will boldly repel the slanderer of his good name, and most strictly respect the chastity of those nearest and dearest to him, in the persons of his wife, his sister, and his child.'

This, it seems to me, invalidates Father Hannah's suggestion in *Darkness Visible* that the comparative triviality of the secrets guarded by the oaths means that amid the religious trappings with which they are administered they are profane. The point, of course, is only one of many in Father Hannah's carefully constructed case.

The report of the Church of Scotland's panel on doctrine into societies involving secret ceremonies was made to the Assembly in May 1965. It found that secrecy, although it might be 'practised, observed and even paraded in a provocative and un-Christian fashion' was sometimes necessary or permissible. It could also be desirable in a large part of married life and in certain spheres of business and law. Of secrecy and Freemasonry, 'the movement chiefly in view', the reports says:

The secrecy of what is called speculative Masonry seems to be a relic of the secrecy of operative Masonry in the craft guilds of the Middle Ages, and to survive as part of the symbolism characteristic of the movement.

It is true that the modern world has witnessed the use of secrecy and of secret oaths to cloak evil and sinister activities (Kenya, South

Africa, USA): but secrecy may likewise be used and has been used to counteract and defeat these activities. Secrecy in itself seems to be neutral; but it can be said in general that where there is secrecy and so an immunity from the criticism and judgment of others the obligation to self-criticism is all the more stringent.

It should be said that the Church of Scotland had the help of Masons when it carried out its investigation of 1964–5. The panel on doctrine included Freemasons and there was a degree of co-operation in the investigation from the Grand Lodge of Scotland. The panel restricted its attention to Freemasonry as practised in lodges under the jurisdiction of the Grand Lodge of Scotland. The decision meant that the inquiry was confined to the first three degrees of Masonry only; for in Scotland the Royal Arch is not regarded, as in England for example, as the completion of the degrees of Master Mason. The Grand Lodge of Scotland controls lodges which administer only the three Craft degrees and the Royal Arch organisation is entirely separate and independent of the Grand Lodge. Some conclusions of the Church of Scotland's inquiry were:

Of Freemasonry in this sense one principal feature is that members of the movement are required to take solemn vows on the Bible or, according to their religious beliefs, on some other Holy Book, and these give rise to a variety of issues. For one thing, it may not after all be a simple matter for a conscientious man to withdraw from the movement; and this is an aspect of the subject which ministers should bear in mind when dealing with those who seek their counsel. On the other hand it seems clear that any expectation the movement may have of its members is a 'moral' expectation unsupported by any sanctions or reprisals; and further it is understood that there is no vow to remain a lifelong and practising Mason and that the expectation in this respect is rather that so long as a man remains a member of the Craft he will obey summonses, and that if he ceases to belong to the Craft he will refrain from disclosing Masonic secrets.

There are two other features of Masonic vows which are often the occasion of concern and perplexity, their content and their penalties.

262

By these vows it is understood that Masons undertake to preserve the cloak of secrecy and to assume certain obligations to fellow Masons and their dependants. On the content of these vows several comments are possible. (I) It is not unreasonable for the Masonic movement to expect ex-Masons to honour a vow of secrecy since secrecy derives from the essential symbolism of the movement. (II) The formation of a brotherhood involves mutual obligations between members and there is nothing reprehensible in the fact that Masons make special provision for the orphans of Masons or for their own elderly and infirm. (III) The situation would of course be different if Freemasonry not only imposed obligations to Fellow-Masons, but also *denied* obligations to non-Masons. (IV) Plainly, the individual Mason may in practice emphasise the receiving rather than the giving of benefits, and may seek to advance his own interests in this way in competition with those of the non-Mason; but if an individual so behaves this is bad Masonry and its is the individual and not the movement that ought to be condemned. (V) Moreover it must always be emphasised that the Christian, whether a Mason or not, is under an obligation to love those with whom he has no natural bond, with whom his only tie is that Christ died for them too.

The penalties attached to the vows are fantastically blood-curdling and fearsome; and it has been argued that anyone making them seriously is guilty of rash swearing, while anyone making them not seriously is guilty of vain swearing. As against this argument it may be thought that its validity depends on the assumption that whether made seriously or not the penalties will be *literally* intended and are not symbolic, whereas there is such a thing as serious symbolism. On the other hand, it would seem that the particular symbolism in question is inappropriate and it is noteworthy that nowadays Masonic lodges are being encouraged to depart from the formulations which embody the traditional penalties.

The remaining difficulties largely stem from what may be called the religious overtones of Freemasonry due to the fact (I) that Masons must believe in God but not necessarily in Christ, (II) that vows are taken on the Bible or sacred book of another religion, (III) that much of the symbolism and ritual consists of a combination of Old Testament material and legend, (IV) that the Bible or other sacred book is open at the Lodge meeting and is regarded as the rule of life and conduct, (V) and that prayer is offered though not in the name of Christ.

Several points seem to be clear and beyond controversy. (a) If Freemasonry is a religion it must be condemned[1] as a religion of works which is at variance with the Christian Gospel. (b) Freemasonry itself, however, claims to be a system of morality which makes free use of allegory and symbol, and which, as a movement, deliberately stands back in neutrality so far as religion, revelation and redemption are concerned. (c) In practice, there are individual Masons who make a religion of their Masonry and there have been a few who in print have offered an interpretation of the movement as a religion or 'super-religion'; but in the light of the official view which Freemasonry has of itself such people must be regarded as in error, even if the ritual seems to lend itself to these misconceptions.

The Presbyterian Church of Victoria, Australia, investigated the theological implication of Freemasonry in 1957–8 and, like the Church of Scotland, was permissive so far as the first three degrees are concerned; but both churches' committees reflected certain reservations in their final recommendations, which are similar. The Presbyterian report reads:

Because of the danger, freely acknowledged by both sides in the debate between Church and Lodge, that members of the Church may come to regard Freemasonry as a legitimate competitor with the Church of Christ for their loyalty and service, the committee concludes its report by affirming strongly that:

(a) Christian Masons are urged to remember that the supreme revelation of God is in Jesus Christ, and that such titles as the Great Architect of the Universe do not make this clear. There can, therefore, be no idea of a super-religion above Christianity.

(b) Salvation is in and through Jesus Christ alone; not in some mystic understanding or by our own merits.

[1] I think 'condemned' is too strong a word. As a religion, Freemasonry can only be said to be in error or condemned if it teaches the doctrine of 'justification by works *alone*'—Luther's famous addition. Then it is at variance with the Christian Gospel. To my mind it is only inadequate and dangerous, for it might lead a member to believe that he can be justified by works alone.

264

(c) Freemasonry is sub-Christian, and must never be accepted by members of the church as a substitute for Christian belief, worship and service.

The report presented to the Assembly of the Church of Scotland expressed the same fears:

The Church has the right to remind those of its members who are Masons that their Masonic vows are not intended to be in any way at variance with their more solemn vows of membership in the Body of Christ, that in Jesus Christ alone is there salvation for men, that His Incarnation and Atonement are the source of a higher and more profound conception of the Godhead than is otherwise available, and that the standard of all Christian living is to be found nowhere else than in Him who thinking it not robbery to be equal with God ... made Himself of no reputation and took upon Him the form of a servant ... and became obedient unto death, even the death of the Cross, and whose followers are commanded to love their neighbour without restriction in respect of race, class, condition, creed or other bond.

A minority of members of the panel on doctrine wanted to go beyond this, and so the last paragraph of the report reads:

While the Panel as a whole agreed with the foregoing, some of its members would make this additional comment. In their view total obedience to Christ precludes joining any organisation, such as the Masonic movement, which seems to demand a whole-hearted allegiance to itself, and at the same time refuses to divulge all that is involved in that allegiance prior to joining. To these members of the Panel it appears that the initiate is required to commit himself to Masonry in the way that a Christian should only commit himself to Christ.

The assurances of Scottish Masonry and Christian ministers who are Masons failed to convince these members of the panel that there was no competition or conflict between their faith and Freemasonry. The debate was confined to consideration of the first three degrees and, although the majority of Freemasons progress no further, many other issues are presented by the rituals or Royal Arch and the additional degrees, some of which are open to Christian Masons alone.

The name given to the Supreme Being in the rituals of the Royal Arch was considered the most serious theological objection to Freemasonry by the Faith and Order Committee of the Methodist Church. A report to the Methodist Conference of 1985 said that the word Jahbulon, which appears within a triangle on top of the altar in the centre of every Royal Arch Chapter, is a composite derived from the names of gods in different religions.[1] As such, the word is an example of syncretism, an attempt to unite different religions in one, which Christians cannot accept.

The committee also noted that the exaltation rites for the Royal Arch degree include a dramatic enactment of the rediscovery of secrets claimed to be lost, and commented:

The references to these secrets carry clear implications of a secret knowledge whose posssession helps one to obtain immortal life, but there is no explicit reference to salvation and no claim that this is the only way to immortality. Christians believe that the knowledge of the sure way to salvation, which includes eternal life, should be freely available to all and must be offered to all.

The rites of Freemasonry raise further questions for Christians and the questions are made more difficult by the different interpretations of the rituals offered by Freemasons themselves. Freemasonry concerns itself with spiritual values and many Masons regard their progress in the society as a spiritual journey marked by the various rites.

In the rite of initiation for the first degree the candidate is blindfolded, and is required to ask for the restoration of light. The explicit reference is to material light, but the context of the ritual, and the accompanying charge to the candidate suggest strongly a spiritual passage from darkness to light as well. During the exaltation ceremony for the Royal Arch, the candidate is blindfolded and

---

[1] According to Stephen Knight, *The Brotherhood*: JAH is Jahweh, the God of the Hebrews; BUL is Baal, the ancient Canaanite fertility god; and ON is Osiris, the ancient Egyptian God of the underworld.

required to ask for light; this time there is no reference to material light and the candidate is congratulated on being admitted to the light of the order.

The rite of raising to the third degree includes the symbolic death of the candidate and a raising from this figurative death by ritual means. In Christianity the Symbolic rite of passing from death to life is the rite of baptism in the name of Father, Son and Spirit; and the passage from darkness to light is through faith in Jesus Christ. Freemasonry thus provides ceremonies which on some Masonic interpretations are equivalent to essential parts of Christian practice and offer alternatives to important elements of Christian faith.

The Methodists' committee also found the oaths included in the initiation rituals extravagant and full of blood-curdling penalties. They were the more objectionable as they were sworn with the candidate placing his right hand on the Bible. These objections were valid at the time because, although in 1964 United Grand Lodge of England had given lodges permission to vary the wording of the oaths to make them more acceptable, most lodges continued with the traditional forms. The year after the Methodist Conference of 1985, Grand Lodge directed that lodges should omit all references to the physical penalties from the oaths sworn by candidates in the three degrees and by a Master Elect at his installation; but references to the penalties were moved to other parts of the ceremonies.[1]

Masonic rituals include prayers offered to a Supreme Being which reflect the claim of Freemasonry to draw together men of different religions who respect one another's religious beliefs. Christians, said the report, must be concerned that the Supreme Being is not equated by all with God as Christians acknowledge Him, and prayer in Craft and Royal Arch Freemasonry is never offered in the name of Jesus Christ. There were documented cases of Masonic services in Christian churches in which Christian prayers had been alerted to remove the name of Christ.

[1]See Chapter XI, The Ordeal of a Master Mason.

The committee decided that there was a great danger that the Christian who became a Freemason would himself be compromising his Christian beliefs or his allegiance to Christ, perhaps without realising that he was doing so. The committee's 'guidance' to the Methodist people that Methodists should not become Freemasons was overwhelmingly approved.

In 1987 the Church of England's General Synod endorsed a report from a working group which stopped short of recommending that Anglicans should renounce Freemasonry. In spite of many theological objections the group as a whole concluded nothing more than that Christians who are Freemasons faced 'clear difficulties'. Members not Freemasons thought that the report pointed to 'a number of very fundamental reasons to question the compatibility of Freemasonry with Christianity'.

As with the Methodists, the most important theological difficulty arose from the ritual of the Royal Arch and the explanation of the word Jahbulon.[1] For many years there has been a conflict among Freemasons about the interpretation of this word. Some argue that it is a sacred and mysterious name for God; others that is is a word containing descriptions of God. A letter Grand Lodge sent to lodges in 1985 quoted an address given to members of the Supreme Grand Chapter of England of Royal Arch by Canon Richard Tydeman, Grand Superintendent 'in and over Suffolk', in which he gave his explanation of the word Jahbulon:

The first syllable indicates eternal existence, the continuing and never-ending I AM. The second syllable, as we are told later (unfortunately only as an alternative) really does mean in Hebrew, 'in heaven' or 'on high' and the third syllable is a Hebrew word for Strength or Power.
Thus we do not need to go into apologies for faulty scholarship in the past, and we can leave Syria and Egypt and Chaldea out

[1]See p. 283.

of it altogether; for what we are pronouncing are not three names of God (or worse still the names of three gods, as some would suggest) but we are pronouncing three aspects of qualities of the Diety which are well known and well used, in Christianity and in other religions, namely His Eternal Existence, His Transcendence, and His Omnipotence. In other words we are describing The True and Living God – Most High – Almighty. It is as simple as that.

The Church of England's working group rejected Canon Richard Tydeman's suggestion that the word Jahbulon describes only the qualities of God. If the word derived solely from the Hebrew, they pointed out, the question of whether it is a name for God, or a description of God, was unresolved because in 'Hebrew, description and name are interlocked, the description *is* the "name"'. The group went on to consider the Hebrew characters set at the angles of the triangle containing the word Jahbulon which are said in Royal Arch ritual to refer to the Deity or some divine attribute:

Take the Aleph and the Beth, they form AB, which is Father; take the Beth, the Aleph and the Lamed, they form BAL, which is Lord; take the Aleph and Lamed, they form AL, which means Word; take the Lamed, the Aleph, and the Beth, they form LAB, which signifies Heart or Spirit. Take each combination with the whole, and it will read thus: AB BAL, Father, Lord: AL BAL, Word, Lord; LAB BAL, Spirit, Lord.

The working group found that the juggling of the Hebrew characters emphasised the formation of BAL, the name of a Semitic deity bitterly opposed by Elijah and the later Hebrew prophets. Any association of this name with that of Jehovah would have deeply shocked them. The teaching about the characters also supported the view that the name on the triangle, far from being a means of describing God, was a syncretistic name for God made out of the names of Yahweh, Baal and Osiris. Discussions by the Supreme Grand Chapter of proposed changes to Royal Arch ritual, including revision of the explanation of the word Jahbulon

269

and the characters around it, were noted, but the report added:

JAHBULON (whether it is a name or description), which appears in all the rituals, must be considered blasphemous: in Christian theology the name of God (Yahweh/Jehovah) must not be taken in vain, nor can it be replaced by an amalgam of the names of pagan deities.

The working group saw these difficulties – the interpretation of Royal Arch ritual and the definition of the Masonic God placed at the centre of the ceremonial – as insignificant when the main Christian difficulty was faced. A Christian must already know the name of God and have no need of its revelation in a ritual drama of this kind. The group found offensive the pretence that the Holy Name was the property of Royal Arch, and a secret to be revealed only to Masons. However, despite these objections, the report gave no direct answer to the question: Freemasonry and Christianity; are they compatible?

This made it possible to continue the long-standing theological truce between Freemasonry and the Church of England. One factor which must have influenced the group was the belief that some merit resides in Freemasonry's claim to unite men from every religious denomination or creed who believe in a Supreme Being. The simple Deism in which Freemasonry is rooted seems more acceptable late in the twentieth century, when many Christians cannot believe that those who live and die without Christ are without all hope of salvation, and to the strains of the ecumenical movement to unite the Christian world have been added the stresses of inter-faith services for believers of different religions. The report made no attempt to deal with the issue raised by these inter-faith services and simply posed these two questions:

Only last year, the Bishop of Rome himself was in Assisi praying for peace alongside Buddhists, Sikhs, Jews and medicine men North American Indian tribes. When he listened attentively to

270

their prayers was he joining in them or unobtrusively dissociating himself from what was going on? Was the whole affair, in which the Archbishop of Canterbury was himself prominent, just an exhibition of Spiritual sleight-of-hand or ecclesiastical hypocrisy?

The Methodist and Church of England examinations of Freemasonry were followed in March 1989 by another report from the Church of Scotland's panel on doctrine. The working party, unlike the group responsible for the report to the Assembly in 1965, did not confine its inquiry to the first three degrees of Masonry. Meetings were held with senior Masons from the Supreme Grand Royal Arch Chapter of Scotland and the Supreme Council for Scotland of the Thirty-third Degree of the Ancient and Accepted Scottish Rite as well as with the Grand Lodge of Scotland of Ancient, Free and Accepted Masons.

In its discussions with Grand Lodge the working party was referred to avowedly Christian degrees of Masonry, and Craft Masonry was said to be like an open door which invited members to progress further into the Christian degrees. Council members of the Thirty-third Degree claimed that Scottish Rite is a system of Christian morality as distinct from the universal morality offered by the Grand Lodge. The working party examined the rituals of two of the degrees of the Scottish Rite[1], the eighteenth (or Rose Croix), and the thirtieth. Quoting a booklet entitled *The Eighteenth Degree – An Exegesis*, the report says:

In the course of the degree working, 'the Candidate is led by the three theological virtues (Faith, Hope and Charity) to the Calvary Chamber and his own symbolic death to the re-born, with the assistance of the Word, from death-in-sin to eternal life. Still veiled and carrying the embodiment of the three virtues, the Candidate now goes on a triumphal journey. In the gloriously lighted Chapter Room he has revealed to him that through these virtues he may come closer to God and the Word and the veil is stripped from his eyes'.

[1]See Chapter XV, The Side Degrees.

In this degree the candidate is promoted from speculative Masonry to become a Ne Plus Ultra Mason of Heredom, a Knight of the Eagle and Pelican and a Sovereign Prince Rose Croix. The ceremony concludes with a symbolic meal which, the booklet is at pains to point out, is an AGAPE and not a EUCHARIST.

The working party report on thirtieth degree ritual quotes a booklet, *The Thirtieth Degree – An Exegesis*, and records:

The candidate for the thirtieth degree 'is taught that only by overcoming the fear of death, in lending no credence whatever to superstition and by denying self-interest, can he attain to man's crowning achievement which is the dedication of his life to the Glory of Almighty God and the advancement of His Kingdom among men. This solemn vow of dedication is sealed by an offering of incense upon the altar'.

At the conclusion of the thirtieth degree working and having symbolically ascended and descended a ladder representing moral tenets and 'the material labours in the study and practice of the Arts and Sciences', the candidate is created a Grand Elect Knight Kadosh, 'obligated to eradicate from his own nature the vices of cruelty, fanaticism, superstition and greed'. He is exhorted to 'equip himself with the qualities demonstrated in the mysterious ladder so that he may be able 'boldly to withstand the evils of fanaticism and superstition, wheresoever guise they may found, knowing that the Lord of Truth Himself will be with him in that hour to guide him in all that is true'.

Quoting Ephesians 6: 12–18, the booklet concludes, 'Thus armed a Grand Elect Knight Kadosh need fear no enemy of the soul and he may hope, after life's conflict is over, to find a place at the footstool of the Throne on High.'

The working party concludes that the Scottish Rite does not contain a clear and unambiguous allegiance to orthodox Christian doctrine. They find that the central facts of the Gospel are 'theorised and emasculated' to fit the Masonic system and the so-called Christian degrees of Freemasonry are 'less than aptly named'.

Much of the report is written as a letter to Masons within the Church of Scotland and this advises them to consider

272

their involvement. Craft Masonry, as a system of morality claiming to be based on the Bible but shunning all mention of Christ, is bound to be for the Christian 'seriously deficient'. The letter describes suppression of the Christian gospel and a selective use of the Bible as 'unworthy' of Christians. Also 'unworthy' are the bypassing of Jesus Christ as a mediator and high priest, and seeking a foundation of the Brotherhood of man apart from Christ. The working party writes that it was told that limitation to belief in a Supreme Being permitted inter-faith contacts and goes on:

Now it might be right for a Christian in certain circumstances to be party to the use of some minimalist formula and attendant devotions, as a preliminary to a subsequent witness to Christ and to God's mighty act of salvation through Christ, salvation of all men and of their world and of their universe. In inter-faith dialogue it is important that the participants be open and frank about their different perspectives and beliefs and that these differences should not be ignored and suppressed. But this stage cannot be reached in Freemasonry because discussion of religion in your gatherings, we understand, is not permitted!

Then you seem to suggest that your 'brotherhood' and 'companionship' extended to those of other faiths are more promising things than Christianity, for the sake of which greater good, on the subject of Christ the Lord, the light of the world and the light of men, you will be silent. Certainly as the Church we have fragmented the brotherhood we have in Christ most lamentably and the quality of fellowship we display to those of other faiths is very poor, but we do not believe that there is any foundation for the brotherhood of man other than the one that is laid – Jesus Christ. Not to confess Christ before men is again unworthy of you as Christians.

CHAPTER XIV

Royal Arch

The qualifications of Craft Freemasonry open to Master Masons several avenues of Masonic progress through additional degrees.

The majority of Masons go no further than the third degree; but the step most commonly taken from the Craft lodge is into Royal Arch Masonry, where Master Masons are 'exalted' to join the 'Companions' who meet, not in lodges, but chapters. In England the degree is regarded as the completion of the Master Mason's degree, and more than one-third of the members of all English lodges throughout the world are Royal Arch Masons.[1] Within the pattern of Masonic orders Royal Arch is of special importance as the gateway to advancement.

Historically, Royal Arch workings are mentioned in documents of the 1730s, but the date of the creation of the degree is unknown. Some authorities consider it was fabricated in France: others that it was an elaboration of part of the rituals, possibly a lodge Master's degree, used during the early days of speculative Masonry. Royal Arch was established by the middle of the eighteenth century in England, Scotland and Ireland as a new separate working. The minutes of the Grand Lodge of the Antients (1752) suggest it had been worked for some time and the Antients, who made Royal Arch Masons in their Craft lodges, came to regard the ceremonial as a fourth degree. When, in 1756, the Antients' Grand Secretary, Laurence Dermott, published their constitutions[2] he

---

[1] *Masonic Record*, June 1964.
[2] Under the title *Ahinian Regon*.

referred in a typical phrase to Royal Arch as 'the root, heart, and marrow of Masonry', making it clear that for Antient Masons Royal Arch had become the summit of English Craft Masonry.

Ironically enough, the earlier English grand Lodge, which Dermott dubbed the 'Moderns', was officially opposed to Royal Arch, regarding it as an innovation. The Grand Secretary wrote in 1758 that 'our Society is neither Arch, Royal Arch, or Antient'. As late as 1792, Grand Lodge declared that it had 'nothing to do with the proceedings of the Society of Royal Arch Masons'. The policy was mistaken. Interest in the Royal Arch degree was widespread and shared by influential Masons both Modern and Antient.

The 9th Lord Blayney, Grand Master of the Moderns 1764–6, was exalted to Royal Arch and became automatically the Society's Grand Master. He, and a number of other distinguished Masons, including Thomas Dunckerley, a natural son of King George II, founded the first Grand Chapter of the Royal Arch of Jerusalem in the world. Yet, once again, the Moderns were to find that they had competition. About five years later, the Antients formed a Grand Chapter for Royal Arch.

To complicate matters even further, the new wave of interest in the degree revived the Grand Lodge of All England, founded in York in 1725. One of the rivals to both the Antients' and Moderns' Grand Lodges for jurisdiction of the Craft, from 1761 until its end in 1792, the York Grand Lodge sanctioned the conferment of the Royal Arch degree. Also, York has another important claim to an honoured place in Masonic history, for one of the earliest separate Royal Arch lodges was established there. The original members, according to Bernard E. Jones,[1] 'were all actors and members of the York Company of Comedians'. This lodge became in turn a Royal Arch Chapter and a Grand Chapter. The York Grand Lodge, with the agreement of the York Grand

[1]*Freemasons' Guide and Compendium.*

275

Chapter, in 1780 confirmed its authority over five degrees of Masonry—the Craft degrees, Royal Arch, and the order of Knights Templar.

Apart from the competition provided by the Antients and York, the Moderns' first Grand Chapter of Royal Arch also faced a difficulty of its own making. It had decided, in line with past tradition, that the Royal Arch degree was to be confined to Masters and Past Masters. This so restricted the number of eligible candidates, particularly in the provinces, that a degree was invented to qualify Masons as Past Masters. The device was simply to put candidates for Royal Arch into the lodge chair for a single occasion and the rigmarole was aptly called 'Passing the Chair'. Something similar is still worked in America, where admission to Royal Arch is open only to Masters and Past Masters.

When the two main contenders for authority over English Masonry, the Moderns and the Antients, formed the United Grand Lodge of England in 1813, they agreed that Royal Arch was the completion of the third Craft degree and in 1817 the two English Grand Chapters became one. Scotland and Ireland refused to unite in a British Grand Chapter. Scotland founded its own in 1817 and Ireland followed suit in 1861.

Today the Supreme Grand Chapter of English Royal Arch Masons is administered by United Grand Lodge. The First Grand Principal Supreme Grand Chapter, his deputy, the Grand Scribe, Grand Treasure and Grand Registrar, all hold corresponding positions in Grand Lodge. The headquarters of Grand Lodge, Freemasons' Hall, also accommodates the Supreme Grand Chapter and there are no separate Royal Arch charities. In recent years Royal Arch Masonry on the English pattern has spread to Finland, Holland, Switzerland and, during 1965, India.

The Royal Arch rituals vary a great deal. Also qualifications for entry into Royal Arch differ in Britain. All English Master Masons of four weeks' standing are eligible; but candidates for the principal offices must be lodge Masters. In Scotland, before a Master Mason can be accepted for

Royal Arch he needs to take two degrees in Mark Masonry, a system which takes its name from the time-honoured practice of masons' carving their marks on stone buildings. In Ireland the first Mark degree is a necessary qualification for a Master Mason, who must be of six months' standing. English Royal Arch Chapters are attached to Craft lodges; but in Scotland and Ireland the Chapters are separate. Scotland's Grand Lodge sanctions Mark Masonry as well as the three Craft degrees, and the first Mark degree may be taken in Craft lodges. The Supreme Grand Chapter of Royal Arch of Scotland is separate from Grand Lodge and controls eighteen degrees, among them the degrees of Mark Masonry. In Ireland the position is similar, but the dual control over the first Mark degree does not exist; the Supreme Grand Royal Arch Chapter there completely controls the first Mark degree. England has a Mark Grand Lodge independent of both Grand Lodge and the Supreme Grand Chapter of Royal Arch.

Apart from the confusing differences of qualifications and administration, there is another complication: British Royal Arch Masons have two different themes for their rituals, both springing from the story of King Solomon's temple. Before examining these legends it is useful to review some history.

Solomon in order to build his temple and palaces taxed the Jews almost beyond endurance and introduced forced labour. When he died the people's leaders pleaded with his son, Rehoboam, for relief from these crushing oppressions. Rehoboam replied: 'My father chastised you with whips, but I will chastise you with scorpions.' The rebellion that followed spilt the kingdom into two parts. The southern tribes, Judah and Benjamin, remained loyal to Rehoboam and became known as the kingdom of Judah with Jerusalem remaining the capital city. The ten northern tribes, led by Jeroboam, who had been one of Solomon's officers, set up the new kingdom of Israel with Samaria as its capital. Both small states were throughout their history ground between powerful neighbours: first Syria, then Assyria, and then Babylon, to the north; and Egypt to the south.

Israel was swept away by the Assyrians in 722 BC, but Judah survived until King Josiah was defeated and killed in battle with the Egyptians at Megiddo in 608 BC. Egypt's triumph was short-lived, for sweeping in from the north Nebuchadnezzar the Great became Judah's next conqueror and deported its people into captivity at Babylon. There they remained until 539 BC, when Cyrus, the King of Persia, took Babylon and set the Jews free to return to Jerusalem.

The two legends of Royal Arch are woven around episodes in the history of Solomon's temple during all this time. The first legend, chronologically, is that of the repairing of the temple during Josiah's reign and the discovery of the Book of Law. This legend forms the basis of the ceremonies of Royal Arch in Ireland. It is recounted in II Kings 22: 3–13, and II Chronicles 34:8–21, and the principal figures involved are the King, Josiah; the Priest, Hilikah; and the Scribe, Shaphan.

In England and Scotland, Royal Arch rituals derive from the account of the rebuilding of the temple in the time of Cyrus given in the Book of Ezra,[1] and the principal figures are Zerubbabel, Prince of the People; Haggai, the Prophet; and Joshua, the High Priest. The ceremonies also reach beyond the Bible to re-enact the discovery of a vault amid the ruins of the temple where has lain hidden a scroll and an altar. No mention of such a vault is made in the Bible, but the legend may originate from the *Apocrypha. The Second Book of Maccabees*, 2: 4–7, tells of the prophet Jeremiah hiding the tabernacle, the ark and the altar of incense in a hollow cave, presumably just before the sack of Jerusalem by Nebuchadnezzar.

The three most important officers of a Royal Arch Chapter take their titles from the Biblical Principals of whichever legend is favoured. So in England and Scotland they are: Most Excellent Zerubbabel, Excellent Haggai, and Excellent Joshua. There are ceremonies of installation

---

[1]American rituals also use this account, but with the names of the Principals taken from Ireland!

during which further secrets are imparted, but these do not comprise separate degrees.

In the Chapter these Principals have in front of them a single altar and not the individual pedestals seen in a Craft lodge. The altar is a double cube and upon it are inscribed the initials: *S.K.I.* (Solomon King of Israel), *H.K.T.* (Hiram King of Tyre), and *H.A.B.* (Hiram Abiff). As well as these letters is the triple tau. The tau, a Greek letter, is the 'T' of our alphabet and the triple tau of Arch Masonry is the 'T' placed over the letter 'H'. According to Thomas Dunckerley and others it is an abbreviation for *Templum Hierosolymae*, a Latin term for the Temple of Jerusalem. Less prosaic explanation is offered by the Masonic authors Pick and Knight:

After the Union when regalia tended to become standardised, the 'T' became joined with the 'H' and some enterprising manufacturer, eliminating the serifs, found he had the equivalent of three taus, or levels, and an entirely fanciful explanation was grafted on to the ritual.[1]

On top of the altar is a device familiar to every British motorist, a triangle within a circle. When the Chapter is open the word Jahbulon is spelt by letters within the triangle and the word Jehovah by letters within the circle. Also within the circle at the three points of the triangle are the Hebrew characters Aleph, Beth, and Lamed.

As well as the three Principals, each Royal Arch Chapter has these officers: three Sojourners; two Scribes, Ezra and Nehemiah; and a Janitor, or Tyler. The casting of Ezra and Nehemiah among the officers is an anachronism, for both arrived in Jerusalem many years after the temple had been rebuilt; and one may well ask who or what is a Sojourner?

The answer, according to Masonic legend, is that they were pious Jews, who after lingering in Babylon arrived at Jerusalem late; in fact, not until the foundations were being

---

[1] *The Pocket History of Freemasonry.*

dug for the second temple. Such new arrivals on the site were carefully examined, as the Royal Arch ceremony suggests. The Babylonian colonists, known as Samaritans and living in the former state of Israel, were fiercely opposed to the building of the temple. Also they were not without guile, and the Jews were determined to make sure that no idolatrous Samaritans polluted the holy work by helping with the building (Ezra: 4).

In this country the candidate for Royal Arch is joined by two of the Sojourners when the ritual requires them to ask the Chapter for permission to take part in the rebuilding of the temple. In America, the three Sojourners are represented by candidates, and only their chief is an officer of the Chapter, the Principal Sojourner. The American Royal Arch legend is the English one (but with the names of the Principals from Ireland) and yet another difference is that American Royal Arch Chapters have retained and elaborated an old English Royal Arch ceremony, 'Passing the Veils', as a preliminary to exaltation. Bernard E. Jones writes:

In England the candidate was required to pass three veils, each guarded by passwords, each passing being associated with certain Biblical instances and peculiar signs. . . . Numerous symbolic allusions occur in the ceremony, the veils having a general, and each one of them a particular, symbolism related to the colour of the veil—blue for universal friendship and benevolence, purple for union, scarlet for fervency and zeal, and white for purity.[1]

Authorities differ about the interpretation of the overall symbolism of the ceremony. Apart from the theory that it represents the trials and difficulties to be overcome in the search for truth, there is the suggestion that it represents the hazards facing Zerubbabel, Joshua and Haggai on the journey back to Jerusalem from Babylon, where they had gone to persuade Darius to renew the authority to build

[1]*Freemasons' Guide and Compendium.*

the temple granted by Cyrus. Another interpretation of the Passing of the Veils concerns a different journey, that of the repatriated Jews from Babylon to Jerusalem. The ceremony is widely practised in America, where it is part of the contemporary Royal Arch rituals, but preserved as something of a curiosity in Scotland, Ireland and Bristol.

In England the Chapter is opened by Zerubbabel with the Collect from the Communion Service in the Book of Common Prayer; but one phrase is omitted, the final words 'through Christ our Lord'. After this prayer, the three Principals, their hands supporting a Bible, say together: 'We three do meet and agree in love and unity the sacred word to keep and never to divulge the same unless when three such as we do meet and agree.' Then, each utters syllables of the words Jehovah and Jahbulon. The opening ceremony concludes with the unveiling of the Chapter altar and the three Principals take their seats. Each wears a robe over his regalia. Zerubbabel's is crimson, Haggai's purple, and Joshua's blue. They also carry sceptres, and following four evenly spaced knocks upon the floor with these, Zerubbabel says: 'Companions, in the name of the True and Living God Most High, I declare this Holy Royal Arch Chapter duly opened.'

The prospective Companion is accepted by ballot and the Principal Sojourner sent out of the Chapter to examine him. He also gives to the Candidate the password for entry into the Chapter: *Amm Ruhamah*, meaning 'My people have found mercy'. The Candidate is blindfold and led around the Chapter by the Principal Sojourner. Before taking the Royal Arch oath, he is told by Zerubbabel: 'As you seek to participate in the light of our mysteries, we must call upon you to advance towards the Sacred Shrine, in which they are deposited, by seven steps, halting and bowing at the third, fifth, and seventh, for at each step you will approach nearer to the Sacred and Mysterious Name of the True and Living God Most High.'

At the altar the Candidate hears that he has arrived 'at the crown of a vaulted chamber' into which he must descend.

He is given a crowbar with which to make a couple of levering movements, as if to remove two archstones, and then made to kneel. The Chapter Principal Joshua reads Proverbs 2: 1–9 and 3: 13–20. Told he now has to find something in the vault, the Candidate, with the help of the Principal Sojourner, picks up a scroll from the floor.

CANDIDATE. (*Prompted throughout by the Principal Sojourner*.) It is found.

ZERUBBABEL. What is found?

CANDIDATE. Something like a scroll of vellum or parchment.

ZERUBBABEL. What are its contents?

CANDIDATE. For want of light I am unable to discover.

(*The Principal Sojourner takes the scroll and either lodges it against the Candidate's chest or replaces it on the floor.*)

ZERUBBABEL. Let that want of light remind you that man by nature is the child of ignorance and error, and would ever have remained in a state of darkness, had it not pleased the Almighty to call him to light and immortality by the revelations of his Holy Will and Word. Rise, wrench forth the Keystone and prepare to receive the light of the Holy Word.

Once more the Candidate is given the crowbar and, after another levering movement, kneels again and the Principal Haggai reads Haggai 2: 1–9. Then the Candidate, with an open Bible between his hands, takes the oath of secrecy with its penalty of 'suffering loss of life' by having his head struck off. The Candidate's blindfold is removed and he reads from the scroll the first three verses of Genesis.

After this the Candidate leaves the Chapter to prepare for the second part of the ceremony, during which he and two of the Sojourners apply to the Chapter for permission to join in the work of rebuilding the temple. This granted, the Candidate and the Sojourners retire, only to return again and report the discovery of a vault containing a scroll and the altar of incense. As a reward, the Candidate is robed in the surplice of a Companion of the Royal Arch and invested with the degree's jewel, sash and apron. He is also handed

282

temporarily a staff bearing the ensign of the tribe of Judah and told that the secret words of the degree are Jehovah and Jahbulon and that these are to be given in syllables. There is no Royal Arch grip.

Each of the three Principals of the Chapter then delivers a lecture. Zerubbabel speaks last and offers this explanation of the device and letters upon the top of the Royal Arch altar.

'On this plated of gold are a circle and a triangle; these mathematical figures have ever been selected as referring to the Deity or some Divine attribute. The circle is an emblem of eternity, for as it has neither beginning nor end it may justly be deemed a type of God, without beginning of days or end of years, and it continually reminds us of that great hereafter, when we hope to enjoy endless life and everlasting bliss.

'The word on the circle is Jehovah, that great, awful, tremendous and incomprehensible Name of the Most High. . . . In times of antiquity, names of God and symbols of divinity were always enclosed in triangular figures . . . the word on the triangle is that Sacred and Mysterious Name you have just solemnly engaged yourself never to pronounce, unless in the presence and with the assistance of two or more Royal Arch Companions, or in the body of a lawfully constituted Royal Arch Chapter, whilst acting as First Principal. It is a compound word, and the combination forms the word Jahbulon. It is in four languages, Chaldee, Hebrew, Syriac and Egyptian. Jah is the Chaldee name of God, signifying His Essence and Majesty Incomprehensible. It is also a Hebrew word, signifying I am and shall be, thereby expressing the actual, future, and eternal existence of the Most High. Bul is a Syriac word denoting Lord or Powerful, it is in itself a compound word, being formed from the preposition Beth, in or on, and Ul, Heaven, or on High; therefore the meaning of the word is Lord in Heaven, or on High. On is an Egyptian word, signifying Father of All, thereby expressing the Omnipotence of the Father of All, as in that well-known prayer, Our Father, which art in Heaven. The various significations of the words

283

may be thus collected: I am and shall be; Lord in Heaven or on High:

> Father of All: In every age,
> In every clime adored
> By saint, by savage, and by sage,
> Jehovah, Jove, or Lord.

'The characters at the angles of the Triangle are of exceeding importance, though it is immaterial where the combination is commenced, as each has reference to the Deity or some Divine attribute. They are the Aleph, the Beth, and the Lamed of the Hebrew, corresponding with the A, B, and L of the English alphabet. Take the Aleph and the Beth, they form AB, which is Father; take the Beth, the Aleph and the Lamed, they form BAL, which is Lord; take the Aleph and the Lamed, they form AL, which means Word; take the Lamed, the Aleph, and the Beth, they form LAB, which signifies Heart o' Spirit. Take each combination with the whole, and it will read thus: AB BAL, Father, Lord: AL BAL, Word, Lord; LAB BAL, Spirit, Lord.'

Mark Masonry, which for many Masons is a prelude to acceptance by a Royal Arch Chapter, derives from two sources: the ancient practice of operative masons to carve marks on stone which served as signatures, and a legend concerning a missing keystone for King Solomon's temple. The importance attached to masons marks finds early reflection in the Schaw Statutes (1598 and 1599), named after William Schaw, master of work to the Crown of Scotland, which lay down conditions for the registration of masons marks. Early speculative 'gentlemen' Masons in Scotland also adopted marks, and the Laird of Auchinleck placed his upon the minutes of a meeting of the Lodge of Edinburgh in 1600.

Mark Masonry was prevalent in the eighteenth century, but the date when degrees first emerged to form the basis of today's rituals is unknown. There were two degrees and a link between these and Royal Arch Masonry by 1769. A minute of a Royal Arch Chapter at Portsmouth in that year reads:

The Pro[1] Grand Master Thomas Dunckerley bro't the Warrant of the Chapter, and having lately rec'd the 'Mark' he made the Bre'n 'Mark Masons' and 'Mark Masters,' and each chuse their 'Mark'.

There is plenty of evidence also of other lodges making Mark Masons during the remainder of the century and beyond; but Mark Masonry was rejected, at least officially, at the time of the union of Antients and Moderns in 1813.

Regarded as an unwanted child and without a central organisation, Mark Masonry drifted into a causal chaos during the early nineteenth century. There was a Travelling Mark Lodge of Ashton-under-Lyne which met on Sunday afternoons at various Craft lodges and made men Mark Masons. A Mark lodge was started in London with the authority of the Bon Accord Royal Arch Chapter of Aberdeen. The Supreme Grand Royal Arch Chapter of Scotland contended that the Bon Accord Chapter had acted illegally, but the defaulting Arch Masons stood firm and the Chapter was suspended with all its members in 1855.

The Bon Accord Mark Lodge in London continued the struggle for recognition. As a result the United Grand Lodge accepted in 1856 a resolution granting Craft lodges the authority to confer the two Mark degrees; but this was not confirmed at the next meeting and so the position remained as before. A few weeks later the Bon Accord Mark Lodge, with others, set up a Mark Grand Lodge and went into competition with the Supreme Grand Royal Arch Chapter of Scotland as a licensing body for Mark Masonry. Both prospered by constituting Mark Lodges in England and abroad, and the solution was left until 1878. The peace talks resulted in the formation of a single authority for Mark Masonry within the jurisdiction of the English Grand Lodge. The title of the new authority, known today as the Mark

[1]An abbreviation for Provincial.

Grand Lodge, was 'Grand Lodge of Mark Master Masons of England and Wales and the Dominions and Dependencies of the British Crown'. At last, Mark Masonry was officially acceptable.

In the English rituals the Master Mason is given his Mark during the first part of the ceremony. In the second part he comes back into the lodge with the two Deacons, the three men symbolising workmen returning from the quarries with stones for the Temple. The model of a keystone offered by the Candidate is rejected and he is ordered back to the quarries: he simply sits and waits in a corner of the lodge. All then hear that building work is delayed because a keystone 'for the Sacred Arch' is missing. It is the Candidate, of course, who produces the stone, the one previously rejected.

There are important differences in the Irish workings. The two main portions of the rituals are reversed and the stone produced by the candidate is not his own work but that of Hiram Abiff. In the English ritual there are rather cumbersome and unconvincing explanations of the fortuitous skill of the candidate in fashioning the required stone, suggesting that he may have had sight of the plans or remarkable foresight of what might be needed.

CHAPTER XV

The Side Degrees

Royal Arch and Mark Masonry are but two popular extensions of Masonic experience pursued by men who have taken the first three Craft degrees. Other systems of additional degrees and orders are also open to Master Masons and of such variety that they cater for almost every ambition of the Masonic status-seeker and his craving for dramatic make-believe. The bewildering proliferation of Masonry can also provide a means of satisfying the innocent sceptic. A man disappointed with the secrets received after earlier initiations may be persuaded that a worthwhile secret is roosting in the next degree above, and he can never complete the Masonic search. Even a totally dedicated lifetime of effort, suitably financed would be insufficient and, in the higher reaches of Masonry, advancement is frustrated by a lack of patronage, some degrees being conferred only on specially selected candidates and in strictly limited numbers.

The additional, or 'side degrees' as Masons prefer to call them, are divided into Christian and nonChristian, or those of merely occult fascination. It is impossible to reveal all the ceremonies carried out by 'advanced' Masons, because copies of rituals are restricted by the small numbers of men involved. Freemasonry's Craft rituals are shared by about four million men across the world and so are comparatively easy to discover and confirm, while the contemporary secrets of the more remote strata of Masonry are kept by only a few hundred Masons. But enough information is available to discuss some of the additional degrees and Masonic orders of chivalry.

Most of them were concocted by Continental Masons, although there have been attempts to attribute much of the responsibility to the Jacobite exiles who fled abroad from Ireland and Scotland. One refugee to France was Chevalier Andrew Michael Ramsay, who, while in Paris, was tutor to the two young princes of the exiled House of Stuart. In 1737 he was the Chancellor, or Orator, of the Grand Lodge of France, and in a speech reviewed a great deal of the historical and legendary material which has filled the ragbag of Free-masonry. On the evidence of this oration, and in spite of the fact that following it he disappeared from the Masonic scene, Ramsay is often singled out as the significant contributor to the present labyrinth of higher degrees. All that may be safely said is that his words may have fired the imaginations of some of his audience; from this time on extra degrees and chivalric orders become the fashion in Freemasonry and the new systems grow increasingly complex until one embraces ninety-five degrees.

It has also been suggested that Jacobite influence was strong upon the whole early development of speculative Masonry, the movement providing suitable secret meeting-places and the opportunity to develop, through the invention of further degrees, a source of income for an exclusively Jacobite society within the movement. The theory suffers from lack of historical proofs.

Certainly the group of degrees now known as Ancient and Accepted Rite were popular with the Jacobite exiles in Paris. A Chapter of twenty-five degrees was constituted at Clermont in 1754 by the Chevalier de Bonneville. Many of the members were Scotsmen and one of the degrees was known as Scottish Master, a fact which explains why today in many Latin countries and in America Freemasons speak of the Ancient and Accepted Scottish Rite.

The system became a powerful rival to Craft Masonry and in 1758 was adopted by the German Grand Lodge of the Three Globes. It also enjoyed a revival in Paris and in 1761 Stephen Morin was sent from there to take the new degrees to America. He made his headquarters at San Domingo in the West Indies and he succeeded brilliantly. In 1801 the first American Supreme Council of the Ancient and Accepted Scottish Rite was formed at Charleston, South Carolina, with authority over a thirty-three degrees system. The extra eight degrees had been imported from Europe and the Supreme Council claimed that its constitution had been ratified in 1786 by Frederick the Great, King of Prussia. A Supreme Council of the Northern District of America was set up twelve years later (1813).

Meanwhile, the Stephen Morin story was being played out in reverse. A landowner from San Domingo, de Grasse-Tilly, who had received thirty-three degrees in North America, went to Paris and, ignoring Grand Orient, set up a Grand Scots Lodge and a Supreme Council.

Today the Rite has a firm hold in most countries. It has been established in Britain for more than a hundred years: Ireland's Supreme Council was constituted in 1824; and the Supreme Councils of England and Scotland in 1846, all three under American authority. In England the degrees are open to candidates who are Christians and have been Master Masons for at least a year. The degrees are: Entered Apprentice; Fellow Craft; Master Mason; Secret Master; Perfect Master; Intimate Secretary; Provost and Judge; Intendant of the Buildings; Elect of Nine; Elect of Fifteen; Sublime Elect; Grand Master Architect; Royal Arch of Enoch; Scotch Knight of Perfection; Knight of the Sword or of the East; Prince of Jerusalem; Knight of the East and West; Knight of the Pelican and Eagle, the Sovereign Prince Rose Croix of Heredom; Grand Pontiff; Venerable Grand Master; Patriarch Noachite; Prince of Libanus; Chief of the Tabernacle; Prince of the Tabernacle; Knight of the Brazen Serpent; Prince of Mercy; Commander of the Temple; Knight of the Sun; Knight of St Andrew; Grand Elected Knight Kadosh, Knight of the Black and White Eagle; Grand inspector Inquisitor Commander; Sublime Prince of the Royal Secret; and Grand Inspector General.

The first three overlap the Craft degrees and are not worked and the fourth to seventeenth inclusive are conferred upon candidates during the eighteenth degree with the minimum of ceremonial. The eighteenth degree, worked in full, is known as the Rose Croix of Heredom[1] and is so much a focus of Masonic ambition that the whole Ancient and Accepted Rite is often referred to simply as Rose Croix. Without special dispensation, no member of the Rose Croix can progress further until he has become Most Wise Sovereign of his Chapter and has been a member of the eighteenth degree for at least three years. If he is then recommended by the Chapter for promotion, and this proposal approved, he receives the next eleven degrees without further ceremonial. The thirtieth degree, Knight Kadosh, is given with ritual in a Chapter of Grand Elected Knights, and the next three degrees conferred only after unanimous vote of approval by the Supreme Council.

In America many of the Ancient and Accepted Rite degrees not worked in this country are demonstrated before candidates in what are called Scottish Rite Cathedrals. These are equipped as theatres and from comfortable seats in an auditorium Master Masons by the hundreds watch performances of ceremonies with embellishments from a chorus and orchestra. These big-scale productions of the rituals frequently provide the material for a week or more of Masonic theatre.

The most commonly sought-after degree of the Ancient and Accepted Rite, the Rose Croix, has attracted the bitter condemnation of anti-Masonic Christians. Father Hannah in *Darkness Visible* concedes:

The Craft degrees, however objectionable, are based on comparatively harmless fables in an Old Testament context.

[1]Heredom: widely believed to derive from the Greek *hieros domos*, holy house.

But the Rose Croix, he adds, bases its working on the Crucifixion and is 'particularly obnoxious and worthy of ecclesiastical condemnation'.

Father Hannah outlines the ceremony of the degrees in *Darkness Visible* and gives the full ritual in *Christian by Degrees*. He says that his personal collection of authentic rituals printed privately for the Supreme Council contains editions of dates between 1876 and 1952, as well as a manuscript of earlier date.

If Father Hannah, and others, are to be believed, the stage directions alone depict a world of fantasy belonging to a theatre of the macabre. Conferment of the degree requires a 'Black Room', a 'Chamber of Death' and a 'Red Room'. In the east of the Black Room is an altar and above it a transparency showing three crosses. The central cross, higher than the other two, has on it the black Mystic Rose surrounded by a crown of thorns; the other two have a skull and crossbones at the foot. On the altar are a Bible, a pair of compasses and a sword.

The Black Room opens into the Chamber of Death containing among other emblems of mortality a figure in a winding-sheet laid out as a corpse. Torches burn within the skulls on the floor to supplement light from lamps burning spirits of wine. The Red Room, brilliantly lit and adorned with red roses, contains a white cubic stone in the centre and an altar on the south side upon which are the letters *INRI*, a Bible, an alms-dish and a taper.

Further justification for Father Hannah's revulsion would appear to come early, in the ceremony opening the Chapter.

MOST WISE SOVEREIGN. Excellent and Perfect First General, what is the hour?

FIRST GENERAL. The ninth hour of the day.

MOST WISE SOVEREIGN. Then it is the hour when the veil of the Temple was rent in twain and darkness overspread the earth, when the true light departed from us, the Altar was thrown down, the Blazing Star was eclipsed, the Cubic Stone poured forth Blood and Water, the Word was lost, and despair and tribulation sat heavily upon us. (*Solemn pause.*)

Since Masonry has experienced such dire calamities it is our duty, Princes, to endeavour by renewed labours to retrieve our loss. May the benign influence of Faith, Hope and Charity prosper our endeavours to recover the lost Word, for which purpose I declare this . . . Chapter of Princes Rose Croix of Heredom duly open in the Name of the Great Emmanuel.

Richard Carlile in his exposé of 1825[1] gives a similar form or words:

MASTER. Most excellent Brother Senior Warden, what hour is it?

SENIOR WARDEN. The hour of a perfect Mason.

MASTER. What is the hour of a perfect Mason?

SENIOR WARDEN. The instant when the veil of the Temple is rent, when darkness and consternation spread upon the face of the earth, the light is obscured, the tools of Masonry are broken, the blazing star disappears, the pointed cubic stone sweats blood and water, and the word is lost.

MASTER. Most excellent Brother, since Masonry undergoes so great a preparation, let us employ our diligence in fresh labours for the recovery of the word.

The degree ceremony ends with a ritual meal in the Red Room partaken from a table in the centre. This is Richard Carlile's description of the scene:

A sideboard is prepared. This is covered with a tablecloth, and on it are placed as many pieces of bread as there are Knights, and a goblet of wine. The paper with the sacred initials (*INRI*) upon it is deposited upon the altar. Every Knight has a white wand in his hand. The Most Wise strikes his upon the earth thrice,

[1] *Manual of Freemasonry.*

and declares that the Chapter is resumed. Then he leads seven times round the apartment, and is followed by all present, each stopping in front of the transparency to make the sign. At the last round each Knight partakes of the bread; and still preserving the form of a circle, the Most Wise takes the goblet, drinks out of it, and passes it round. When it comes to him again, he places it upon the altar, and the Knights give each other the grip. The paper, with the sacred word upon it is put into the empty goblet and burnt. The Knights make the sign, and the Most Wise says, *Consummatum Est.*

The similarities of the ceremony with that of the Eucharist are more strongly emphasised in Father Hannah's version. The circle of Princes of the Order around the table is addressed by the Most Wise Sovereign:

MOST WISE SOVEREIGN. Princes, we now invite you, according to oriental custom to break bread and eat salt with us; at the same time pledging to each other our fidelity and friendship in the goblet of fraternal affection; and let us invoke the blessing of Him who is the Rose of Sharon and the Lily of the Valley, by whose assistance we hope to progress here on earth towards that perfection which can be consummated only when, rising from the tomb, we ascend to join our great Emmanuel and are united with Him for ever in a glorious and happy Eternity.
(*The Director of Ceremonies presents the platter to the Sovereign, who takes a piece of wafer and presents it to the Prelate on his left, who breaks off a portion. Both dip their pieces into salt and eat them. The Prelate repeats these actions with his next neighbour, and so on round the Circle. Then the Director of Ceremonies hands the chalice to the Sovereign, who turns to the Prelate and faces him. The Sovereign says* Emmanuel, *and the Prelate gives the sign of the Good Shepherd, saying* Pax Vobiscum. *The Sovereign drinks and passes the chalice to the Prelate, who repeats the ceremony with the Brother on his left, and so on. The Prelate lights the spirit in the other cup with a taper kindled from the altar candles. When all have partaken,*)

293

MOST WISE SOVEREIGN. All is consumed.

PRELATE. *Gloria in excelsis Deo, et in terra Pax Hominibus bonae voluntatis.*

MOST WISE SOVEREIGN. Princes, we rejoice to have united in this Feast of Fraternal affection. May we henceforth treasure up the sacred doctrines of the Order in the secret repository of our hearts.

Excellent and Perfect Prelate, I now request you to remove the Sacred Word, that it be not exposed to the eyes of the profane, but be consumed according to ancient custom as a perpetual memorial of our veneration of Him who came to consummate the redemption of all those who faithfully and sincerely put their trust in Him, our risen Emmanuel.

(The Prelate removes the Word from the altar, passes to the west side of the table, faces east, and burns it in the cup of burning spirits. The fire is not extinguished but allowed to die down.)

PRELATE. *Consummatum est.*

The chapter is then closed with a very short ceremony, consisting almost entirely of these exchanges between the Most Wise Sovereign and the Prelate, which also come from Father Hannah's version of the Rose Croix rituals:

MOST WISE SOVEREIGN. Excellent and Perfect Prelate, what is the hour?

PRELATE. It is the first hour of the third day, being the first day of the week, the hour of a perfect Mason.

MOST WISE SOVEREIGN. What is the hour of a perfect Mason?

PRELATE. It is the hour when the Sacred word is found and the Cubic Stone is changed into the Mystic Rose. The Blazing Star has reappeared in all its splendour; our Altars are renewed; the True Light restored in our eyes, the clouds of darkness dispersed; and the New Commandment is given to love one another.

MOST WISE SOVEREIGN. Let us then observe this New Commandment to love one another, the result and perfection of all preceding Masonry, which will enable us to erect an edifice in our hearts to the Glory of the Lamb; to whom belongeth Might, Majesty, Dominion and Power, who liveth and reigneth world without end, Amen.

Royal Arch and Ancient and Accepted Rite are considered Christian degrees; so, too are the following Masonic orders practised in this country: Royal Order of Scotland, *Societas Rosicruciana in Anglia*, Order of Eri, Holy Royal Arch Knight Templar Priest, Knight Templar and Knight of Malta, Red Cross of Constantine, and Knight of the Holy Sepulchre.

The two degrees of the Royal Order of Scotland are the Heredom of Kilwinning and Knight of the Rosy Cross. Once again there is a ritual theme of a lost word and both degrees have been ascribed to Chevalier Andrew Ramsay. Tradition, and nothing more, associates the first degree with David I, King of Scotland (1124–53),[1] and the second with King Robert the Bruce (1306–1329),[1] who is said to have instituted it after the battle of Bannockburn.

Whatever residue of truth may linger in those inviting possibilities, the fact is that there are now Chapters of this once very exclusive order in several parts of the world. They are ruled from Scotland. As well as being Christian, candidates also have to be Master Masons of five years' standing. In London the Metropolitan Provincial Grand Lodge of the Order further stipulates that candidates must be members of the thirtieth degree of the Ancient and Accepted Rite. This would make the Order rather select there, but for the fact that London Masons without the thirtieth degree may apply to other Provincial Grand Lodges and need only go as far as Windsor to do so.

The *Societas Rosicruciana in Anglia* is a curious appendage of Masonry. It is not strictly a Masonic order, but its membership is confined to Freemasons, its origins are at one and the same time comparatively modern and older

[1]Dates of reign.

295

than Freemasonry itself. The Society was founded in 1886 by two Masons, Robert Wentworth Little and Kenneth R. H. Mackenzie. Little claimed to have found the rituals of the order in the vaults of Freemasons' Hall and Mackenzie to have met descendants of the old Rosicrucians in Germany, one of whom passed on ancient secrets to him. A candidate must be

A man of sufficient ability to be capable of understanding the revelations of philosophy, theosophy and science, possessing a mind free from prejudice and anxious for instruction; he must hold the fundamental principles of the Christian doctrine, be a true philanthropist and a loyal subject.[1]

There are nine grades of members: First Order: Zelator, Theoricus, Practicus, and Philosophus. Second Order: Adeptus Junior, Adeptus Major, and Adeptus Exemptus. Third Order: Magister and Magus. The Order of Eri, which offers three degrees, is open to fifth-grade members by invitation only. There are Colleges of the Society in England, Scotland, Australia, New Zealand and America.

Within the world of Masonry it is an honour to be invited to seek membership of the Knights Templar. Powerful romanticism surrounds the orders of Knighthood founded during the Crusades and the legends of Masonry have found golden embellishment among those able to accept the so-called traditional links between the two movements. The full title of the Masonic Knights Templar is indeed imposing: The United Religious and Military Orders of the Temple and of St John of Jerusalem, Palestine, Rhodes and Malta.

Several theories have been put forward in support of the Masonic take-over of the Knights Templar. One says that when the Order was suppressed members took refuge within the secrecy of Freemasonry, so making Masons heirs to their ceremonies and traditions. An elaboration of this is the suggestion that the Knights Templar were not suppressed

---

[1]Society's Ordinances.

at all in Scotland and, in recognition of their valour during the battle of Bannockburn, were admitted to the Royal Order of Scotland by Robert the Bruce, at Kilwinning. Further embroidery of the Scottish history of the Knights Templar brings in the Jacobite Movement with the election in 1745 of Prince Charles Edward, the Young Pretender, as Grand Master of the Order in Scotland; and there is always the possibility that the Masonic degree associated with the Order was worked by the Jacobite exiles in France.

Finally, there is the theory that the Master of the Knights Templar, Jacques de Molay, appointed a successor and the line of Grand Masters continued unbroken with clandestine appointments. The first successor is alleged to have been one Johannes Marcus Larmenius and there exists to this day a spurious charter—it is kept at Mark Masons' Hall—purporting to record the names of the Grand Masters.

A Dublin newspaper of 1774 yields the first firm evidence of a Knights Templar Masonic degree being worked in the British Isles. An advertisement informs readers that the Knights Templar amd other Masonic organisations are to hold a St John's celebration. In England it is Thomas Dunckerley, a pioneer of additional degrees, who provides the first evidence of the existence of the degree. In a letter to the Royal Arch Chapter of Friendship at Portsmouth (1778) he gives authority to members to make Knights Templar. The Grand Lodge of All England at York also embraced the Knight Templar degree and in the south-west Bristol Freemasons were working it by 1780 and had formed a 'Supreme Grand Royal Encampment'.

Today there are two degrees, Knight Templar and Knight of Malta. The first is conferred in a Preceptory and the Second in a Priory, and in those countries where the Order flourishes it is governed by a Grand Priory. In England membership is restricted to Christian Master Masons of one year's standing who must also be Royal Arch Masons and find unanimous approval in the ballot for membership. A candidate for Knight of Malta can only be accepted if the ballot is unanimous and, of course, he is already a Knight Templar.

Both Richard Carlile and Father Hannah have exposed the ritual of the Knight Templar degree and agree that its symbolism is not of a particularly intricate or edifying order. Carlile's comment:

The whole ceremony is purely Christian, according to the vulgar notions and the literal sense of Christianity.[1]

And Father Hannah's view:

Its ritual is an imaginary, naïve, and rather Boy-Scoutish reconstruction of ancient orders of Knighthood with plenty of clashings of swords, military drill, secret passwords, and the most magnificent and pretentious costume of any English Masonic order, but unlike the Rose Croix its legend does not concern our Lord himself.[2]

In fact, it places the candidate in the role of a pilgrim, who after various symbolic trials of fortitude is accepted into the Knighthood.

Both the rituals of Carlile and of Father Hannah, who uses the sixth reprint of a 1936 edition issued from Mark Masons' Hall, testify to the same grotesque features. The penalty of the oath of secrecy is that of 'my skull sawn asunder', and the candidate is given a skull during the ceremony. He is also given a taper; Carlile's explanation is that this is used 'to perambulate the encampment five times in solemn meditation'. Father Hannah's ritual says that the candidate proceeds round the Preceptory with the skull and the lighted taper which is not extinguished until the following ceremonial has been performed:

EMINENT PRECEPTOR. You will now repeat after me these inprecations: May the spirit which once inhabited

---

[1] *Manual of Freemasonry*, 1853 edition.
[2] *Christian by Degrees*.

298

this skull rise up and testify against me, if ever I wilfully violate my obligation of a Knight Templar. Seal it with your lips seven times on the skull.

(*The Candidate does so. The Marshal then replaces it on the Sepulchre.*)

May my light also be extinguished among men, as was that of Judas Iscariot for betraying his Lord and Master, and as I now extinguish this light.

(*The Candidate blows out the taper, which is replaced, unlighted, by the Marshal.*)

Even without promotion to the next degree of Knight of Malta or to the offices of Eminent Preceptor in Knights Templar Preceptory, a Knight Templar can, if he has also been a Master of a Craft lodge, advance to the Order of Holy Royal Arch Knight Templar Priest. This is an order of thirty-two degrees, but thirty-one of them are not worked, merely conferred titularly. The degree of Knight Templar Priest is performed with full ceremonial under a principal officer known as High Priest of the Tabernacle.

Little publicity attaches to Masonic Knights Templar in Britain, where sophisticated status seeking rarely demands extrovert display for satisfaction. In America, the Knight Templar wears an ornate uniform frequently seen in public. Parades of the Knights are common and sometimes they march in the form of a Passion Cross, six abreast for the upright and twenty-two abreast for the crosspiece.

For Christian Masons in England who are also Royal Arch companions there is yet another group of chivalric orders. These are the Red Cross of Constantine, and the orders of the Holy Sepulchre and St John the Evangelist. The first degree was worked towards the end of the eighteenth century, but the present orders owe a great deal to the enthusiasm of R. W. Little, the co-founder of the modern *Societas Rosicruciana in Anglia*. Knights of the Red Cross of Constantine meet in a Conclave, and knights of the other orders in a Commandery. A single Grand Council controls the orders.

No profession of the Christian faith is required of English Freemasons who wish to enter the following Masonic orders and systems: Order of the Secret Monitor; the Allied degrees; Royal and Select Masters also known as the Cryptic degrees, the 'Operatives'; and Royal Ark Mariners. The order of the Secret Monitor was at one time part of the Allied Degrees, but is now a separate and independent organisation administering three degrees based on the legend of the brotherly friendship of David and Jonathan. The three Secret Monitor degrees of Member, Prince and Supreme Ruler are open to all Master Masons. The Allied degrees in their present form are most probably of American origin and consist of the Order of St Lawrence the Martyr, the Knights of Constantinople, the Grand Tyler of King Solomon, the Red Cross of Babylon and the Grand High Priest. Mark Master Masons are eligible for the first three degrees, but to take the remaining two candidates must also be Royal Arch Masons. The system of degrees is governed from Mark Masons' Hall by a Grand Council of the Allied Masonic Degrees.

The Cryptic degrees are so called because their legend concerns a crypt or vault beneath King Solomon's temple containing secrets which contribute to those of the Royal Arch degree. They are also thought to preserve the working of the old ceremony of Passing the Veils, still part of Royal Arch ritual in some chapters, notably in Bristol. A legend attributing the degrees to Frederick the Great is dismissed by R. F. Gould as 'a fairy tale, pure and simple'. The four degrees, Most Excellent Master, Royal Master, Select Master, and Super Excellent Master, are open to Mark Masons and Royal Arch Masons.

The 'Operatives' is a brief description of the Worshipful Society of Free Masons, Rough Masons, Slaters, Paviors, Plasterers and Bricklayers. Primarily interested in the working of old operative masonic rituals, the Society has dubious claims to an ancient ritual of York masons. Men who are both Mark Master Masons and Royal Arch Masons are eligible for five of the seven degrees: Apprentice,

Fellow, Super-Fellow, Fitter, and Marker; Super-Fellow, Setter, and Erector; Intendant and Superintendent. The sixth degree, Certified Masters of Harodim, is open only to Installed Masters in both Craft and Mark Masonry; and the seventh degree, Grand Master, is conferred by the Three Grand Master Masons as an honour on selected candidates.

Finally, there is a Masonic degree with a nautical flavour, the Royal Ark Mariners. Lodges are open to Mark Master Masons and must be 'moored' to Mark Lodges. The degree was worked by Thomas Dunckerley at Portsmouth in 1780 and Dunckerley was Grand Commander of the Masonic Mariners in 1794. Today Ark Masonry aims to offer a sanctuary from 'the storms and tempests of life': the Mariners' Lodge is a place where ceremonies conducted by Worshipful Commander Noah commemorate the deliverance of Noah and his family from the Flood and God is styled the Supreme Commander of the Universe.

CHAPTER XVI

Masonic Charity

If money is used to measure charity, Masonry has plenty of it. The Masonic benevolent institutions deserve unstinted admiration and have encouraged the widespread belief that Masons are members of a mutual benefit club wealthy enough to mitigate the worst consequences of death, old age, ill health, or simply a run of bad luck. They also have the seal of royal patronage. All the Masonic benevolent institutions in England are allowed the prefix 'Royal' in their titles and the Queen is Grand Patron of three of them, the Girls' and Boys' Institutions and the charity for the aged. The Royal Masonic Hospital, open to Masons, their wives, widows and dependent children, has no patron; in 1989 its President was the Grand Master, the Duke of Kent.

The tradition of royal patronage for Masonic charities is a lengthy one. The Royal Masonic Institution for Girls, the oldest of the four foundations, had as its original patron the Duke of Cumberland, Grand Master of the 'Moderns' from 1782 to 1790. Queen Victoria agreed to become the Institution's Chief Patroness in 1882 and, no doubt, was influenced by the enthusiasm of the Prince of Wales, Grand Master of England's Masons from 1874 until his accession to the throne as Edward VII in 1901.

Probably no one person has contributed more to the establishment of Freemasonry in Britain as we know it today than Edward VII. He gave it a fashion among the influential and, during his long rule of the Craft, Masonry was able to attract the highly placed and the affluent from among the professions, the established Church, and the armed services. More than 1,300 new lodges were founded

302

during his reign as Grand Master and his prestigious assurance of the worthiness and respectability of the movement was reinforced by the active participation of his brother, the Duke of Connaught, who became Provincial Grand Master for Sussex and succeeded him as Grand Master.

From the time he became Grand Master, Edward VII was President of the Royal Masonic Benevolent Institution for the aged and became its Grand Patron in 1901. At the centenary festival of the Girls' Institution in 1888, over which he presided as Prince of Wales, more than £50,000 was collected and over £140,000 was raised at a similar function ten years later in aid of the Institution for Boys. A Royal Charter of Incorporation was given the Boys' Institution in 1926, and the continuance of royal patronage was marked with the opening by King George V, who was not a Mason, and Queen Mary of the Royal Masonic Hospital in 1933. A year later Queen Mary opened the girls' school at Rickmansworth.

Financial help for the needy Mason and dependants today is more readily available than care, and it can come from three sources, the Royal Masonic Benevolent Institution, the Grand Lodge Board of Benevolence and the charity chests of the lodges.

The Royal Masonic Benevolent Institution, not to be confused with the Grand Lodge Board of Benevolence, is financed by voluntary donations; the Board by income from the Craft. The Institution provides money for aged Freemasons, their widows, spinster daughters and spinster sisters. As well as offering accommodation, the Institution also gives annuities to people all over the world who have been recommended by lodges within the English jurisdiction.

The history of the Institution includes at least one recorded clash of personalities and a confrontation between one of the earliest protagonists of the charity and the Grand Master. There was opposition when, in the 1830s, the idea of a home was first put forward; but the suggestion found a staunch advocate in a Dr Robert Crucefix. It seemed that

the project for an 'Asylum for Worthy and Decayed Freemasons', as it was described then, had found official support
in 1835 with a governing committee including the Deputy
Grand Master and the Grand Treasurer as trustees; but the
Grand Master, the Duke of Sussex, had various reasons for
opposing the plan.

There were already other charities for the children of
Masons, and the Grand Master feared that not only would
support be diverted from these but that the proposed home
for the aged might attract into Masonry 'an improper class
of individuals'. He also wished to see an annuity fund
established rather than a home. Dr Crucefix was undeterred
and, although suspended for remarks made at a committee
meeting, got deeper into trouble by publishing some of the
proceedings of Grand Lodge in the *Freemasons' Quarterly
Review*, a journal which he had started to further the cause
of the new charity. As a result, in 1840, it was proposed to
expel him and only a humble apology averted the punishment. Two years later the Grand Master's annuity plan
came into operation and in 1849 was extended to provide
a widows' fund. That same year the foundation stone for the
first Masonic Asylum was laid on a site at Croydon, and the
two charities were amalgamated in 1850 to form the Royal
Masonic Benevolent Institution for Aged Freemasons and
their Widows. It was a victory for the early pioneers, but one
which Dr Crucefix did not live to see.

The Grand Lodge Board of Benevolence in one form or
another has been in existence ever since the formation of
the Grand Lodge of England in 1717 and was officially a
Committee of Charity by 1724. It derives its income from
capitation fees and dues received from those promoted to
ranks of honour.

The Royal Masonic Institution for Girls is the oldest of
the benevolent institutions and was founded in 1788 on a
site St Pancras Station, thanks in great measure to the efforts
of Chevalier Bartholomew Ruspini, an Italian dentist. At that
time there was accommodation for fifteen children between
the ages of five and ten. In 1795 a new school was built in

St George's Fields, and another new building opened in Wandsworth in 1851. A junior school was established at Weybridge in 1918 and was sold about twenty years ago. The senior school, built at Rickmansworth in 1934, has been opened for day girls, who need not be the daughters of Freemasons, in order to fill vacancies. The Institution continues to maintain girls at different schools throughout the world and to make grants to the daughters of Freemasons towards university education and for special courses.

The Royal Masonic Institution for Boys began in 1798 as the 'Institution for Clothing and Educating the Sons of Indigent Freemasons', established by William Burwood and other members of a lodge under the jurisdiction of the 'Antients' Grand Lodge. Like other Masonic charitable foundations, it was to become available to all English Freemasons. As the number of pupils grew the school was provided with new premises, the last being at Bushey Park, Herts. These were opened in 1903 and in 1929 a junior school was added. Rising costs forced the sale of the school in 1977 when it was bought for more than £2 million by an American university[1] and turned into a co-educational campus. The 450 boys at the school were moved to other schools and the Institution paid their fees in part or in full. The Institution continues to use other schools to educate the sons of Masons who have died or are from homes in difficult financial circumstances.

The Royal Masonic Hospital was first suggested in 1911 and approved by Grand Lodge in 1913. During the First World War there were at different times three Masonic nursing homes and they were open to wounded soldiers, whether Masons or not. The old Chelsea Women's Hospital served as a nursing home during the twenties and early thirties, but with a capacity of only fifty beds the waiting list was always long. The present Royal Masonic Hospital was officially opened in 1933, free of debt. The hospital is intended for patients of modest means and a Samaritan Fund

[1] The United States International University (Europe), San Diego, California.

helps cases of hardship. Over the years it has been extended and modernised and continues to enjoy a fine reputation despite financial problems. In 1984 these led the board of management to recommend that the hospital be sold to an American company. The offer, from American Medical International, of Los Angeles, which includes the Harley Street Clinic in its British holdings, was of £20,200,000. Under the offer, the hospital would have kept existing staff and sufficient funds would have been available to subsidise the treatment of poorer Masons. The board asked a meeting attended by 950 governors, Masons who have subscribed a minimum sum to the hospital, to approve the deal, but it was rejected.

The charitable foundations of English Masons have been reorganised during the past ten years following a committee of inquiry under the chairmanship of Mr Justice Bagnall. One of the concerns of the committee was the widespread belief that Masonic charity was too concentrated on the needs of Freemasons and their dependants, unlike organisations such as Rotary and Round Table whose charitable works are not so limited. Following the acceptance of the Bagnall Report in 1980, the Grand Charity was established with a Council and Petitions Committee to allocate grants and funds to non-Masonic organisations and institutions. Masonic charity is now administered by Grand Lodge through Grand Charity, the Masonic Trust for Boys and Girls, and the Foundation for the Aged and Sick. Freemasons also support local appeals from many different sources and, of course, it is impossible to measure how greatly the teachings of Freemasonry may enhance the generosity of individual Masons.

It may fairly be said, however, that in this country the main charitable effort of Freemasonry is narrowly directed towards the needs of members of the movement and their families, while in America, for example, the Masonic charities appear more broadly humanitarian. This may be due in part to the highly developed social and health services which Britain enjoys; it could also reflect the development in America of subsidiary Masonic organisations so that women and young people may support the movement, which is more conscious of the public impression it creates.

The charities supported by the Grand Lodge of the State of New York illustrate the situation. Masons there are called upon to support: the Masonic Medical Research Laboratory, the Masonic Home in Utica, the Masonic Youth Foundation, the National Masonic and New York Children's Drug and Alcohol Abuse Prevention Programs, Military and Veterans Hospitals, the Livingston Library and Museum, DeMolay Foundation, Washington National Shrine (Tappan), Washington National Shrine (Alexandria) and the Grand Master's Benevolent Fund.

The Order of Knights Templar maintains an Eye Foundation for those in need of eye treatment, regardless of race, colour, creed, age or nationality. The only condition of treatment imposed by the Foundation is that the applicant must be unable to afford to go elsewhere. Each Knight Templar in the United States pays a small annual fee to maintain the work, and the foundation gives grants towards research and is active in the establishment of cornea banks.

Among the allied organisations of America Freemasonry are: the Grotto and Tall Cedars of Lebanon, open to Master Masons; girls with a Mason in the family can join Job's Daughters or the Rainbow Girls; women, the Eastern Star; and boys the Order of DeMolay. The élite of the allied organisations in the sense that it is open only to thirty-two-degree Masons or Knights Templar is the Ancient Arabic Order of the Nobles of the Mystic Shrine, and a 'Shrine's' wife can be a Daughter of the Nile.

The largest of the women's organisations is the Eastern Star and most of its chapters in America and Canada accept men and women as members, while in New York any Mason who takes an oath of secrecy may visit an Eastern Star Chapter whether he is a member of the Order or not. The Order promotes charity and Masonic goodwill and is for women relatives of Master Masons, who may also advance to the Order of Amaranth or the Order of the White Shrine of Jerusalem. The Order of the Amaranth takes its name from an imaginary flower which never fades and its ritual is believed to be of Swedish origin, deriving from an Amaranther Order established in 1653 by Queen Christina. The White Shrine of Jerusalem devotes itself to social and religious activities and is claimed to be a wholly Christian degree.

The Order of Job's Daughters is for girls between the ages of twelve and twenty who are related to Master Masons, and it has a social purpose. The Order of the Rainbow for Girls invites the membership of girls from twelve to eighteen years of age who are related to Masons or Eastern Stars, or friends of these girls, and it aims to teach right living. The equivalent organisation for boys between the ages of fourteen and twenty-one years is the Order of DeMolay, designed to develop character, teach citizenship and love of parents.

The Grotto (full title: the Mystic Order of Veiled Prophets of the Enchanted Realm) and the Tall Cedars of Lebanon are both open to Master Masons and are primarily social organisations. The Grotto supports cerebral palsy clinics and 'Forests' of the Tall Cedars of Lebanon collect funds to fight muscular dystrophy.

The most publicised of American Masonic orders is the purely playground Order of the Shriners for thirty-two degree Masons or Knights Templar; but its serious charitable purpose is known throughout the United States, where few people can have failed to be made aware of the Crippled Children's Hospitals of the Shrine. These have won deserved admiration and praise for their work among unfortunate children, who are treated regardless of race, creed, or Masonic connection. The annual conventions of the Shrine are affairs of ballyhoo and publicity on a Hollywood scale that leaves English Masons sick with embarrassment.

The Order's ritual is said to be based on the Koran and its members are organised within 'Temples' each ruled by a 'Potentate'. The central authority is an Imperial Council and the chief officer is styled 'Imperial Potentate'. The membership of the Shrine has include three Presidents, Warren G. Harding, Franklin D. Roosevelt and Harry S. Truman.

Only a few of the organisations which are allied to American Freemasonry have been reviewed here, but sufficient, I believe, to establish the more widely based nature of the movement as a whole and of its charitable endeavours in particular. Comparison with British Freemasonry is interesting rather than invidious, for many aspects of Freemasonry in America strike the Britisher as brash, if not adolescent and naïve: but it is undeniable that behind the garish costumes and the drama of many American varieties of Masonic organisations is the same earnest devotion to charitable purposes.

CHAPTER XVII

South Africa Investigates

Any man empowered to be the sole judicial commissioner to inquire into secret organisations and their influence upon the life of a nation has a forlorn task; but such an appointment was made by the Government of South Africa in 1964. The man chosen was Judge of Appeal D. H. Botha, and his terms of reference were wide enough to sanction the most comprehensive investigation in the history of the country. He was instructed to decide, among other matters, whether secret societies were guilty of any form of treason, unlawful influence on the Government, acquisition of funds from hostile sources, nepotism or interference with public appointments, and subversion of the morals, customs and way of life of the people. His authority enabled him to summon, swear and interrogate witnesses; call for documents; visit offices, and take whatever further action seemed necessary to him in order to complete his inquiry satisfactorily. He was to report on the secret activities of any organisation he came across, or which was brought to his attention, but was specifically asked to investigate three organisations. These were: Freemasonry; the Afrikaner Broederbond, a movement devoted to the preservation of Afrikaner traditions and culture; and the Sons of England, a society occupying itself with the maintenance of the English language and English traditions in South Africa.

To a task of daunting responsibilities, Judge Botha brought formidable forensic equipment. He had joined the public service in 1927 and was promoted to Senior Law Adviser in 1953. Three years later he became a judge in the Orange Free State Provincial Division of the Supreme

Court of South Africa, and in 1958 Judge-President of the same Division. Since 1961 he had been Judge in the Appellate Division. When his appointment as Commissioner was announced in the South African Parliament by the Prime Minister, Dr Verwoerd declared that Judge Botha had never taken part in politics, did not belong and had never belonged to any secret organisation.

On the face of it there was a strong likelihood that Judge Botha's investigations might go on for years. Both the press and the radio were used to invite people who wished to give evidence to come forward. To protect witnesses from the glare of publicity, the Commissioner was instructed to sit in private and, further, that in making his inquiries and drafting his report he was not to violate the confidential nature of anything revealed, unless it formed part of findings disclosing guilt on the part of any organisation or person. In the event, the judge began work officially on 1st August 1964, and so few people offered any evidence that he was able to sign his report before Christmas. It is a document of nineteen pages, nearly half of which are given over to an examination of Freemasonry.

In fact, the judge investigated only the three organisations named in the terms of reference and Freemasonry is the largest of them. In South Africa at that time 20,000 members formed about 500 lodges within the jurisdictions of the Grand Lodges of England, Scotland, Ireland and South Africa.[1] Not surprisingly, much of the evidence reviewed reflects Masonic attitudes similar to those in Britain. Nevertheless, because of the co-operation given by Masonry in South Africa to Judge Botha, in the way of access to documents and examination of witnesses both formally and informally, I think it proper to reproduce the following extracts from his report. The paragraphs selected concern charges frequently levelled at British Freemasonry.

[1] The Grand Lodge of Southern Africa was established in 1961 to replace the nominal government of some of the lodges by the Grand Lodge of the Netherlands.

311

'One of the principal questions to which I endeavoured to find an answer was what happens at a meeting of Freemasons. Such meetings take place behind closed doors, however, and no non-Freemason is admitted to them. I had therefore in the first place to rely upon the evidence of Freemasons themselves. Four members of the order gave evidence before me. I also informally questioned other senior office bearers of the order. Because of the exceptionally high esteem in which each of these persons is held in society and also because of their obvious integrity, I entertain no doubts about the acceptability of their evidence. They gave me the assurance that, except for the rituals and symbolic ceremonies such as the ceremonial opening and closing of the lodges, as well as the ceremonial initiation of members of the order and the discussion of administrative, financial and other questions relating to the lodge and its charitable institutions, only lectures on some Masonic subjects are given. The principles of Freemasonry are constantly taught and illustrated in the lodges through the medium of its rituals and by means of symbols and allegory. At the end of every meeting a collection for charity is taken.

'It was asserted in evidence before the Commission that Freemasonry pledges its members to interfere in the administration of justice and to defeat the ends of justice where such action is necessary to assist a brother Freemason in distress. It is admittedly the duty of a Freemason to render assistance to a brother Freemason who is in need of help. Against that no objection can be raised. It was asserted further, however, that, where a Freemason is in distress as a result of his having committed a crime, his brother Freemason is obliged to assist him in such circumstances as well. If this is so, then no objection can be raised against that either, but now the further allegation was made that, where assistance can be given by interfering in the administration of justice or defeating the ends of justice, it is the duty of a Freemason to provide assistance in that form as well. The implications of this allegation are that the obligation resting upon a Freemason to assist a brother Freemason requiring

312

help also includes the obligation, where necessary, to do so in an irregular or improper manner or even to transgress the country's laws. I cannot read such an obligation into the Masonic duty of a Freemason under such circumstances.

'Transgression of the country's laws by a Freemason is also a Masonic offence which, in appropriate cases, can result in his expulsion from his lodge or even from the order. I am not prepared to accept that the order compels its members under any circumstances to commit an offence which can lead to their expulsion from their lodges or from the order itself.

'There were assertions of a general nature that members of the order in the Police Service, in compliance with their duties as Freemasons, sometimes fail to perform their police duties properly in order to protect and help a brother Freemason who has committed an alleged offence. If this were the case, such a member of the order in the Police Service would at least be guilty of a contravention of the Police Service Regulations, if not of defeating the ends of justice, which could prejudice his position not only as a police officer but also as a Freemason. In the absence of definite proof, I cannot accept the assertion that a member of the order in the Police Service is bound by such a Masonic obligation. If a Freemason in the Police Service were to protect and assist a fellow Freemason under such circumstances and in such a way, he would do so on his own initiative and not in pursuance of his Masonic duties.

'The obligation which a Freemason assumes in his oath upon admission to the third or master mason's degree (no such obligation being assumed in the other two Craft degrees) reads as follows:

That my hand given to a master mason shall be a sure pledge of brotherhood; that my feet shall traverse through dangers and difficulties to unite with his in forming a column of mutual defence and support; that the posture of my daily supplications shall always remind me of his wants and dispose my heart to succour his weakness and relieve his necessities. . . .

'This obligation is subject, however, to the ensuing words, namely "*as far as may fairly be done without injury to myself or my family*". In my opinion these words support the conclusion to which I have come above.

'Although it was asserted in general both in evidence and in memoranda that, in their police investigations, Freemasons in the Police Service protect and favour brother Freemasons who have clashed with the country's laws, no proof of such conduct was submitted to the Commission, and the Commission was also not able to find any such evidence. A few alleged cases to which reference was made, were investigated further by the Commission and found to be without any grounds whatever.

'It was alleged that, in the Police Service in particular, members of Freemasonry are favoured in so far as appointments and promotions are concerned. It was even asserted that the feeling exists among members of the Police Force that they cannot advance unless they become members of the order. The allegations were of a general nature and it was therefore difficult to investigate them. I am convinced, however, that Freemasonry does not in any way concern itself with appointments and promotions in the Police Service, the Public Service or the Defence Force.

'The Grand Lodge under the Scottish constitution pointed out in a document addressed to master Masons that any attempt on the part of Masonic bodies, *inter alia*, to secure the election or appointment of public servants would not only be contrary to the fundamental principles of Freemasonry but that it would also endanger its unity, strength, usefulness and welfare. Witnesses on behalf of the order emphatically rejected the allegation that Freemasonry concerns itself with appointments and promotions in the Public Service and drew my attention to pamphlets which are made available to candidates for membership of the order before they are admitted to it. In these pamphlets candidates are warned, *inter alia*, that:

It cannot be too strongly emphasised that Freemasonry is not to be entered upon in the hope of personal gain or advancement.

314

Admission to the order must not be sought for mercenary or other unworthy motives. Anyone so actuated will be bitterly disappointed, and in all friendship we warn you. . . .

Freemasonry offers no pecuniary advantages, nor does there exist any obligation, or implied understanding, for members of the fraternity to deal with one another or to support each other in any way in the ordinary business relations of life. . . .

'Not one of the witnesses who made general allegations against Freemasonry in this connection was able to mention a single example where any person's appointment or promotion in the Public Service, the Police Service or the Defence Force had been influenced by the fact that he was a member of the order. In view of the prescribed procedure and statutory provisions which have to be followed and observed in respect of appointments and promotions . . . it is clear to me that it is not reasonably possible for any organisation to exert any influence when such appointments and promotions are made.

'It was difficult to check the assertion that a feeling exists among members of the Police Force that they cannot advance unless they become members of the order. The Commission was unable to find any evidence of such a feeling. The chief of the police, whose assistance was invoked, could also not find any evidence of the existence of such a feeling. If it does indeed exist, statistics appear to show that it has little, if any, effect on the number of members of the Police Force who join Freemasonry. Out of a total membership of 5,533 in the case of lodges under the Transvaal District Grand Lodge under the English constitution, only 55 are members of the Police, i.e. less than one per cent. And out of a total membership of 4,971 in the case of the lodges under the Transvaal and Orange Free State District Grand Lodge under the Scottish constitution, only 47 are members of the Police, this figure also representing less than one per cent. More or less the same percentage is encountered in the other grand lodges. Apart from the consideration that the order recruits no members, these figures also adequately refute an allegation made in another connection, namely that

315

Freemasonry concentrates on the Police Force in particular. The police representation in Freemasonry is, according to the statistics, one of the lowest. With an average of more than 40 per cent, the representation of the business world, which includes the trades, is one of the highest.

'In the evidence against Freemasonry, it was asserted that it subverts the morals, customs, and ways of life of the people of South Africa on the grounds:

> (I) that it administers an oath to its members to preserve the secrets of the order even before they know what the secrets are which they are thus pledged to preserve;
> (II) that it maintains a dual morality because it administers to a member an oath in which such a member undertakes not to violate the chastity of the wife, daughter or sister of a brother Freemason;
> (III) that the oaths administered are disgusting, unethical and uncivilised; and
> (IV) that by means of its prescribed oaths and obligations Freemasonry pledges its members to discriminate against non-Freemasons and in favour of members of the order in an unethical manner.

'Before a candidate joins the order he is enlightened in great detail on what Freemasonry is and what it is not, but it is of course true that, at the time when he takes the oath to preserve the secrets of the order, he does not yet know what those secrets are. It would, however, be an unacceptable risk for the order first to disclose to the candidate the secrets which he must preserve, before the oath of secrecy is administered to him. The question was asked, however, why any oath of secrecy at all should be administered.

'It is extremely difficult for me to give any decisive answer to the question whether or not the administration of the oath of secrecy is unethical under the above-mentioned circumstances. The taking of an oath can in itself hardly be unethical unless it imposes an immoral obligation, this certainly not being the case in a Masonic oath. I find it difficult to understand how the fact that the secrets to be preserved are, at the time of the administration of the Masonic oath, not yet known to the person taking the oath, can make the taking of the oath unethical. If such a person subsequently discovers that the preservation of the secrets which have now been revealed to him, are incompatible with his civil, moral or religious duties, he cannot possibly consider himself bound by his oath, the reason being that he joined the order and took the oath on the very assurance that there is nothing in Freemasonry which is incompatible with the above-mentioned duties. It is also clear that nobody is obliged to take the oath unless he is desirous of becoming a member of the order. Under all these circumstances I do not consider it possible to say that the morals, customs and way of life of the people of South Africa, or any appreciable part of them, can be subverted by taking the Masonic oath of secrecy. No evidence of any such subversion was submitted to the Commission.

'It is common cause that a Freemason, upon his admission to the third degree or Master Mason's degree, gives this pledge:

I will not injure or revile a Master Mason myself, or knowingly suffer others to do so, if in my power to prevent it, but on the contrary, will boldly repel the slanderer of his good name, and *will ever most strictly respect the chastity of those nearest and dearest to him in the persons of his wife, his sister and his daughter.*

'The italic part of the pledge does not occur in the present ritual of the Grand Lodge of Southern Africa. Viewed in its context this italic part ... is obviously not intended as the maintenance of a dual morality but as a measure instituted in an attempt to prevent any wrong being done to a brother Freemason through the violation of the chastity of his wife, daughter or sister which could seriously prejudice the unity existing among brother Freemasons.

'As little as the pledge, in the same context, 'that I will not injure a Master Mason myself', allows a Freemason who has taken the oath to do an injustice to anyone else with impunity,

317

just as little does the explicit undertaking not to violate the chastity of the wife, daughter or sister of a brother Free-mason allow a Freemason to dishonour any other woman with impunity. In so far as such a woman is concerned, he continues to be subject to the moral laws which have always applied to him. The fact that violation of the chastity of certain particular women can, after a Freemason has given his pledge, possibly have more serious consequences for him than the dishonouring of some other women, cannot in my opinion subvert either his own morals or those of the people.

'The assertion that the oaths taken by the members of Freemasonry are disgusting, unethical and uncivilised has its origin in the nature of the penalty—death in a gruesome manner—which the person taking the oath calls down upon his own head if he violates his oath. That part of the oath on which the assertion is based had already disappeared from the ritual in use in the lodges under the Scottish constitu-tion and those under the Grand Lodge of Southern Africa. I was informed that it is also on the way out in the case of the rituals in use in the lodges under the English and Irish constitutions.

'It should be borne in mind that the Masonic oaths are centuries old and that they were introduced at a time when perjury was not so much an offence against society, as is the case today, as an offence against the gods, and when the punishment for it was supposed to be left to the gods. The penal provision in an oath was therefore essential in order to give it strength and gravity. Today it has only a symbolic significance. The Masonic oath itself imposes no moral obligations on the person who takes the oath.

'I was unable to find anything in the Masonic oath which pledges a Freemason to discriminate in an unethical way against non-Freemasons and in favour of members of the order. As I have already said, the solemn undertaking of a Freemason to aid a brother Freemason in distress does not bind him to advance a brother Freemason or to promote his interests above those of a non-Freemason in an improper

318

manner or at the expense of a non-Freemason. No evidence was submitted to show that Freemasons discriminate against non-Freemasons in an unethical manner or in favour of members of the order.'

The most common allegation against Freemasonry, and other secret societies, is that its members are guilty of nepotism and interference with public appointments. While Judge Botha was at work in South Africa, the *Irish News* and *Belfast Morning News* reported (13 November 1964) that in the Northern Ireland Parliament Mr Tom Gormley (Nat.) had asked that senior Civil Servants be forbidden to join a secret society. Some Civil Servants, he said, were members of a secret society and he could give instances of favouritism. He thought it should be realised that some of these people felt so secure in their positions that it could lead to inefficiency in a department. Too much promotion was being given to inefficient people. Another member, Mr Harry Diamond (Rep.-Lab.) told the House a Protestant official in the building had complained to him that every appointment from the level of porter to senior Civil Servant was carried out via the Masonic Order. Mr James O'Reilly (Nat.) said that there was wide dissatisfaction among Civil Servants because only those closely associated with the Masonic Order could get promotion.

The Minister of Home Affairs, Mr Brian McConnell, in his replies declared that the Civil Service upheld the British tradition of impartial administration and he rejected any implication to the contrary. Some people were very quick to find some excuse when they did not measure up to the promotion they wanted. Within the Civil Service promotion was on merit and nothing else and was normally carried out by a board which considered the merits and records of the candidates.

Similar accusations were implied in the House of Commons in April 1951 when Mr Fred Longden (Labour) asked a question suggesting that a Royal Commission be appointed to inquire into Freemasonry to discover what influence it might have in personal appointments and if it was guilty of interference in constitutional institutions. The proposal was rejected by Mr Herbert Morrison and there the matter rested.

It cannot be argued, of course, that Judge Botha's report exonerates Freemasonry in any other country even if it is considered that it does so in his own; but it does provide salutary warning of two difficulties placed in the way of any examination of Freemasonry. Firstly, that it is extremely difficult to persuade witnesses to come forward; and secondly that much of the evidence which is offered is unacceptable.

Introducing his report, Judge Botha says that at least four people refused evidence because the organisations were entitled to be represented at sittings and to interrogate them. In all only ten people volunteered to appear. Another twenty-two submitted memoranda and some of them were summoned before the judge. The number of witnesses appears the more inadequate when related to the three secret organisations concerned, and when it is revealed that so few members of the movements thought it necessary to come forward and defend them. Seven of the ten willing witnesses were against the movements, four opposed Freemasonry and three the Afrikaner Broederbond. No one gave any evidence against the Sons of England and among the memoranda were eight against the Bond and eight complaining of Free-masonry.

The prelude to the setting up of the Commission was a spate of newspaper publicity about secret organisations. The Afrikaner Broederbond movement, fashioned to further the interests of South African descendants of the early European settlers who now form more than half of the country's white population, was a particularly popular target. An Associated Press report[1] of a debate in the South African Parliament on the influence of secret societies said:

[1]Published *South Wales Echo*, 26th February 1964.

Opposition members got some amusement from the image of the stern Dr Verwoerd helping in some of the initiation ceremonies of his society—Dir Broederbond (The Brotherhood or Bond of Brothers). According to newspaper disclosures, the Prime Minister would have to dress in his best black suit and sit in a dark room beside a 'corpse' swathed in a black shroud, lying on a bier, and with the word 'betrayal' written on it in blood.

He might even have to switch on a light to show a dagger being plunged into the 'body' while the initiate would hear a chaplain intone: 'He who betrays the bond will be destroyed by the bond.' Cartoonists in anti-Government newspapers depict the Broeders as funny little men wearing Ku Klux Klan-type hoods and cloaks. Serious critics claim the Broederbond is a much more sinister and influential society that the Klan ever was.

Among these serious critics were, of course, members of the House of Assembly in South Africa, but the Opposition refused to associate itself with Judge Botha's inquiry because the Government would not agree to the Commission sitting in public. In addition, the leader of the Opposition, Sir de Villiers Graaff, considered the terms of reference to have been draw up badly[1] and to prevent investigation of Broederbond activities in municipalities and in the South African Broadcasting Corporation. As a result of these criticisms, Judge Botha found that when he came to inquire into the allegations made in speeches against the Afrikaner Broederbond by Members of Parliament they had resolved not to volunteer evidence.

Judge Botha says that he decided not to compel the MPs to give evidence and then goes on to make some devastating observations about the value of the evidence contained in them.

The charges made in the speeches in question were of a general nature and it appeared to me that the charges were not based on facts which the various speakers had at their disposal. . . . This impression was in fact confirmed by the principal critic of the Bond in the House of Assembly who, in correspondence which I

[1]*Daily Telegraph*, 10th June 1964.

321

conducted with him in regard to the matter, readily admitted that his allegations against the Bond were based mainly on copies of parts of documents published from time to time in a Sunday newspaper. It was therefore clear to me that he would not be able to give any acceptable evidence before the Commission. The documents in question furthermore constituted part of the records submitted to me by the Bond, and from them I was able to draw my own conclusions.

The judge found none of the three organisations guilty of any of the allegations contained in the terms of reference. The exculpations were inevitable in view of the few witnesses available and because of the nature of the evidence they gave. Both circumstances conspired to cause the Commissioner to rely extensively upon documents provided by the organisations themselves and the testimony of their senior officers. Clearly, the official character of any organisation may not be the one consistently adopted by every member of that society and, while this is in no way the fault of the movement, it can cause genuine concern and complaint. Judge Botha's findings are a reflection of the fact that however widespread that concern and complaint may have been in South Africa no evidence was forthcoming or could be discovered by the judge to provide any legal ground for censure.

It is extremely unlikely also that such grounds might be provided in Britain. In 1952 when considerable public interest was focused upon Freemasonry in this country by the widespread newspaper publicity given to Walton Hannah's book *Darkness Visible*, the *Sunday Pictorial* invited readers' letters on the subject. On 6 July it reported the results of the invitation:

Letters have cascaded from every corner of Britain, from Europe, India, Burma and Africa. Arguments on both sides have been presented by Masons and their wives, by non-Masons, by former Masons. They have come from all professions and every walk of life.

The most fiercely argued question was this: How influential are the Masons? Is it true they sometimes operate as a closed shop in affairs which have nothing to do with Freemasonry? On this the Masons speak with two voices. (1) The great majority of their letters deny that the Brotherhood has any influence at all outside the lodges. They dismiss with scorn allegations that Masons help each other in professional life, in promotion inside the Services, and in business deals. (2) A small number of Masons admit that favouritism is practised. For this they blame the black sheep who must inevitably be found inside any big movement. Only a few among Britain's Masons, they say, are guilty, and it is wrong that the Brotherhood as a whole should be attacked. They point out that the Masonic oaths specifically forbid Masons to seek such material advantages. Any Mason who does so is therefore disloyal.

From non-Masons there were many charges of favouritism amongst Masons. They allege that Masons 'pass business round', that non-Masons are 'squeezed out'; that small cliques of Masons in the professions, the Services and some trade unions protect and help each other. Most complaints came from the police, the Army, particularly regarding officers and warrant-officers, local government officers and commercial travellers. Many correspondents used similar words: 'If you're not "on the Square"—a Masonic phrase—you haven't got a chance.'

The *Sunday Pictorial* went on to point out, however, that many of the letters were anonymous and my own experience of such correspondence supports the probability that none of the 'evidence' offered would have stood the test of presentation in a court of law or of examination by a judicial commission. Indeed, it is naïve to expect evidence of this kind to be forthcoming in view of the nature of Freemasonry itself and the hostility, often irrational, that it arouses. There is also the emotional need of many men to find a scapegoat to blame for failures in the quality of the national life, or personal and business careers. The most popular of these whipping boys have been the Jews and the Freemasons.

CHAPTER XVIII

Masonry and Motive

Men become freemasons for a variety of reasons. The simplest is the wish to join a social organisation to which a number of one's friends belong. More complex is the case of the man who knows that some men with whom he has an ambition to associate are Freemasons. When either of these motives inclines a man towards Freemasonry, he may put up with its rituals and doctrines as the price for enjoying its social benefits and the protection the movement could extend to his family should he die. Such considerations are so mundane, so businesslike even, that they hardly call for any explanation.

Other, more subtle, reasons which often come into play in attracting men to Freemasonry spring from the aura of mystery around the movement and are reinforced by the character of its rituals. Some of these motives reflect an immaturity of personality which seeks satisfaction in membership of an exclusive group, an élite which possesses some kind of superiority or privilege. This is what draws some people to the smaller, more eccentric religious bodies, where they are assured that they belong to the Chosen Few who know the Truth and please God, while everyone outside their ranks dwells in darkness and is doomed. Certainly, the large number of men from all walks of life who are attracted to Freemasonry strengthens the impression that grown men often retain the schoolboy's fondness for the gang that not everyone can join and that they find in it this bolstering conviction of superiority.

There are also, it seems clear, many men incapable of making rewarding social contacts except within a group where they can share in the experiences of a dramatic ritual. Even the most humdrum bodies are prone to set forms for opening and closing their meetings, introducing new members, and so forth. Obviously, Freemasonry, with its elaborate rituals, its special props and bag of magic symbols, and its invented secrets, fills the bill infinitely better. The shared secrets, like the common ritualistic experience, bind Masons together. Those who are ostentatious about Masonic secrets emphasise the necessity of secrecy as a unifying force within the movement. These Masons also reveal the compensation they find in membership for their inability to build satisfactory relationships with their fellows under normal conditions. The secret society had been with us ever since the earliest communities and is a support for the individual until the stage is reached in adult life when the conspiratorial element can be rejected along with the childish attitudes of gang membership.

Not the least important of these attitudes is the demand for reinforcement of the vital sense of individual worth, which is satisfied on a different plane by religion. In a non-religious and purely social context, the bare fact of election to Freemasonry may be important to a man. As far as his ego is concerned, the value of it is enhanced by the fact that if he has sought admission and gained it he has passed some test; if he has been invited to join, he appears to be offered a flattering reward. Professional men who become members in either circumstance may feel that they are better within their profession in some peculiar way than the rest of their colleagues, because they know of those who have been refused admission or have never been asked to join. The illusion may be most comforting and it may be gratifyingly reinforced when the new Mason takes part in subsequent ballots for admission.

Most comforting possibly is the Masonic ritual which it is the main purpose of the lodges to perform. Freemasons will argue, of course, that this cannot be valued by the outsider, and in terms of a subjective judgement this is true. All rituals offer those who take part in them private

325

and secret experiences. One of the purposes of ritual is to provide a framework within which the individual may seek these; and symbolism, to be widely effective, must be capable of broad interpretation. The Eucharist, for example, offers to Christians who believe in the doctrine of transubstantiation an experience which cannot be shared by those who do not. The ambitions of Masonic rituals are not of the same high order as religious ceremonies; but they have important characteristics in common.

Probably the most important of these common ingredients are the catechetical element and certain sensuous aspects; the flow of words, the shared situation of congregation, music, and sometimes incense. Many people are attracted to religious ceremonies for these experiences and men will find them in Masonry along with special advantages. Apart from the exclusiveness of Freemasonry there are other appeals within lodge rituals: uniformity of dress; the prospect of promotion to authority and an important part 'on stage' in the ceremonial; and the opportunity for every man to be his own priest.

The fact that Masonic ritual owes more to invention than evolution broadens the possible interpretations of its symbolism. Within the symbols of Freemasonry there is no relevance to theological definitions and historical sources comparable to that which resides in Christian counterparts. This can add to the comfort of Masonic ritual. Its formulae, although less meaningful than the religious, still provide a support, a feeling of solidity and consolation, particularly if experienced frequently enough. This is to say, of course, that the Masonic ritual is a conditioning; and this is a general truth of any ritual. It does not deny that some Masonic ritual is relevant to the aspirations of good men. Lodge ceremonies are more powerful, however, in conditioning attitudes of the individual because of the dramatic experiences of initiation. Through his ritualistic trials the Mason is the more likely to develop a warm feeling that he is not only different from his fellow men who are outside the brotherhood but better.

326

To be effective, conditioning of this kind demands the inducement of awe and mystification within the candidate. Masonry achieves this by the manner of its initiations and the fact that, as with entrance into any secret society, the candidate should have no opportunity to discover the ceremonies and to go over them beforehand. Unlike most religious ceremonies, these initiation rituals are highly physical in their symbolism. Blindfold, the candidate is literally 'in a state of darkness'; his breast, a leg and a forearm are bared; there is the noose about his neck; and, having left everything of metal outside the lodge, sometimes even his braces, his temporary state of poverty is as real as his appearance is abject. Lodge members watching the ceremonies must feel powerful emotions as they recall their own initiations and yet are free now to enjoy the rituals with the relish of a sense of superiority. The new boy has to go through it, has no knowledge of what is happening, and will emerge imbued with a respect for the elders and betters who have graduated.

The Masonic initiation ceremony is full of suggestions of rebirth, and has much in common with the atmosphere of the evangelical conversion situation. There is the entry in humility into a highly charged emotional atmosphere, the repeated questions and answers, and the specially emphasised phrases of a liturgical language. All this forms part of the reception of a candidate whose degradation has been physically stressed and who has been kept waiting in a room outside the lodge for the ceremony to begin. His suggestibility has almost certainly been heightened so that he will be more ready for a change in his beliefs and an acceptance of the ritual as something of great importance. It would be surprising if the candidate did not feel at the end of it all that he had been given something upon which he could depend, a feeling reinforced by the idea that it was a socially acceptable thing upon which to rely. What the ritual achieves is the close identification of the newcomer with the group.

Identification with any group at depth is, of course, a form of protection and provides some stability for the psyche. It is a reinforcement of the value the individual places upon himself. Religions often provide this stability of group feeling, but, in addition, many of them—including Christianity—seek through their rituals to promote identification with a theologically defined God. Furthermore, in Christian churches these aims are sought within ceremonial sufficiently restrained to allow the ritual to be examined by all those taking part as it occurs. The participant in Christian ritual is not meant to be in a state of shock, as is the initiate into Freemasonry. Christian ceremonies are open to inspection beforehand and so there is shelter in foreknowledge against the brain-washing effect of confrontations with frightening unknowns. Again, at Christian ceremonies, it seldom happens that a lay member is the sole focus of the ritual for any length of time as the candidate is during Masonic rituals; and, if the practice of confession is considered to offer similar focus and himiliation, it is a private humiliation. Christian ceremonies also introduce prayers of intercession and with them general considerations outside the intimate concern of the group, and so release some of the emotion built up within the members.

It can be as inhibiting to be a Mason as to be a religious person, for in both circumstances men should feel their conduct under the special scrutinies of God and fellows of a chosen group. Yet Masons, unlike those who give their allegiance to a religion, cannot really know why they join Mansonry. They are not given an opportunity critically to decide this. They can only seek assurance that it confirms and supports the broad ideals they favour and that it will benefit them. When they consent to undergo the initiation ceremonial, Masonic candidates cannot have the same awareness as religious converts or novices have that they are walking into a highly charged situation nor that this will require of them either instant submission or great strength of character if rejection is to be on the spot.

For the man who decides to join Freemasonry, the rituals of initiation may have such an impact upon him that his original motives for membership are obscured. The Mason repelled or disillusioned by the ceremonial must realise with chagrin that he has been persuaded by his friends to join an organisation with good purposes and ideals which he could have accepted happily without the additional ties derived from shared experiences of humiliating initiations.

The Mason who is disappointed and critical may find a defence for the rituals in the charitable activities of Freemansonry: these serve to answer both external and internal critics. Within the organisation the achievements of Masons' good works assuage apprehensions of a sense of inadequacy; provide a ready-made and favourable answer to the questions: Why am I doing this? Should I feel guilty about belonging to a secret society and having made myself look absurd by undergoing its rituals? The reply 'for charitable works', however, begs the larger question that a great many organisations, such as drapers and licensed victuallers, maintain similar charitable foundations without resort to ritual or secrecy. But again, upon some Masons the effect of the ceremonies may be such as to make the word 'charity' a more highly charged emotional cue for repeated action. Maybe this explains why some relatives of Masons complain that they find themselves poor by comparison with the wealth they might have enjoyed if their menfolk had not been obsessively devoted to Masonry.

Many other Masons probably have no doubts at all and accept the rituals without question or reservation, even continue to look for the promised 'secret'. Maybe for them the secret is the achievement of a new start in life, something clearly suggested by the symbolic poverty with which they have to approach their first initiation. A lot of people yearn for the promise of a clean start, a stripping off of the trappings of the past in preparation for a new journey towards spiritual understanding or perhaps, more mundanely, material success. Masonry in its ceremonies puts each member back to square one. This encourages the feeling of rebirth within the newcomer into the society, so that the answers to life approved by Freemasonry can be planted more easily and the candidate started on the road to what the proper, selected Mason ought to be.

It could be that the men most likely to become Freemasons from idealistic motives are the more intelligent, sensitive people from close family backgrounds. Such families have special codes and secrets and a great deal of communication between the members is on a private, secret level. Certainly an appetite for secrecy is formed within families; but there is an important difference between the secrecy of close family relationships and that of Freemasonry. Within the family, or between man and wife, the secret sharing is based upon the revelation to one another and, possibly, the discussion together of deeply rooted attitudes. Freemasons, barred from exchanging views about politics and religion, do not talk about similar problems, even superficially, at their meetings. Masonic secrecy is not of the kind to encourage people to share personal secrets, which is one of the ways of developing personality. Indeed, the cultivation of approved Masonic etiquette helps to obscure their individuality.

Masonic secrecy may also interfere with the full development of marriage. The danger was probably non-existent until comparatively recently, for at any rate up to 1914 the middle-class father was expected to belong to a private masculine world beyond the family circle and was free to move in and out of it without question. Today, apart from the great advances towards the emancipation of women, there is a new family pattern of living in which the father has an enlarged and more important role. Masonry can not only prove disruptive of marriage because of the resentment many women feel nowadays towards a husband who marks off an important part of his life as a secret territory; but also because of the wider impact of this on the family for today the essential family unit of parents and children is so often isolated from grandparents and the wider circle of relations. Frequently, too, the substitute tribe formed by the old-fashioned street community has disappeared. As a result,

330

anything which takes father away and puts him in a specially important position to which he does not seem entitled cannot be helpful.

There may be no damage, however, particularly if the wife of a Mason merely regards his membership as a logical step in his career. Also, if the husband finds no deep esoteric experience in the ritual this may lessen disruptive influence on the marriage. He may regard the third-degree initiation ceremony, for example, as figurative assurance that Masonry can pull him out of any difficulty. Membership may give him the comfort of sought-after status. In this way the man who joins Masonry might become an easier character to live with as his feeling of acceptance by those whose approval he prizes becomes reinforced during a series of meetings and perhaps by progress to official positions in the lodge.

Among the problems that puzzle an outsider who is trying to understand what men find in Freemasonry is a basic one posed by the rituals. It concerns any decision to change one's whole outlook, make a new start, be born again, for any such decision to be effective has to be taken by the person himself; yet, as we have seen, would-be Masons may approach the movement with only a vague idea that it strives to be an experience of this kind. Unlike a convert who has been listening to the expositions of an evangelist, the candidate for Masonry often has no inkling of what precisely this important change may be.

The symbolism of the ceremonies of the first three degrees is concerned with life and death. There are daggers and a halter, a mock lowering into the grave and raising from it. Within the rituals the candidate is put through dramatic reconstructions of many of the essential experiences of life. One is still left wondering what it is that Masons need from these ceremonies, and why it is that so many men who do not join Freemasonry are able to fulfil all their needs in other forms of clubs or in marriage, or by joining a church, or by pursuing their career.

The status conferred by a special group's approval would seem to be a large part of the answer. This is emphasised

331

by the number of clergymen who are members, for they are frequently great self-doubters and the career itself often carries little money or power. Also, when a clergyman goes to an area today he has to appeal to his parishioners very much by his own personality. He can no longer rely on traditional attitudes towards the collar and the cloth. It may seem to clergymen that it is particularly helpful to join the organisation offering contact with men who could be most influential.

The sense of isolation which may be a very powerful one for a clergyman also suggests that it is loneliness which accounts for some of the support Freemasonry gets from academics.[1] A great deal of loneliness among a wide variety of men is countered by Freemasonry. Men of different walks of life know that they are going to meet together in circumstances with which they are all familiar and there is no question of anyone being a wallflower. Members all take part and are all accepted.

The rituals are also heavily loaded with the details of the special Masonic communication system, something of great value in the outside world as the means to identify fellow Masons. The phrases of the ritual are one aspect of this and, slipped into ordinary conversation, have the significance of code. So frequently is Masonic language used in this way that many of its words have become part of the ordinary language. Phrases from Masonry in common currency include expressions such as 'on the level', 'third degree' and 'black ball'. A great deal of the content of the rituals is therefore a social training in the special recognition systems of words and grips and signs.

It is a reward for the sacrifice of dignity inherent in the initiation ceremonies and for time and money after acceptance. Here is a communication system that, unlike a public school tie, will operate through a great variety of social strata. The Freemason, at his lodge meetings watching or participating in the ceremonies, is learning to communicate not just

[1]As evidenced by the existence of University lodges.

with words, but with signs and grips which are a worldwide deaf and dumb language. Equipped with this knowledge he can be recognised and received by fellow Freemasons anywhere as a specially favoured stranger. He is enabled to make demands upon the membership of an international club and to find someone who will befriend him and who often is also a person most likely to be in a position where he can help.

This is vastly more valuable a reward than membership of the present-day city guilds and trade companies can offer. From the craft organisations which had secrets they desperately sought to preserve, these livery companies have come down as a perquisite for top managements in the new industries founded upon the old skills. The most a contemporary city company member can expect is an annual banquet, and the Freedom of the City. The latter is a status gift to be greatly prized no doubt; but in terms of practical privilege offers little in London, for example, except some protection from police arrest within the boundaries of Westminster. What the Masons have succeeded in doing is to change the character of the operative mason's craft organisation into something of much greater value. Freemasonry today is a movement which has had the imagination to leave the craft behind. It has substituted for it an international club of much broader purposes which merely retains a collection of symbols drawn from the ancient craft.

There it would seem the imagination has run out, or been diverted to the foundation of higher degrees, for the prospect of further development is remote. Maybe in order to retain the intrinsic conditioning nature of the ceremonies and the middle way of the organisation in this country, change is virtually impossible. Development is confined to the individuals who join.

This implies that, consciously or not, men join Freemasonry in the hope of personal advancement, and this, of course, is true not only of Masonry, but of any group or club. But that Freemasons seek special advantages from their form of club is clear from many standpoints. The secret nature of the organisation, for example, is quite different from the

333

secrecy necessary to protect real secrets of state or business, and indicates that Masons want from the movement something that other people do not have and cannot qualify for except through selection by other Masons.

Among candidates there must be a strong predisposition to join this kind of society. Many men are not attracted to ritualistic and secretive groups for their own sake. It is significant that Judge Botha's investigations into the membership of lodges in South Africa established that more than forty per cent of the members were drawn from men in the business world. This is clear evidence that Freemasonry appeals to the man who is looking for a super-Rotary, an organisation offering more useful and, therefore, more influential support.

If this is the case, then the ritual, for all it achieves in welding the group more closely together, is an instrument of deceit. So much so that it could condition Masons to accept a dual morality, one for their relationships with fellow Masons, the other for men who are not. Even the pretensions of a single Masonic brotherhood are shattered by the exploitation of the same motivations in the additional degrees which provide élites within the Craft elect. It is difficult also to believe that the vast majority of intelligent people who go through the processes of Masonic initiation are really impressed by it or go on being impressed by it. One would have thought for most men the conditioning effects achieved would wear off.

Maybe at first men are irritated by the ceremonies, but the thing that is uppermost in their minds is that they have been accepted by a powerful group with important advantages to offer that far outweigh the temporary inconvenience of the ridiculous and debasing situations in which the candidate is placed. No one presumably chooses to become a Mason for the sake of enjoying ceremonies about which he knows nothing—about which, indeed, he may have heard intimidating rumours. What candidates hope for must be the sympathy and mutual support that Masonry is understood to afford, and the prospect of getting on friendly terms with people who are in positions to offer patronage of one kind of another. A motive of this kind is needed to explain the fact that many Masons come from intelligent and privileged groups unlikely to want or need a comradeship overlaid with the superficial trappings of a religion.

CHAPTER XIX

Conclusions

The main concern of people who are not Masons is the secret power and influence that the Freemasonry network may exercise against social justice and legitimate government. Some people find it impossible to believe that Freemasonry in many countries has as its sole purpose nothing more than the preservation and propagation of Masonic principles. Incredible though it may seem to some, there is not a shred of reliable evidence to suggest that British Freemasons, and those in other countries recognised by Grand Lodge, do anything more at their lodges than go through the ceremonies, discuss the charitable and Masonic business associated with the lodge and, if there are no candidates for initiation, listen to a lecture on a Masonic subject. Freemasonry, by the very kind of man it attracts in Britain, is an instrument for the defence of the existing order. Most British Masons are middle-aged, respected and respectable.

Fears about Freemasonry, however exaggerated they may appear, are justified by the secrecy with which the movement surrounds itself. As its leaders are of the Establishment, British Freemasonry may influence the conduct of national affairs, but pressure groups, overt or hidden, will always be close to those with power. If Masonry's leaders in this country form such a group, it certainly competes with other groups, and the identification of men of power within Freemasonry is not by itself evidence of Masonic manipulation. Freemasonry in Britain is continually emphasising its nonpolitical character and it is only a remote possibility that its membership across the country could secretly be marshalled for some political purpose.

The political innocence of British Freemasonry has long been accepted and agreed to be in sharp contrast with the activities of some forms of Masonry abroad, particularly on the Continent. So it is not surprising perhaps that Clerks of the Peace have been relieved of the obligation, dating back to the Unlawful Societies Act of 1799, to keep yearly returns of the names, addresses and occupations of local lodge members.

The House of Comments was told in December 1985 that nowadays the justices' clerks keep no such records. This can only be deplored, for the provision seemed to offer some safeguard against Masonic conspiracy to interfere with legitimate government, if only because of the slight prospect that Freemasons involved could be identified as such. Lodge membership lists compiled by justices' clerks should be reintroduced and under a Freedom of Information Act the media should have access to them.

The lists might also provide policemen with some helpful insight into the membership of any lodges that they might consider joining. As neither priests nor policemen are excluded from Freemasonry at the moment, it can be argued that the movement is overlooked by both the Church and the police. Unfortunately, the membership of both clergy and police has done nothing to dissuade the general public from the belief that Freemasonry is little more than a large Old Boys' network used by Masons to advance their own and fellow Masons' self-interests. On this ground alone policemen and clergymen should not become Masons, but there are other reasons, special to each group, which support such a ban.

In the case of the police it is a reputation which has been considerably tarnished during recent years, not least by the exposure of corruption among a few Masonic police officers. Of course, compared with the thousands of policemen who are Freemasons, these men are a very small minority and would probably have committed their crimes had they not been Freemasons. Their membership of the movement does not mean that Freemasonry itself is corrupt and public fears of it justified; but those fears, justified or not, have been reinforced. On appointment all policemen undertake to carry out their duties 'without fear or favour, malice or ill will', but many people believe that some Masonic policemen may not always be impartial towards other Freemasons because of the oaths they have sworn in the lodge.

Understandably, this conclusion causes deep offence among thousands of honourable policemen. They feel insulted by the implication that they will not stand by their oath of allegiance on appointment and find nothing in their Masonic oaths which conflicts with it. The resentment overlooks the secrecy which surrounds Freemasonry and the signs and codewords by which Mason recognise each other. These are responsible for the widespread suspicion that Freemasonry may be used to assist criminal conspiracy. Policemen are already obliged to be circumspect about the company they keep, and are not able to strike, nor take part in party politics, nor to join a trade union. A ban on being a Mason would be a further grievous intrusion into their rights as citizens; and the founding of the Lodge of St James for former and present officers of the Metropolitan Police was notice that many policemen have no intention of giving up Freemasonry voluntarily. They will only do so if compelled by Parliament.

The Synod of the Church of England, and the Methodist Conference of 1985, evaded an important responsibility when they failed to rule that Christianity and Freemasonry are not compatible. The Methodists were simply given 'guidance' that they should not become Freemasons and the Synod decided it was sufficient to point out that there are 'clear difficulties' to be faced by Christians who are Freemasons. The compromising nature of both verdicts leaves a great many Christians who are not Masons not knowing where they stand; and Masonic Christians remain under fire from both within the Church and without.

A considerable Catholic literature expounds both theological and social arguments against Freemasonry, which was first condemned by Rome in 1783. Surprisingly, in July

1974, a more open attitude seemed to be expressed in a confidential letter sent to a number of bishops' conferences by the Sacred Congregation for the Doctrine of the Faith, the former Holy Office. The letter offered an interpretation of Canon 2335, which lays down excommunication as the punishment incurred by Catholics who become Freemasons. It made clear that the Canon was directed against Catholics belonging to associations actually engaged in conspiring against the Roman Catholic Church or the State, and some bishops' conferences thought that a reconciliation had been signalled between the Church and those Masonic movements not guilty of plots against Church or State. Subsequently, a number of men were given permission by their bishops to be Freemasons.

Until 1973 works expressing the traditional objections of the Roman Catholic Church towards Freemasonry on both theological and political grounds were available from the Catholic Truth Society. The literature was withdrawn then because it was thought that a change in the policy of the Church was imminent. Among the material freely available from the Society before 1973 was a book entitled *Freemasonry and the Anti-Christian Movement*, by the Rev E. Cahill, first published in 1929. Father Cahill says at one point: 'Limits of space and other reasons preclude us from discussing the deeper and far more intimate nature of the Masonic secret: how far, namely, the Masonic cult is to be identified with the *formal* worship of Satan, the arch-enemy of mankind, and how far Satan physically co-operates in Masonic activity.'

One can only regret the limits of space, imposed from I know not where, and the 'other reasons'. It is an extreme allegation to present without detailed evidence from some source. Reviewing the Papal condemnations of Freemasonry, Father Cahill sees much in history to support them:

The systematic war against religion and Christian morality in France which threatens the final ruin of that great nation; the persistent campaign of assassination waged by the secret societies against the Catholic dynasty of the Hapsburgs, as well as the attempts on the life of the Catholic King of Spain; the revolution in Portugal, with all the horrors and excesses that accompanied it; the revolution in Spanish America, in Cuba, and the Philippines; the various anarchical attempts in Spain itself, and especially the anarchical rising in Barcelona (July 1909), and the subsequent agitation aroused by the Masonic and Jewish controlled press all over the world for the organisation of an international *Kulturkampf;* the awful tragedy of Russia; the whole course of the revolutions and persecutions in Mexico, with all their accompanying horrors; the irreligion, immorality, race suicide, divorce, juvenile crime, destruction of home life; the spirit of unrest and dissipation, which was now affecting the very springs of life over the whole civilised world, all traceable in large part directly or indirectly, to the influence and activities of the same sinister but half-hidden power which, in the opinion of many, is to be identified with the Anti-Christ foretold in Holy Writ, or is at least the herald of his coming.

The pamphlets obtainable from the Catholic Truth Society in England until 1973 contain the same heavy implication that Masons plot against the State and that the majority of members are in some way dupes of a select international Masonic set which pulls strings to affect the destinies of nations.

The pamphlet *Catholics and Freemasonry* by Dr L. Rumble,[1] alleges Masonic participation in revolutionary movements in France, Austria, Italy, Switzerland, Spain, Portugual and Sweden. Revolutions occur, however, to which the Roman Catholic Church has not been able to ascribe direct Masonic influence. Revolutionaries are by definition a danger to the existing State, but they may or may not menace the Church; surely, much depends upon the closeness of the ties between the State and the Church concerned.

Nor can Dr Rumble's assertion that Masons are used for policies of which they know nothing pass unchallenged. It cannot seriously be argued, for example, that Freemasons in America knew nothing of the policies behind the War of

[1] My copy dated September 1962; at that time 120,000 had been printed.

Independence or the American Civil War, when Masonic leaders were on both sides. The course of history is influenced by many factors, and, while revolutionary movements may be engineered from time to time by secret societies, they have depended for their effectiveness, at least in more recent times, upon a broad conviction among large numbers of people that upheaval and sacrifice will produce something they want.

According to Father Cahill, behind the manipulators of Freemasonry are those other arch-manipulators, the great Jewish International Financiers, who, of course, have almost complete command of the world's newspapers and control practically all of the world's cinema. There was nothing malodorous about opinions of this kind in the twenties and thirties and they have a currency today, in spite of the more recent pitiful chapters in the history of that scapegoat nation.

There was another fashionable bogey of which Father Cahill wrote, the intimate connection of Socialism with Freemasonry. He judged the fundamental aims and ideals of the two to be closely akin, and found both to be international, anti-patriotic, disruptive and materialistic. The founders of Socialism, Marx, Engels and Lasalle, he declared, were Jews and Freemasons. Perhaps the Communists themselves have provided the most damaging evidence against any suggestions of a link between them and Freemasonry by the mere fact that membership of Masonry is forbidden in Communist-controlled countries. Freemasonry has concepts which are meant to have international application, but the majority of its members lack the will to provide an organisation to pursue these. The idea of a 'Comintern of Masonry' is hardly likely to appeal to the Duke of Kent.

The possibility of secret movements planning to gain power by stealth obsesses the minds of many and such fears were widespread at the time of the P2 scandal in Italy. The press revealed in May 1981 that the members of this Masonic lodge were nearly a thousand men, the most powerful and influential in the land, and that they included

341

financial advisers to the Vatican who were involved in the crash of Banco Ambrosiano.

P2 was exposed as a secret group of Masons, some of whom conspired to combine business and politics with the intention of destroying Italy's constitutional order. It was a Masonic Lodge in name only. P2 had never been officially constituted, and there were no regular meetings of all members, but the P2 scandal raised embarrassing questions for British Freemasons. They arose because the United Grand Lodge of England had recognised the Grand Orient of Italy in 1972, believing that its long tradition of political intrigue had at last been abandoned.

There was embarrassment too for Rome. A few days before the headlines a Vatican statement criticised 'mistaken and tendentious interpretations' of the letter to bishops in 1974. It emphasised that excommunication and other penalties prescribed for Catholics who become Freemasons had not been abrogated. Many journalists saw the declaration as an attempt to distance the Church from the imminent P2 scandal. The extent of the involvement of Rome in that scandal has yet to be determined. The full company of those within and without the Vatican involved in corrupt financial dealing is unlikely to be known following the death under Blackfriars Bridge in London of Roberto Calvi, president of Banco Ambrosiano. Nevertheless, the letter to bishops in 1974 was more than an attempt to dissociate the Church from the P2 scandal. It was a reassertion of Rome's opposition to Freemasonry.

Historically, many of the fears surrounding Freemasonry have been generated by the Roman Catholic Church, particularly those concerning the threat to the State. Yet Rome's antipathy remains deeply rooted in the Church's need to exert its own authority. The secrecy of Freemasonry shields it from the inspection of the Church. Rome regards the Masonic creed of brotherhood as a challenge to its position as the sole guardian of true Christianity.

The worst pretension of Freemasonry is that it offers men esoteric truths which cannot be revealed until they have become members of a special brotherhood. The idea that religious and moral truth should be the preserve of only those accepted for membership of a secret society is as offensive to committed Christians as the theological objections to Masonic ritual. This argument alone should compel those Churches which tolerate Freemasonry to ban the clergy from membership.

For many critics the social objections to Freemasonry far outweigh the theological ones, which the Churches of England and Scotland and the Methodists cannot find conclusive enough to demand that Christians should give up the Craft. Candidates for Freemasonry are only initiated if they have an acceptable social standing in the eyes of existing members of the lodge and their admission depends on a unanimous or near unanimous vote in favour. Any movement proclaiming universal fraternity cannot discriminate without falling lamentably short of true brotherhood.

In Britain Masons confidently assert that there is no colour bar within the organisation, but one can be forgiven for imagining that a coloured man finds it harder to obtain sponsors and the votes required for election into the lodge. The official ban on religious and political discussion is designed not only to prevent the movement being used for subversive ends, but also to ensure the harmony of the lodge. So an official ruling which can be used to keep out coloured men is readily to hand and has been grasped by Freemasons in America. Craft lodges there will not initiate a black man and the only one of the fifty State Grand Lodges to recognise the legitimacy of a black lodge is the Grand Lodge of New Jersey.

Any movement with the aspirations to promote individual and public good proclaimed by Freemasonry cannot today justify its exclusion of women, and it is no reply to this challenge for Freemasons to point to the excommunicated organisations which exist for women. The continued exclusion of women from Freemasonry and the strong reservations about its compatibility with Christianity expressed by the Synod of the Church of England must also call into question the Royal seal of approval which English Masons have enjoyed for generations. It no longer seems appropriate that the Queen should be Grand Patroness of the Free-masons.

Down the centuries Masonry in England has had Royal patronage and leadership, but changing times and social attitudes make the distancing of the Royal Family from Freemasonry inevitable, as the men who might be invited to become its leader find that ridicule rather than prestige comes with the role. Prince Philip has been a member of Lodge No. 2612[1] since 1952, when he was a serving naval officer, but is believed to have given up going to lodge meetings; and Prince Charles has not become a Freemason.

The secrecy of Freemasonry and some aspects of its rituals and Masonic sign language all make it easy to ridicule. These elements of Freemasonry attract much unfavourable criticism and antipathy despite the fact that most Masons are admirable men, and the movement properly claims to bring them together for fellowship and the promotion of integrity and good citizenship. It would be unrealistic not to expect some Freemasons to seek whatever advantages they can from Freemasonry: members of other groups behave in the same way. What members of other groups do not feel compelled to do is to meet in secret or to pay lip service to the ideal of international brotherhood while hoping for patronage from their Brotherhood.

The secret of British Freemasonry is unworthy of the fear aroused by different brands abroad and is locked not in Masonic temples up and down the country but in the minds of its members: it suits our national love of hypocritical compromise. Freemasonry is capable of offering the best of all possible worlds. The Mason belongs to a society which professes universal brotherhood, but is exclusive; the move-ment condemns patronage, but is capable of conferring it; and, while it maintains it is not a religion, it apes religious

[1]The lodge in which King George VI, then Duke of York, was initiated in 1919, and the Duke of Kent in 1928.

ceremonies. Freemasonry exploits deeply rooted desires for true brotherhood and religion, yet offers neither. Its continued existence as a sad shadow across our national life is an advertisement of the fact that many men have stopped searching for true brotherhood and religion and appear to have lost the vision of what these might be.

APPENDIX 1

Aims and Relationships of the Craft

Accepted by Grand Lodge, 7th September 1949

In August 1938 the Grand Lodges of England, Ireland and Scotland each agreed upon and issued a statement identical in terms except that the name of the issuing Grand Lodge appeared throughout. This statement, which was entitled 'Aims and Relationships of the Craft', was in the following terms:

1. From time to time the United Grand Lodge of England has deemed it desirable to set forth in precise form the aims of Freemasonry as consistently practised under its Jurisdiction since it came into being as an organised body in 1717, and also to define the principles governing its relations with those other Grand Lodges with which it is in fraternal accord.

2. In view of representations which have been received, and of statements recently issued which have distorted or obscured the true objects of Freemasonry, it is once again considered necessary to emphasise certain fundamental principles of the Order.

3. The first condition of admission into, and membership of, the Order is a belief in the Supreme Being. This is essential and admits of no compromise.

4. The Bible, referred to by Freemasons as the Volume of the Sacred Law, is always open in the Lodges. Every candidate is required to take his Obligation on that book or on the Volume which is held by his particular creed to impart sanctity to an oath or promise taken upon it.

5. Everyone who enters Freemasonry is, at the outset, strictly forbidden to countenance any act which may have a tendency to subvert the peace and good order of society; he must pay due obedience to the law of any State in which he resides or which may afford him protection, and he must never be remiss in the allegiance due to the Sovereign of his native land.

6. While English Freemasonry thus inculcates in each of its members the duties of loyalty and citizenship, it reserves to the individual the right to hold his own opinion with regard to public affairs. But neither in any lodge, nor at any time in his capacity as a Freemason, is he permited to discuss or to advance his views on theological or political questions.

7. The Grand Lodge has always consistently refused to express any opinion on questions of foreign or domestic State policy either at home or abroad, and it will not allow its name to be associated with any action, however humanitarian it may appear to be, which infringes its unalterable policy of standing aloof from every question affecting the relations between one government and another, or between political parties, or questions as to rival theories of government.

8. The Grand Lodge is aware that there do exist Bodies, styling themselves Freemasons, which do not adhere to these principles, and while that attitude exists the Grand Lodge of England refuses absolutely to have any relations with such Bodies, or to regard them as Freemasons.

9. The Grand Lodge of England is a Sovereign and Independent Body practising Freemasonry only within the three Degrees and only within the limits defined in its Constitutions as 'pure Antient Masonry'. It does not recognize or admit the existence of any superior Masonic authority, however styled.

10. On more than one occasion the Grand Lodge has refused, and will continue to refuse, to participate in conferences with so-called International Associations claiming to represent Freemasonry, which admit to membership Bodies failing to conform strictly to the principles upon which the Grand Lodge of England is founded. The Grand Lodge does not admit any such claim, nor can its views be represented by any such Association.

11. There is no secret with regard to any of the basic principles of Freemasonry, some of which have been stated above. The Grand Lodge will always consider the recognition of those Grand Lodges which profess and practise, and can show that they have consistently professed and practised those established and unaltered principles, but in no circumstances will it enter into discussion with a view to any new or varied interpretation of them. They must be accepted and practised wholeheartedly and in their entirety by those who desire to be recognised as Freemasons by the United Grand Lodge of England.

348

The Grand Lodge of England has been asked if it still stands by this declaration, particularly in regard to paragraph 7. The Grand Lodge of England replied that it stood by every word of the declaration, and has since asked for the opinion of the Grand Lodges of Ireland and Scotland. A conference has been held between the three Grand Lodges, and all unhesitatingly reaffirm the statement that was pronounced in 1938: nothing in present-day affairs has been found that could cause them to recede from that attitude.

If Freemasonry once deviated from its course by expressing an opinion on political or theological questions, it would be called upon not only publicly to approve or denounce any movement which might arise in the future, but would sow the seeds of discord among its own members.

The three Grand Lodges are convinced that it is only by this rigid adherence to this policy that Freemasonry has survived the constantly changing doctrines of the outside world, and are compelled to place on record their complete disapproval of any action which may tend to permit the slightest departure from the basic principles of Freemasonry. They are strongly of opinion that if any of the three Grand Lodges does so, it cannot maintain a claim to be following the Antient Landmarks of the Order, and must ultimately face disintegration.

APPENDIX 2

The Relationship of Masonry and Religion

(Extract from Report of Board of General Purposes to Grand Lodge, 12th September 1962)

The Board has been giving the most earnest consideration to this subject, being convinced that it is of fundamental importance to the reputation and well-being of English Freemasonry that no misunderstanding should exist either inside or outside the craft.

It cannot be too strongly asserted that Masonry is neither a religion nor a substitute for religion. Masonry seeks to inculcate in its members a standard of conduct and behaviour which it believes to be acceptable to all creeds, but studiously refrains from intervening in the field of dogma or theology. Masonry, therefore, is not a competitor with religion, though in the sphere of human conduct it may be hoped that its teaching will be complementary to that of religion. On the other hand, its basic requirement that every member of the Order shall believe in a Supreme Being and the stress laid upon his duty towards Him should be sufficient evidence to all but the wilfully prejudiced that Masonry is an upholder of religion, since it both requires a man to have some form of religious belief before he can be admitted as a Mason and expects him when admitted to go on practising his religion.

The Board hopes that Grand Lodge will agree that this is a valid statement of the Masonic position, and in the practical application of these principles will lay down:

(I) that Masonic rites, prayers and ceremonies be confined to the Lodge room, and that dispensation to wear regalia (which term includes white gloves) in public be granted only in exceptional cases;

(II) that elements of vocal music normally associated with religious worship be not included in Masonic ceremonies, all other items being subject to the approval of the Masonic authorities;*

(III) that there be no active participation by Masons, as such, in any part of the burial service or cremation of a Brother and that there be no Masonic prayers, readings or exhortations either then or at the graveside subsequent to the interment, since the final obsequies of any human being, Mason or not, are complete in themselves and do not call in the case of a Freemason for any additional ministrations. That if it is wished to recall and allude to his Masonic life and actions, this can appropriately be done at the next Lodge Meeting in the presence of his Brethren, or at a specifically arranged Memorial Service;

(IV) but that while no obstacle should be put in the way of Masons wishing to take part in an act of corporate worship, only in rare and exceptional cases should they be granted dispensation to do so wearing regalia; moreover that the order of service should in all cases be such as the officiating Minister or his superior consider to be appropriate to the occasion.

*This sub-paragraph was withdrawn by leave of Grand Lodge.

APPENDIX 3

Opening and Closing the Lodge in the Three Degrees

OPENING THE LODGE IN THE FIRST DEGREE

(Brethren may sing a hymn. Worshipful Master gives one knock with gavel, answered by Senior and Junior Wardens.)

WORSHIPFUL MASTER. Brethren, assist me to open the Lodge.

(All rise, if not already standing after hymn.)
To Junior Warden. Brother . . ., what is the first care of every Mason?

JUNIOR WARDEN. To see that the Lodge is properly tyled.

WORSHIPFUL MASTER. Direct that duty to be done.

JUNIOR WARDEN *(To Inner Guard.)* Brother . . ., see that the Lodge is properly tyled.
(Inner Guard goes to door and without opening it gives First Degree knocks, answered from outside by Tyler.)

INNER GUARD. Brother . . . *(to Junior Warden.)* The Lodge is properly tyled.

JUNIOR WARDEN. *(Gives First Degree knocks.)* The Lodge is properly tyled.

WORSHIPFUL MASTER. *(To Senior Warden.)* Brother . . ., the next care?

SENIOR WARDEN. To see that none but Masons are present.

WORSHIPFUL MASTER. To order, Brethren, in the First Degree.
(Worshipful Master and Brethren take step and First Degree sign.)
Brother Junior Warden, how many principal officers are there in the Lodge?

JUNIOR WARDEN. Three: the Worshipful Master, and the Senior and Junior Wardens.

WORSHIPFUL MASTER. Brother Senior Warden, how many assistant officers are there?

SENIOR WARDEN. Three, besides the Tyler or Outer Guard; namely the Senior and Junior Deacons and the Inner Guard.

WORSHIPFUL MASTER. (*To Junior Warden.*) The situation of the Tyler?

JUNIOR WARDEN. Outside the door of the Lodge.

WORSHIPFUL MASTER. (*To Junior Warden.*) His duty?

JUNIOR WARDEN. Being armed with a drawn sword, to keep off all intruders and Cowans to Masonry, and to see that the Candidates are properly prepared.

WORSHIPFUL MASTER. (*To Senior Warden.*) The situation of the Inner Guard?

SENIOR WARDEN. Within the entrance of the Lodge.

WORSHIPFUL MASTER. His duty?

SENIOR WARDEN. To admit Masons on proof, receive the Candidates in due form, and obey the commands of the Junior Warden.

WORSHIPFUL MASTER. (*To Junior Warden.*) The situation of the Junior Deacon?

JUNIOR WARDEN. At the right of the Senior Warden.

WORSHIPFUL MASTER. His duty?

JUNIOR WARDEN. To carry all messages and communications of the Worshipful Master from the Senior to the Junior Warden, and to see that the same are punctually obeyed.

WORSHIPFUL MASTER. (*To Senior Warden.*) The situation of the Senior Deacon?

SENIOR WARDEN. At or near to the right of the Worshipful Master.

WORSHIPFUL MASTER. His duty?

SENIOR WARDEN. To bear all messages and commands from the Worshipful Master to the Senior Warden, and await the return of the Junior Deacon.

WORSHIPFUL MASTER. Brother Junior Warden, your place in the Lodge?

JUNIOR WARDEN. In the south.

WORSHIPFUL MASTER. Why are you placed there?

JUNIOR WARDEN. To mark the sun at its meridian, to call the Brethren from labour to refreshment, and from refreshment to labour, that profit and pleasure may be the result.

WORSHIPFUL MASTER. Brother Senior Warden, your place in the Lodge?

SENIOR WARDEN. In the west.

WORSHIPFUL MASTER. Why are you placed there?

SENIOR WARDEN. To mark the setting sun, to close the Lodge by command of the Worshipful Master, after having seen that every brother has had his due.

WORSHIPFUL MASTER. (*To Senior Warden or Immediate Past Master.*) The Master's place?

SENIOR WARDEN or IMMEDIATE PAST MASTER. In the east.

WORSHIPFUL MASTER. Why is he placed there?

SENIOR WARDEN or IMMEDIATE PAST MASTER. As the sun rises in the east to open and enliven the day, so the Worshipful Master is placed in the east to open the Lodge, and employ and instruct the Brethren in Freemasonry.

WORSHIPFUL MASTER. The Lodge being duly formed, before I declare it open, let us invoke the assistance of the Great Architect of the Universe in all our undertakings, may our labours, thus begun in order, be continued in peace, and closed in harmony.

IMMEDIATE PAST MASTER. So mote it be.

WORSHIPFUL MASTER. Brethren, in the name of the Great Architect of the Universe, I declare the Lodge duly open (*all cut sign*) for the purposes of Freemasonry in the First Degree.

(*Worshipful Master gives First Degree knocks, answered by Senior Warden, who raises his column, and by Junior Warden, who lowers his. Inner Guard and Tyler give the knocks on Lodge door. Immediate Past Master opens the Volume of the Sacred Law and arranges the Square and Compasses on it with the points of the Compasses beneath the Square. Junior Deacon puts out First Degree tracing board. Brethren sit when Worshipful Master does so.*)

OPENING THE LODGE IN THE SECOND DEGREE

(*Entered Apprentices leave the Lodge. Worshipful Master gives a single knock, answered by Senior and Junior Wardens.*)

WORSHIPFUL MASTER. Brethren, assist me to open the Lodge in the Second Degree.

(*All rise.*)

Brother Junior Warden, what is the first care of every Fellow-Craft Freemason?

JUNIOR WARDEN. To see that the Lodge is properly tyled.

WORSHIPFUL MASTER. Direct that duty to be done.

JUNIOR WARDEN. Brother Inner Guard, see that the Lodge is properly tyled.

(*Inner Guard and Tyler give knocks of First Degree. Inner Guard returns, takes step and First Degree sign.*)

INNER GUARD. Brother Junior Warden, the Lodge is properly tyled.

JUNIOR WARDEN. (*Knocks, takes step and First Degree sign.*) Worshipful Master, the Lodge is properly tyled. (*Cuts sign.*)

WORSHIPFUL MASTER. Brother Senior Warden, the next care?

SENIOR WARDEN. To see the Brethren appear to order as Masons.

WORSHIPFUL MASTER. To order, Brethren, in the First Degree.

(*Worshipful Master and Brethren take step and First Degree sign.*)

Brother Junior Warden, are you a Fellow-Craft Freemason?

JUNIOR WARDEN. I am, Worshipful Master; try me, and prove me.

WORSHIPFUL MASTER. By what instrument in Architecture will you be proved?

JUNIOR WARDEN. The Square.

WORSHIPFUL MASTER. What is a Square?

JUNIOR WARDEN. An angle of ninety degrees, or the fourth part of circle.

WORSHIPFUL MASTER. Being yourself acquainted with the proper method, you will prove the Brethren Craftsmen, and demonstrate that proof to me by copying their example.

JUNIOR WARDEN. Brethren, it is the Worshipful Master's command that you prove yourselves Craftsmen.

(*Junior Warden maintains First Degree sign. Brethren cut it and take step and give Second Degree signs.*)

Worshipful Master, the Brethren have proved themselves Craftsmen, and in obedience to your command I thus copy their example. (*Does so.*)

WORSHIPFUL MASTER. Brother Junior Warden, I acknowledge the correctness of the signs.

(*Worshipful Master gives Second Degree signs.*) Before we open the Lodge in the Second Degree, let us supplicate the Grand Geometrician of the Universe, that the rays of Heaven may shed their influence, to enlighten us in the paths of virtue and science.

IMMEDIATE PAST MASTER. So mote it be.

WORSHIPFUL MASTER. Brethren, in the name of the Grand Geometrician of the Universe, I declare the Lodge duly open (*all cut Hailing sign*) on the Square (*all give Penal sign*) for the instruction and improvement of Craftsmen.

(*Worshipful Master gives Second Degree knocks, repeated by Senior and Junior Wardens. Inner Guard gives knocks on Lodge door and Tyler answers. Immediate Past Master places one point of Compasses above the Square and Junior Deacon puts out Second Degree tracing board. All sit, taking cue from Worshipful Master.*)

OPENING THE LODGE IN THE THIRD DEGREE

(*All Fellow-Craft leave the Lodge. Worshipful Master gives a single knock, answered by Senior and Junior Wardens.*)

WORSHIPFUL MASTER. Brethren, assist me open the Lodge in the Third Degree.

(*All rise.*)

Brother Junior Warden, what is the first care of every Master Mason?

JUNIOR WARDEN. To see that the Lodge is properly tyled.

WORSHIPFUL MASTER. Direct that duty to be done.

JUNIOR WARDEN. Brother Inner Guard, see that the Lodge is properly tyled.

(*Inner Guard and Tyler give Second Degree knocks on door. Inner Guard takes step and Second Degree sign.*)

INNER GUARD. Brother Junior Warden, the Lodge is properly tyled.

JUNIOR WARDEN. (*Gives Second Degree knocks, takes step and Second Degree sign.*) Worshipful Master, the Lodge is properly tyled.

WORSHIPFUL MASTER. Brother Senior Warden, the next care?

SENIOR WARDEN. To see that the Brethren appear to order as Craftsmen.

WORSHIPFUL MASTER. To order, Brethren, in the Second Degree.

(*Worshipful Master and Brethren, take step and Second Degree sign.*)

Brother Junior Warden, are you Master Mason?

JUNIOR WARDEN. I am, Worshipful Master; try me and prove me.

WORSHIPFUL MASTER. By what instruments in Architecture will you be proved?

JUNIOR WARDEN. The Square and Compasses.

WORSHIPFUL MASTER: Being yourself acquainted with the proper method, you will prove the Brethren Master Mason by signs, and demonstrate that proof to me by copying their example.

JUNIOR WARDEN. Brethren, it is the Worshipful Master's command that you prove yourselves Master Masons by signs.

(*Junior Warden keeps up Second Degree sign while Brethren take step and go through the signs of a Master Mason, the signs of Horror, Sympathy, and the Penal sign.*)

Worshipful Master, the Brethren have proved themselves Master Masons by signs, and in obedience to your command, I thus copy their example. (*Does so.*)

WORSHIPFUL MASTER. Brother Junior Warden, I acknowledge the correctness of the signs.

(*Takes step and gives the signs.*)

Brother Junior Warden, whence come you?

JUNIOR WARDEN. The east.

WORSHIPFUL MASTER. Brother Senior Warden, whither directing your course?

SENIOR WARDEN. The west.

WORSHIPFUL MASTER (*To Junior Warden.*) What inducement have you to leave the east and go to the west?

JUNIOR WARDEN. To seek for that which was lost, which, by your instructions and our own industry, we hope to find.

WORSHIPFUL MASTER. (*To Senior Warden.*) What is that which was lost?

SENIOR WARDEN. The genuine secrets of a Master Mason.

WORSHIPFUL MASTER. (*To Junior Warden.*) How came they lost?

JUNIOR WARDEN. By the untimely death of our Master, Hiram Abiff.

WORSHIPFUL MASTER. (*To Senior Warden.*) Where do you hope to find them?

SENIOR WARDEN. With the Centre.

WORSHIPFUL MASTER. (*To Junior Warden.*) What is a Centre?

JUNIOR WARDEN. A point within a circle, from which every part of the circumference is equidistant.

358

WORSHIPFUL MASTER. (*To Junior Warden.*) Why with the Centre?

SENIOR WARDEN. That being a point from which a Master Mason cannot err.

WORSHIPFUL MASTER. We will assist you to repair that loss, and may Heaven aid our united endeavours.

IMMEDIATE PAST MASTER. So mote it be.

WORSHIPFUL MASTER. Brethren, in the name of the Most High, I declare the Lodge duly open (*all cut Penal sign*) on the Centre, for the purpose of Freemasonry in the Third Degree.

(*Worshipful Master gives Third Degree knocks, answered by Senior and Junior Wardens. Inner Guard and Tyler give them on the door. Immediate Past Master places both points of the Compasses above the Square, and Junior Deacon puts out Third Degree tracing board.*)

All Glory to the Most High.

(*All give sign of Joy and Exultation and take their seats.*)

CLOSING THE LODGE IN THE THIRD DEGREE

(*Worshipful Master gives single knock, answered by Senior and Junior Wardens.*)

WORSHIPFUL MASTER. Brethren, assist me to close the Lodge in the Third Degree.

(*All rise.*)

Brother Junior Warden, what is the constant care of every Master Mason?

JUNIOR WARDEN. To prove the Lodge close tyled.

WORSHIPFUL MASTER. Direct that duty to be done.

JUNIOR WARDEN. Brother Inner Guard, prove the Lodge close tyled.

(*Inner Guard and Tyler give the Third Degree knocks on door. Inner Guard takes step and Third Degree Penal sign.*)

INNER GUARD. Brother Junior Warden, the Lodge is close tyled. (*Cuts sign.*)

JUNIOR WARDEN. (*Gives Third Degree knocks, takes step and Third Degree Penal sign.*) Worshipful Master, the Lodge is close tyled. (*Cuts sign.*)

WORSHIPFUL MASTER. Brother Senior Warden, the next care?

SENIOR WARDEN. To see that the Brethren appear to order as Master Masons.

WORSHIPFUL MASTER. To order, Brethren, in the Third Degree.
(*All take step and give Third Degree Penal sign.*).
Brother Junior Warden, whence come you?

JUNIOR WARDEN. The west, whither we have been in search of the genuine secrets of a Master Mason.

WORSHIPFUL MASTER. Brother Senior Warden, have you found them?

SENIOR WARDEN. We have not, Worshipful Master, but we bring with us certain substituted secrets, which we are anxious to impart for your approbation.

WORSHIPFUL MASTER. Let those substituted secrets be regularly communicated to me.
(*The Wardens keep up Penal sign, leave their pedestals and go to the centre of the Lodge, where they face each other about three feet apart, Senior Warden faces south, Junior Warden north. Junior Warden takes step and gives Senior Warden pass-grip leading from Second to Third Degree. They raise their hands and he whispers the password TUBAL-CAIN. They let go hands and both give Penal sign. Junior Warden then takes another step, and goes through the signs of the Third Degree. He also demonstrates the Five Points of Fellowship and whispers the words of the Third Degree, MACHABEN and MACHBINNA. Junior Warden salutes Senior Warden with Third Degree Penal sign, and returns to pedestal, still keeping up sign. Senior Warden goes to centre of Lodge, faces east, and keeps Penal sign.*)

SENIOR WARDEN. Worshipful Master, condescend to receive from me the substituted secrets of a Master Mason.

WORSHIPFUL MASTER. Brother Senior Warden, I will receive them with pleasure, and for the information of the Brethren you will speak the words aloud.
(*Worshipful Master leaves pedestal left and goes to within a yard of Senior Warden. He takes step and is given the substituted secrets by the Senior Warden, who communicates them as the Junior Warden did, but speaks the words aloud. Senior Warden salutes with Penal sign and both return to their pedestals holding sign.*)
Brethren, the substituted secrets of a Master Mason thus regularly communicated to me, I, as Master of this Lodge, and thereby the humble representative of King Solomon, sanction and confirm with my approbation; and declare that they shall designate you

and all Master Masons throughout the universe, until time or circumstances shall restore the genuine.

THE BRETHREN. (*Bending forward.*) With gratitude to our Master we bend.

WORSHIPFUL MASTER. All gratitude to the Most High.

(*All give sign of Joy and Exultation and recover to Third Degree Penal sign.*)

Brother Senior Warden, the labours of this Degree being ended, you have my command to close the Lodge. (*Gives Third Degree knocks with left hand.*)

SENIOR WARDEN. Brethren, in the name of the Most High, and by command of the Worshipful Master, I close (*all cut sign*) this Master Mason's Lodge.

(*All recover, and then drop the hand. The Senior Warden gives the Third Degree knocks.*)

JUNIOR WARDEN. And it is closed accordingly. (*Repeats knocks. Inner Guard repeats them at door and Tyler answers. Immediate Past Master places one point of Compasses beneath the Square. Junior Deacon removes or covers tracing board. The Brethren sit when the Master does. Fellow-Craftsmen are admitted.*)

CLOSING THE LODGE IN THE SECOND DEGREE

(*Worshipful Master gives single knock, answered by Senior and Junior Wardens.*)

WORSHIPFUL MASTER. Brethren, assist me to close the Lodge in the Second Degree.

(*All rise.*)

Brother Junior Warden, what is the constant care of every Fellow-Craft Freemason?

JUNIOR WARDEN. To prove the Lodge close tyled.

WORSHIPFUL MASTER. Direct that duty to be done.

JUNIOR WARDEN. Brother Inner Guard, prove the Lodge close tyled.

(*Inner Guard and Tyler give knocks of Second Degree on the door. Inner Guard returns, takes step and Second Degree sign.*)

INNER GUARD. Brother Junior Warden, the Lodge is close tyled. (*Cuts sign.*)

JUNIOR WARDEN. (*Knocks, step, and sign of the Second Degree.*) Worshipful Master, the Lodge is close tyled. (*Cuts sign.*)

WORSHIPFUL MASTER. Brother Senior Warden, the next care?

SENIOR WARDEN. To see that the Brethren appear to order as Craftsmen.

WORSHIPFUL MASTER. To order, Brethren, in the Second Degree.

(All take step and Second Degree sign, which they hold until Lodge is closed.)

Brother Junior Warden, in this position, what have you discovered?

JUNIOR WARDEN. A sacred symbol.

WORSHIPFUL MASTER. Brother Senior Warden, where is it situated?

SENIOR WARDEN. In the centre of the building.

WORSHIPFUL MASTER. *(To Junior Warden.)* To whom does it allude?

JUNIOR WARDEN. The Grand Geometrician of the Universe.

WORSHIPFUL MASTER. Then, Brethren, let us remember that wherever we are, and whatever we do, He is with us, and His all-seeing eye observes us, and whilst we continue to act in conformity with the principles of the Craft, let us not fail to discharge our duty to Him with fervency and zeal.

IMMEDIATE PAST MASTER. So mote it be.

WORSHIPFUL MASTER. Brother Senior Warden, the labours of this Degree being ended, you have my command to close the Lodge. *(Gives Second Degree knocks with left hand, holding sign with right.)*

SENIOR WARDEN. Brethren, in the name of the Grand Geometrician of the Universe, and by command of the Worshipful Master, I close this Fellow-Crafts Lodge. *(Senior Warden gives Second Degree knocks.)*

JUNIOR WARDEN. Happy have we met.

Happy may we part.

And happy meet again.

(Gives Second Degree knocks. Inner Guard and Tyler repeat them on the door. Immediate Past Master puts both points of Compasses under the Square. Junior Deacon removes tracing boards. Entered Apprentices Admitted.)

CLOSING THE LODGE

(Worshipful Master gives single knock answered by Senior and Junior Wardens.)

WORSHIPFUL MASTER. Brethren, assist me to close the Lodge.
(*All rise.*)
Brother Junior Warden, what is the constant care of every Mason?

JUNIOR WARDEN, To prove the Lodge close tyled.

WORSHIPFUL MASTER. Direct that duty to be done.

JUNIOR WARDEN. Brother Inner Guard, prove the Lodge close tyled.
(*Inner Guard and Tyler give Degree knocks. Inner Guard takes step and First Degree sign.*)

INNER GUARD. Brother Junior Warden, the Lodge is close tyled.
(*Cuts sign.*)

JUNIOR WARDEN. (*With knocks, step and First Degree sign.*)
Worshipful Master, the Lodge is close tyled. (*Cuts sign.*)

WORSHIPFUL MASTER. Brother Senior Warden, the next care?

SENIOR WARDEN. To see that the Brethren appear to order as Masons.

WORSHIPFUL MASTER. To order, Brethren, in the First Degree.
(*All take step and First Degree sign.*)
Brother Senior Warden, your constant place in the Lodge?

SENIOR WARDEN. In the west.

WORSHIPFUL MASTER. Why are you placed there?

SENIOR WARDEN. As the sun sets in the west to close the day, so the Senior Warden is placed in the west to close the Lodge by command of the Worshipful Master, after having seen that every Brother has had his due.

WORSHIPFUL MASTER. Brethren, before we close the Lodge, let us with all reverence and humility express our gratitude to the Great Architect of the Universe for favours already received; may He continue to preserve the Order by cementing and adorning it with every moral and social virtue.

IMMEDIATE PAST MASTER. So mote it be.

WORSHIPFUL MASTER. Brother Senior Warden, the labours of the evening being ended, you have my command to close the Lodge. (*Keeping up sign, gives First Degree knocks with left hand.*)

SENIOR WARDEN. Brethren, in the name of the Great Architect of the Universe and by command of the Worshipful Master, I close the Lodge.

(All cut sign. Senior Warden gives First Degree knocks and lowers his column.)

JUNIOR WARDEN. And it is closed accordingly, until the . . . day of . . . emergencies excepted, of which every Brother will have due notice. (*Gives First Degree knocks, and raises his column. Inner Guard and Tyler give knocks. Junior Deacon removes the tracing board.*)

IMMEDIATE PAST MASTER. (*Takes away Square and Compasses, and closes the Volume of the Sacred Law.*) Brethren, nothing now remains, but, according to ancient custom, to lock up our secrets in a safe repository, uniting in the act of Fidelity, Fidelity, Fidelity.

(All give sign of Reverence each time the word Fidelity is spoken.)

APPENDIX 4

The Seddon Murder Trial 1912

This was a trial during which both the man in the dock and the judge revealed themselves as Freemasons. It has become part of the legend surrounding Freemasonry and a brief account is justified here as it is seen by many anti-Masons as the classic case of an attempt to use Masonry to interfere with the course of justice.

Frederick Henry Seddon was under cross-examination at the Old Bailey about the poisoning of a woman lodger when he made a Masonic sign to Mr Justice Bucknill, whom he knew to be a prominent Freemason. The judge not only reprimanded Seddon but threatened him with a retrial before another judge. When a verdict of 'guilty' was brought in, Seddon said: 'I declare before the Great Architect of the Universe, I am not guilty, my Lord.'

Mr Justice Bucknill sentenced Seddon to death, but before doing so felt constrained to tell him: 'You and I know that we both belong to the same Brotherhood and it is all the more painful for me to have to say what I am saying. But our Brotherhood does not encourage crime; on the contrary, it condemns it. I pray you again to make your peace with the Great Architect of the Universe.'

The trial is regarded by Freemasons as proof that there is no Masonic influence on the true course of justice. Anti-Masons claim that on the contrary, Seddon made his attempt to exploit Freemasonry too late in the trial, as the jury had already declared its verdict. There is also the view that Seddon was not trying to appeal for help, but used the Masonic term for God simply to emphasise his oath to tell the court the truth.

Bibliography

Among the many books, newspapers, periodicals and other sources the author has drawn upon for information, the following short list represents those he has found particularly helpful.

Box, Hubert S., *The Nature of Freemasonry*, Augustine Press, 1952.

Cahill, E., *Freemasonry and the Anti-Christian Movement*, M. H. Gill and Son Ltd, Dublin, 1952.

Carlile, Richard, *Manual of Freemasonry*, London, 1853.

Church of England, *Freemasonry and Christianity: Are they compatible?* Church House Publishing, London, 1987.

Gould, Robert Freke, *The History of Freemasonry*, London, 3rd edition, 1951.

Hannah, Walton, *Darkness Visible*, Augustine Press, 1952; *Christian by Degrees*, Britons Publishing Co, 1954.

Jones, Bernard E., *Freemasons' Guide and Compendium*, Harrap & Co Ltd, 1963.

Knight, Stephen, *The Brotherhood*, Granada Publishing, 1983.

Knoop, D., and Jones, G.P., *The Genesis of Freemasonry*, Manchester, 1947.

Pick, F.L., and Knight, G.N., *The Pocket History of Freemasonry*, Frederick Muller, 1953.

Poole, Rev Herbert, *The History of Freemasonry*, Caxton Publishing Co Ltd, 1951.

Stalker, John, *Stalker*, Harrap, 1988, Penguin Books, 1988.

Yallop, David A., *In God's Name*, Corgi Books, 1988.

Index

371

THE HOLY BLOOD AND THE HOLY GRAIL
BY MICHAEL BAIGENT, RICHARD LEIGH AND
HENRY LINCOLN

The subject of this book could constitute the single most
shattering secret of the last two thousand years.

The first publication, in 1982, of THE HOLY BLOOD
AND THE HOLY GRAIL, sparked off a storm of
controversy, reverberations of which are still resounding
throughout the Western world. The book's conclusions
are persuasive, and to many will be shocking, perhaps
profoundly dangerous. Whatever your own views, it is a
book that you will truly not be able to set aside.

'Probably one of the most controversial books of the 20th
Century.'
U.P.I.

'A book that cannot easily be dismissed.'
Neville Cryer, The Bible Society

'Their quest for knowledge possesses all the ingredients of
a classic 19th Century mystery novel . . . a book that will be
hotly denounced and widely read.'
Financial Times

'A very extraordinary story . . . if you like this sort of detective work on the past you will like the book very much.'
Anthony Powell, Daily Telegraph

0 552 12138 X

A SELECTED LIST OF NON-FICTION TITLES
AVAILABLE FROM CORGI BOOKS.

☐ 12138 X	THE HOLY BLOOD AND THE HOLY GRAIL		
		Michael Baigent, Richard Leigh & Henry Lincoln	£3.99
☐ 13182 2	THE MESSIANIC LEGACY		
		Michael Baigent, Richard Leigh & Henry Lincoln	£3.95
☐ 13296 9	VICARS OF CHRIST	*Peter de Rosa*	£3.99
☐ 13007 9	JOURNEY INTO MADNESS	*Gordon Thomas*	£3.99
☐ 13006 0	THE TRIAL	*Gordon Thomas*	£3.99
☐ 13288 8	IN GOD'S NAME	*David Yallop*	£3.99

All Corgi/Bantam Books are available at your bookshop or newsagent, or can be ordered from the
following address:

Corgi/Bantam Books,
Cash Sales Department,
P.O. Box 11, Falmouth, Cornwall TR10 9EN

Please send a cheque or postal order (no currency) and allow 60p for postage and packing for the
first book plus 25p for the second book and 15p for each additional book ordered up to a maximum
charge of £1.90 in UK.

B.F.P.O customers please allow 60p for the first book, 25p for the second book plus 15p per copy
for the next 7 books, thereafter 9p per book.

Overseas customers, including Eire, please allow £1.25 for postage and packing for the first book,
75p for the second book, and 28p for each subsequent title ordered.